HISTORY OF ENGLAND

VOLUME ONE

GEORGE MACAULAY TREVELYAN was born in 1876 and educated at Harrow and Trinity College, Cambridge. He was Regius Professor of Modern History at Cambridge from 1927 to 1940 and Master of Trinity College from 1940 to 1951. He is the author of *England under the Stuarts*, *British History in the Nineteenth Century*, *Six Centuries of Social History*, *England under Queen Anne*, and A HISTORY OF ENGLAND, which was first published in 1926.

HISTORY
OF
ENGLAND

Volume One: From the Earliest Times to the Reformation
by G. M. TREVELYAN, O.M.
Master of Trinity College, 1940–1951. Formerly Regius
Professor of Modern History in the University of Cambridge

Doubleday Anchor Books
DOUBLEDAY & COMPANY, INC., GARDEN CITY, N.Y.

To President Lowell of Harvard

History of England was originally published by Longmans, Green and Company, Ltd. in 1926. The Anchor Books edition is published by arrangement with Longmans, Green and Co. Inc., New York.

Anchor Books edition: 1953

First Edition, June 1926
Second Edition, July 1937
Second Edition revised, April 1942
Third Edition, October 1945
Reissue (with minor corrections), 1952
PRINTED IN THE UNITED STATES OF AMERICA
DESIGNED BY DIANA KLEMIN

NOTE TO THE REISSUE (1952)

The only substantial addition appears in Volume III, page 231, which records the final settlement with India and Pakistan. Minor corrections and deletions have been made from Volume III, page 225, to the end of the book.

PREFACE TO LATER EDITIONS

In 1945 and again in 1952 a few alterations and additions have been made to the text of this work, and some recent publications have been added to the lists of 'Books for Further Reading.'   G. M. Trevelyan

PREFACE

A book that traverses so vast a field as the whole of English history in the course of seven hundred pages is apt to be either a text-book or an essay. It can in no case be a full narrative of events. This work is an essay in so far as it attempts to analyze the social development of the nation in relation to economic conditions, political institutions, and overseas activities. It is a text-book in so far as it preserves the narrative form in brief, deals in dates, and gives prominence to leading events and persons.

Scottish, Irish, Welsh, and overseas Imperial history are treated, I trust not in all cases from too English a point of view. But what unity the book has, especially in its earlier parts, is necessarily derived from England as the centre. Not to arouse expectations which I may not fulfil, I have called the book merely a History of England.

The original nucleus out of which the work has grown was the Lowell Lectures which I had the honour of delivering in Boston, Mass., in the spring of 1924. I therefore dedicate the book in its present form to President Lowell of Harvard and my other kind hosts on that occasion.

I am greatly indebted to two friends at the older Cambridge, Dr. Clapham of King's, and Mr. Claude Elliott of Jesus: to the former for allowing me to see the early part of his *Economic History of Modern Britain* before it went to press, a privilege of which I have made extensive use; and to Mr. Elliott for reading the earlier half of my work and giving me valuable advice on numerous points.

BERKHAMSTED, *April* 1926.   G. M. Trevelyan

CONTENTS

BOOK ONE

*The Mingling of the Races. From the Earliest Times
to the Norman Conquest*

BOOK TWO

The Making of the Nation. From the Conquest to the Reformation

MAPS

GENEALOGICAL TREES

INTRODUCTION

The history of civilized man in our country is very old; it begins long before the reign of Alfred. But the history of Britain as a leader in the world's affairs is of much shorter date; it begins with the reign of Elizabeth. The reason can be read upon the map. Map-makers, whether in ancient Alexandria or in mediæval monasteries, placed our island on the north-west edge of all things. But, after the discovery of America and the ocean routes to Africa and the East, Britain lay in the centre of the new maritime movement. This change in her geographic outlook was employed to good purpose by her inhabitants, who in the era of the Stuarts made her the chief seat of the new trans-oceanic commerce and of the finance and industry that sustained it. Next, with the aid of modern science, the land of Newton applied machinery to manufacture and began the world-wide Industrial Revolution. Meanwhile, Britain was peopling and giving laws to North America; and after she had lost the Thirteen Colonies, she built up a second Empire, more widely scattered and more vast.

These latter centuries of material growth and leadership correspond with the period of greatest intellectual achievement. In spite of Bede, Roger Bacon, Chaucer and Wycliffe, Britain's contribution to mediæval science and literature is slight when compared to the world of her intellectual creation from the time of Shakespeare onward. The era when London awoke to find herself the maritime centre of the suddenly expanded globe, was also the era of the Renaissance and the Reformation—movements of intellectual growth and individual self-assertion which proved more congenial to the British than to many other races, and seemed to emancipate the island genius.

In the sphere of pure politics Britain is famous as the mother of Parliaments. In answer to the instincts and temperament of her people, she evolved in the course of centuries a system which reconciled three things that other nations have often found incompatible—executive efficiency, popular control, and personal freedom.

It is indeed in the Middle Ages that we must seek the origin of Parliament, and of the English Common Law which the ultimate victory of Parliament over the Royal power has made supreme in all English-speaking lands. The political merit of the Mediæval period lay in its dislike of absolutism in the Temporal sphere, its elaborate distribution of power, its sense of corporate life, and its consultation of the various corporate interests through their representatives. But, although Parliament was a characteristic product of the Middle Ages, the development of its powers in Tudor, Stuart and Hanoverian days, its resistance to the political theories of the Roman law received in contemporary Europe, and its transplantation to America and the Antipodes, are the great events which raised the political history of Britain into a sphere apart from the political life of the continent. For, although France and Spain had a number of mediæval Estates and Parliaments, they failed to adapt them to modern conditions. On the passing of feudalism, the Latin peoples read despotic monarchy as the political message of the new era. Against Machiavelli's princely interpretation of the new nationalism, Britain alone of the great national States successfully held out, turned back the tide of despotism, and elaborated a system by which a debating club of elected persons could successfully govern an Empire in peace and in war. During the commercial and military struggles with foreign rivals which followed between 1689 and 1815, our goods, our ships, and our armies proved that Parliamentary freedom might be more efficient than despotism as a means of giving force to the national will. Nor, in the new era of man's life introduced by the Industrial Revolution, has this verdict yet been reversed.

In the Nineteenth Century the same Parliamentary institutions, while undergoing democratic transformation, were put to the severe test of coping with the new and bewildering conditions of social life created by the Industrial Revolution. At the same time the vast and ever-increasing Empire, of white, brown, and black communities, presented diverse and complicated problems, each one recurring in new guise every few years under the stimulus that modern economic conditions give to social and political change. Parliamentary government for the white races, and the desire to govern justly societies not yet prepared for self-government, have so far preserved this astonishing association of peoples.

Whatever, then, be our chief interest in the past—whether material progress and racial expansion, the growth of political and social institutions, or pure intellect and letters—it is the last four hundred years in British History which stand out. Yet I have not hesitated to devote a third of this work to a survey of the pre-Tudor epochs. The mingling of the armed races poured into Britain from the earliest times until 1066, and the national temper and customs which they developed in the shelter of the island guarded by the Norman and Plantagenet Kings, alone rendered it possible for five millions of people, ruled by Elizabeth, to lay hold on the splendid future offered to themselves and their descendants by the maritime discoveries and intellectual movements of that age. If the hour then came, the men, too, were ready.

Britain has always owed her fortunes to the sea, and to the havens and rivers that from the earliest times opened her inland regions to what the sea might bring. Long before she aspired to rule the waves she was herself their subject, for her destiny was continually being decided by the boat-crews which they floated to her shore. From Iberian and Celtic to Saxon and Danish settlers, from pre-historic and Phœnician traders to Roman and Norman overlords, successive tides of warlike colonists, the most energetic seamen, farmers and merchants of Europe came by the wave-path to inhabit her, or to instil their knowledge and spirit into the older inhabitants. Her east coast lay obvious and open to Teuton and Scandinavian immigrants; her south coast to cultural influences from the Mediterranean by way of France. From Teuton and Scandinavian she acquired the more important part of her population and character and the root of her language; from the South she received the rest of her language, the chief forms of her culture, and much of her organizing power.

The Norman Conquest severed her ties with Scandinavia, which Canute had drawn very close. For several hundred years the Nordic islanders were governed by a French-speaking aristocracy and a Latin-speaking clergy. By a significant paradox it was under this foreign leadership that the English began to develop their intense national feeling and their peculiar institutions, so different

in spirit from those of Italy and France. Already among
the fellow-countrymen of Chaucer and Wycliffe, even
when engaged in the disastrous adventure of the Hundred
Years' War, we see the beginnings of a distinct English
nationality, far richer than the old Saxon, composed of
many different elements of race, character and culture
which the tides of ages had brought to our coasts and
the island climate had tempered and mellowed into harmony. At the Reformation the English, grown to manhood,
dismissed their Latin tutors, without reacting into close
contact with the Scandinavian and Teuton world. Britain
had become a world by itself.

It was at this crisis in England's cultural and political
growth, when she was weakening her ties with Europe,
that the union with Scotland came about, and at the same
time the ocean offered the islanders a pathway to every
corner of the newly discovered globe. The universality of
the Englishman's experience and outlook—quite as marked
a characteristic as his insularity—is due to his command of
the ocean which has for more than three centuries past
carried him as explorer, trader, and colonist to every shore
in the two hemispheres.

Thus, in early times, the relation of Britain to the sea
was passive and receptive; in modern times, active and
acquisitive. In both it is the key to her story.

BOOK ONE

The Mingling of the Races.
From the Earliest Times to the
Norman Conquest

INTRODUCTION

It is a commonplace to say that the British are a people of mixed blood. I hope, in this First Book, to indicate a little how, when and why this mingling of races occurred.

It may be as well to say, at the outset, that the entrance into our island of the races who people it to-day was completed in main outline at the time of the Norman Conquest. With that event, which itself made less racial than social and cultural change, we come to an end of migratory invasions and of forced entry behind the point of the sword. Since Hastings there has been nothing more catastrophic than a slow, peaceful infiltration of alien craftsmen and labourers,—Flemings, Huguenots, Irish and others,—with the acquiescence of the existing inhabitants of the island. To invade Britain was singularly easy before the Norman Conquest, singularly difficult afterwards. The reason is clear. A well-organized State, with a united people on land and a naval force at sea, could make itself safe behind the Channel even against such military odds as Philip of Spain, Louis XIV, or Napoleon could assemble on the opposite shore. In recent centuries these conditions have been fulfilled, and although an invading force has sometimes been welcomed, as when Henry Tudor or William of Orange came over, no invasion hostile to the community as a whole has met with even partial success owing to the barrier of the sea. But, before the Norman Conquest, there had been long ages when neither the island State

nor the island navy was formidable; even in the days of
Alfred and Harold they were inadequate to their task, and
in earlier times they did not exist. Except when protected
by the Roman galleys and legions, ancient Britain was
peculiarly liable to invasion for geographic and other reasons.

The story of the Mingling of the Races in Britain, ending
with the advent of the Normans, covers a thousand years of
history very dimly descried, succeeding to many thousand
more of archæological twilight. The era of Celt, Saxon
and Dane is like Macbeth's battle on the blasted heath.
Prophecy hovers around. Horns are heard blowing in the
mist, and a confused uproar of savage tumult and outrage. We catch glimpses of giant figures—mostly warriors
at strife. But there are ploughmen, too, it seems, breaking
the primeval clod, and we hear the sound of forests crashing to the axe. Around all is the lap of waves and the
cry of seamen beaching their ships.

CHAPTER ONE

Early Man. Iberian and Celt

It is not my purpose to describe pre-insular Britain and the
great geologic changes, the volcanoes, the rise and fall
of mountains, the tropical swamps in which the coal
forests grew, or the industrious building of the chalk downs
under the sea. Nor shall I attempt to distinguish the various races of primitive hunters, from 'Piltdown man' onwards, who may have wandered over the land during the
inter-glacial periods. It was probably at the great spring-
time of Northern Europe, after the glacial epoch, that the
soil of the future Britain was first trodden by 'Homo
Sapiens,' unequivocal man. These early immigrants came
over by the land-bridge from Europe as they followed
northwards the last retreat of the ice; with them, or just
before them, came the commonest of the wild animals,
birds, flowers and trees. These hunters of the mammoth,

the horse and the reindeer, have probably mixed their blood with some of the later races who are certainly among our ancestors. At the time of their coming overland, the chalk downs of Dover and Calais were still united in a continuous range; the majestic Thames flowed into the lower Rhine; and the Rhine itself meandered towards the Arctic Ocean through the marshy plain now submerged beneath the waves of the North Sea, where the bones of mammoth and reindeer are dredged off the Dogger Bank.

Since the flora and fauna which we call native to Britain came northward at this period to replenish a land swept bare by the snow cap of the last ice age, they are, therefore, closely identified with the flora and fauna of Northern Europe—except for the red grouse peculiar to the British Isles. Ireland was cut adrift from England before the piercing of the Dover Straits by the sea, and is, for that reason, poorer in mammals, plants and reptiles.

For many centuries after Britain became an island the untamed forest was king. Its moist and mossy floor was hidden from heaven's eye by a close-drawn curtain woven of innumerable tree-tops, which shivered in the breezes of summer dawn and broke into wild music of millions upon millions of wakening birds; the concert was prolonged from bough to bough with scarcely a break for hundreds of miles over hill and plain and mountain, unheard by man save where, at rarest intervals, a troop of skin-clad hunters, stone-axe in hand, moved furtively over the ground beneath, ignorant that they lived upon an island, not dreaming that there could be other parts of the world besides this damp green woodland with its meres and marshes, wherein they hunted, a terror to its four-footed inhabitants and themselves afraid.

A glance at any physical map will show how Britain has always thrust out towards the continent of Europe a low coast with an undulating plain behind, easy of access through many havens and navigable rivers. It was only

westward and northward, against the Atlantic, that the
island presented a mountainous and iron-bound coast—
though even there the mouths of Severn, Dee, Mersey,
Clyde and other lesser inlets held the makings of future
history. But, from the earliest ages the flat south and east
coastlines with the plains and low ridges behind them
presented, so long as they were unguarded by a fleet, a
standing temptation to the migratory tribes, pirates, plunderers and traders roaming along the continental shores.

The temptation to invade the island lay not only in the
pearls, the gold and the tin for which it seems to have been
noted among certain Mediterranean merchants long before the foundation of Rome; temptation lay also in its
fertile soil, the rich carpet of perennial green that covered
the downs and every clearing in the forest, the absence
of long interludes of frost that must have seemed miracu-
lous in a land so far to the North before men knew the
secret of the Gulf Stream.[1]

[SEE MAP 1.] The forest of Britain swarmed with big
and small game, and early man was a hunter. Whole
districts, long since drained, were then shallow meres filled
with fowl and fish; the greatest of these fen lands stretched
from future Cambridge to future Lincoln; countless generations of early fowlers and fishermen dropped their tools
and weapons of chipped flint in its waters, or on the
sandy heaths round its margin, for the better instruction
of archæologists. In the age of the shepherd the open
chalk downs of the South were his wealth and his delight,
while the more daring swineherd followed the hunter into
the dark forest below.

[1] Both Cæsar and Tacitus remark on the absence of severe
cold in Britain, though Tacitus adds: 'the sky is overcast
with continual rain and cloud.' The rapid changes of
weather and temperature in Britain, a source of bitter
merriment to its inhabitants in every age, stimulate the
physical and mental energies, and 'make us Englishmen.'
It is, in fact, one of the higher values of the land, but it
can hardly have been one of the temptations to would-be
invaders!

Flints lay about in profusion in many regions, but the best of them were buried in the chalk; shafts thirty feet deep were sunk by the earliest island miners, who laboured down at the bottom with stag-horn picks and shoulder-blades for shovels, hewing galleries through the chalk and extracting the precious flints which then made man the master of the world. The 'palæolithic' or 'old stone' age, with its roughly chipped flints, fades by imperceptible degrees into the 'neolithic' or 'new stone' age, when men had learnt to polish their flint tools and weapons with an admirable perfection.

When, some 2000 years before Christ, the age of bronze gradually began in Britain, followed after more than a thousand years by the age of iron, the metals, too, were found in plenty, with timber at hand to smelt them. Timber grew everywhere for housing and fuel. Fresh water was widely distributed; indeed before the age of draining and well-sinking, it was found more plentifully at high levels than in the South England of to-day. And village sites, from primæval hut circles to the Saxon townships of Domesday Book, were always chosen close to fresh water.

Last, but not least, when man took to ploughing and sowing, the soil was found to yield manyfold in the eastern and southern regions, those sunniest parts of the island where wheat-growing is still generally profitable under the very different world conditions of the modern grain market. Agriculture is the greatest change of all in the early life of man, for it enables him to multiply, fixes him to the home and to the soil, draws him into larger village communities, and thereby renders other inventions and changes more easy. The plough made but a slow conquest of Britian. It reached a definable stage in the latter part of the Saxon epoch, by which time the bulk of the present-day villages had come into existence, at least in embryo, as clearings in the forest. But agriculture had been first introduced in prehistoric times, when it could only be practised in certain carefully chosen localities that were neither marshy nor encumbered by dense forest and under-growth, nor yet mere barren heath.[2]

Such were the attractions of this desirable land. And it stood, obvious to all, as centre to the grand semi-circle of the North European shore that stretches for two thousand miles from Norway to Ushant. From times long before the dawn of history until the Norman Conquest, all the various seafaring tribes who succeeded each other as nomads or settlers on any part of that great coastline regarded Britain as their natural prey. And Britain was the more subject to their attacks because the pressure of the folk wanderings was mainly from the East of Europe to the West. It followed, that for several thousands of years, wave after wave of seagoing adventurous races, or of races pushed behind by other adventurers, was flung upon Britain's southern and eastern shore.

Until each set of new-comers was half-way across the island, the worst natural obstacle they could meet was the widespread woodland and marsh. But where the forest was pathless or the valley too wet, the invader could either row up the river or trek round by the heaths and downs. The high-placed camps, roads and dew-ponds of the primitive peoples, often found where only the sheep and

[2] For instance, in Cambridgeshire, successive civilizations of flint-users had congregated on the sandy heath uplands on the border of the fens where Mildenhall now stands. See Map 1., p. 22, below. But when the bronze and iron ages succeeded to the stone age, the centre of population shifted at last to the upper Cam valley, owing to the greater importance of agriculture. The shores of the upper Cam were not water-logged or forest-bound, and were better soil than the Mildenhall heaths; so population gradually followed the plough upstream. But though the forest narrowly cramped the dimensions of this new domain, no attempt seems to have been made to encroach on the forest area till Roman and Saxon times. Yet this forest area occupied the greater part of the upland country which is now so bare of wood and so characteristic of agricultural Cambridgeshire. See the remarkable works of Sir Cyril Fox —*The Archæology of the Cambridge Region,* 1928, and *The Personality of Britain,* 1943.

plovers now congregate, remind us of the greater part which the bare uplands played in the life of man, before the forests were felled and the valleys drained.

The first serious geographic obstacle appeared when the invader, perhaps in the second or third generation of his advance, at length approached the north or west of the island—the mountain ranges of Wales, of North-West England and of Scotland. Here the pursued might rally and the pursuers be forced to halt. If there had been no such mountain ranges, if England had been all one lowland, each successive invasion would have rapidly overrun the whole island. In that case no racial difference might to-day be discernible such as divides so-called Celtic Britain—Wales and the Scottish Highlands—on the one hand, from the Saxon districts on the other, for the primitive Saxons might have swept right over Wales and crossed into Ireland in the Sixth Century. But in fact the great plains of Ireland were only reached by the English of the Twelfth Century, marshalled under the feudal banner of Strongbow; the mountains of Wales and the Pennines had impeded the first rush of the Saxon immigrants. Much the same thing must have happened long before in many unrecorded Celtic and Iberian invasions. History is governed by geography. If the mountain ranges had stood along the southern and eastern shores of England instead of standing far back to west and north, the tribal invasion of the island from the continent would have been so arduous a task that Britain would not have become the early receptacle for so many different races of vigorous barbarians. The physical formation of a country is the key to the history of its early settlement, especially in days before man had the mastery of nature which he now possesses.

And so, owing to these geographic features of Britain, the same phenomena of tribal invasion were repeated again and again on the same general scheme. Again and again, how often we know not, from the early stone age till the Danish invasions, some race of warriors crossing from some part of what we now call France, Holland, Germany or

Scandinavia, has settled on the rich lowlands of southern
and eastern Britain, killed or subjected many of the older
inhabitants, and driven the rest into the mountains of the
north and west or into the barren and remote peninsula of
Cornwall.

It is thus that we must account for the variety and the
present location of the races that were mingled in Britain
so long ago. Cornwall, Wales and the Highlands of Scotland
are inhabited by the oldest stocks; we call them, to-day,
'the Celtic fringe' of the island. But most of them are pre-
Celtic—as also are the Irish. The Celts, late comers into
western Europe, were tall men, fair or red-haired, who
entered Britain and Ireland only a few hundred years before the coming of Julius Cæsar. The bulk of those whom
we miscall 'Celts' are for the most part dark-haired people
whose ancestors had been in the island thousands of years
before the red Celt was ever heard of. They were the folk
whom Matthew Arnold in his poem describes as 'dark
Iberians,' coming down, 'shy traffickers,' to chaffer with the
Phœnician traders on the shore.

We may conveniently speak of these pre-Celtic peoples,
collectively, as 'Iberians,' though in fact they consisted of
many different races, not all of them dark-haired.[3] Some
'Iberian' blood probably flows in the veins of every modern
Englishman, more in the average Scot, most in the Welsh
and Irish. The Iberians were no mere savages. They raised
themselves, during the long stone and bronze ages in Britain, from savagery onto the first steps of civilized life. At
first hunters and users of flint, then shepherds also, they
naturally learnt the uses to which man can turn the dog,
the sheep, the goat, the ox, the pig; they adopted the use
of metals; they became the men of the bronze age skilled
in weaving and in crafts of many kinds, including agriculture. If in earlier times the largest political unit consisted
of a tribe of a few hundred souls, living in dread of wolves
and bears, and of their nearest human neighbours, the

[3] Some of the pre-Celts were of what archæologists call
the 'Mediterranean,' others of the 'Alpine' race.

Iberians acquired in some parts of the country a much higher political organization, designed gigantic earthworks like the Maiden Castle near Dorchester on a scientific military plan, and reared Stonehenge, no mean engineering feat. Although the earliest of them had come over in coracles or canoes, they learnt to build the 'long-ship' or low war-galley.

Many of these improvements, especially agriculture, metal work and long-ship building, were probably taught to the islanders by merchants from the distant South, or by continental tribes who had learnt from those merchants. The Levant was the cradle of European civilization. The inhabitants of Mesopotamia, Egypt and Crete, in days before Tyre, Athens or Rome, evolved agriculture, metalcraft, shipbuilding and many other of the arts of life. Such Promethean secrets, starting on their journey from South and East, handed on from trader to trader and from tribe to tribe ever northward and westward across the forests of barbarous Europe, or travelling more quickly by merchant galleys round the Pillars of Hercules, reached at last those half fabulous 'tin islands' in the mists and tides of the northern seas.

The trade of Britain with the Levant, or rather of the Levant with Britain, is far older than the Celtic Conquest. English jet found in Spain is believed to date from 2500 B.C. and Egyptian beads found in England from about 1300 B.C. So early, perhaps much earlier, the Mediterranean traders had discovered the British islands with their wealth of pearls and gold, to-day long exhausted, and their metals, not yet at an end. But if these eastern merchants have the credit of bringing civilization to Britain, the Iberian tribesmen had the wit to adapt their teaching.

Either the traders, or else some conquering race, brought from overseas the first weapons of bronze that have been discovered in the island. But since copper and tin both lay near the surface in different parts of the island, particularly Cornwall, the natives were soon taught to smelt the two together and so make bronze for themselves. After that, the end of the long stone age was in sight; it was only a

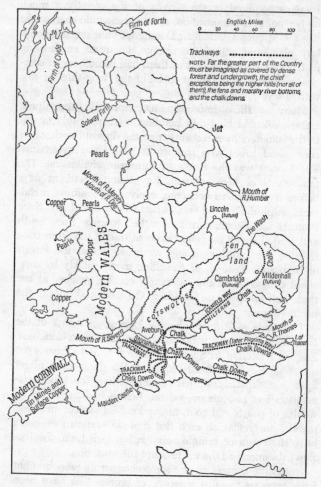

Map 1 Iberian Britain

matter of time before bronze, and iron after it, was lord of all. Some of the islanders attained high technical skill in metal working, and indeed some of the finest enamel work

on bronze that the world contains was produced by these
Iberian ancestors of ours. Many of the centres of this ancient civilization—Stonehenge perhaps—were placed on
sites agriculturally poor, but once famous for the best flints
or for surface gold, tin or copper, long since exhausted.

Trade routes and trade connections grew up within the
island itself between very distant tribes; and there were
ports trading with Ireland for gold, and others that shipped
tin to the continent. Ancient trackways, running along bare
downs and ridges, linked up the various centres of civilization which were otherwise separated by wide morasses and
long leagues of forest. The fortifications were placed chiefly
on the high bare land on the route of the trackways. They
often ran along the edge of the chalk downs below the
top of the tableland but above the marshy and tangled
forest of the plain, like the track along the south edge of
the North Downs, long afterwards called the 'Pilgrims'
Way' to Canterbury, and still at places available to the
pedestrian as it was four thousand and more years ago.

So too, ages before the arrival of the Celt, the Icknield
Way ran along the chalk close under the ridge of the
Chilterns, and was carried on westward by the line of the
downs south of Thames; its object was to join up the fenland and agricultural civilization of East Anglia with the
great downland civilization gathered round the circles of
Avebury and Stonehenge, where man was most thickly
congregated, because there he was most free from the
impediment of forest and of marsh. The forest, still impenetrable save by a few daring hunters, lay deep on both
sides of the Icknield Way. Ideas and arts of vast import
to man have been carried along its springy turf by way-
farers listening anxiously to the noises of the forest, to
distinguish the howl of wolves, the growl of bears or the
yet more dreaded voice of hostile tribesmen.

From the seventh to the third centuries before Christ, the
Celtic tribes, originally occupying North-western Germany
and the Netherlands, were moving across Europe in many
different directions. In the first centuries after Christ the

Teuton tribes, starting from homes rather further to the
East, were destined to move over much the same ground
in much the same manner; but between the folk-wander-
ings of Celt and of Teuton was to be interposed the great
event of the Roman penetration north of the Alps.

The Celts, in their earlier day, showed as much vigour
in migration as any race that came after them. One great
body settled in France and became an important element
in the racial content of the Gaulish nation. A southern wing
settled in the valley of the Po, put an end to the Etruscan
hegemony in Italy, and about 387 B.C. sacked Rome, when
the geese were said to have saved the Capitol. Others
pushed into Spain, others into the Balkans. During the
same centuries a northern wing of this great world movement overran our island and imposed Celtic rule and language on its inhabitants. The Celtic invaders of Britain
came in successive tribal waves, kindred indeed but mutually hostile and each with a dialect of its own. Erse, Gaelic,
and Welsh are still extant variations of the tongues which
they and the Iberians evolved. Wave after wave of Celts,
each entering Britain by the lowlands of south and east,
slaughtered, subdued or chased across the island not only
the Iberians but such of their own kinsfolk as had preceded
them; many of the pursued, as on all occasions in Britain,
found refuge in the mountains to north and west.[4]

[SEE MAP 2.] At least two big waves of Celtic invasion can
be distinguished: first the Gaels or Goidels, still found in
Ireland and Scotland, some of whom may have come over
as early as 600 B.C.; secondly the Cymri and Brythons still
found in Wales. Among the Brythonic peoples were the
Belgæ and other tribes whom Cæsar found spread over
Southern England; they were closely related to the Gauls

---

[4] Professor Chadwick appears to think that the Celts who
came to Britain at various times, probably from Belgium,
Holland and N.W. Germany, were (like the Anglo-Saxons
after them) practically one race, but that they acquired
different cultures and developed different dialects of
Celtic, according to the varying dates of their crossing the
sea, or the variations of their subsequent history and contact with the natives.

beyond the Channel. These Britons seem to have been already settled in the island that is still called by their name, at the time when Pytheas, the Greek traveller from Marseilles, recorded his visit to the 'Pretanic isle' in the days of Alexander of Macedon. [CIRCA 325 B.C.]

The Celts who overran so much of Europe in the last six centuries before Christ were tall, light-haired warriors, skilful in ironwork, which was then replacing bronze, and in arts and crafts of their own, much admired by modern archæologists. Such was the outfit at any rate of the later among the Celtic invaders of Britain. The fair-haired Celts imposed themselves as an aristocracy on the conquered tribes throughout Britain and Ireland. In the end the races mixed, but what proportion the Celtic bore to the old Iberian blood it is impossible to say. In Wales, Cornwall, Ireland and the Highlands of Scotland, the physique and colouring seem chiefly Iberian. The proportion of Celtic to Iberian blood is very small in the Welsh mountains. How far it was the same in the richer eastern portions of Britain at the time of Roman and Saxon invasions, there is no means of determining. It is equally impossible to know what form the Celtic conquerors gave to their economic and social relations with the conquered Iberians. In Wales there long remained traces, which some archæologists at least thought they detected, of a system by which certain hamlets were left to the conquered and others reserved for the conquerors, the former paying a heavier tribute. But it would be rash to conclude that such a system was universal in the island. Slavery or serfdom may have been commoner in the east.

The Celts, like the Iberians before them, remained tribesmen or clansmen, bound together by legal and sentimental ties of kinship as the moral basis of society. Unlike the Saxons after them, they developed no strictly territorial, still less any feudal organization. A thousand years after England had been subjected to Saxon conquests, Wales, Ireland and the Scottish Highlands were in different degrees still governed by the tribal rules of life. And we may be sure that in the palmy day of Celtic lordship in the

British Isles, the Kings were tribal chiefs, rather than territorial or feudal monarchs. Justice was the justice of the clan, which punished and protected its members, exacting on their behalf from other clans either vengeance, or else payment in reparation for injuries done. The Celtic tribes, when the Romans came over, were perpetually at war with one another, but they formed large accretions, each tribe being spread over a considerable area, often equal to several modern counties.

Agriculture continued to progress slowly in the iron age under the Celts, as in the bronze age under the Iberians. Wheat was grown in the south, oats further north—as to-day. The Celt loved to cheer or fuddle his brain with mead—grain fermented with honey. But the acreage under plough was small, for the forests remained unfelled, and those river valleys, like Thames and Trent, where drainage was a necessary prelude to close habitation, remained marshy and sparsely peopled.

Herds of swine wandering by thousands through the virgin oak forests were a feature of Saxon and Norman times and must have been no less a feature of Celtic and pre-Celtic economy. Pig in various forms is still favourite feeding in England, and in primitive times it was the staff of life not only in Ireland but in Britain. Sheep and oxen were perhaps the chief source of accumulated wealth and the chief means of barter. Horses were bred to drag the war chariots of the Celtic chiefs to battle, but the plough was drawn by oxen.

Taking the Celtic island as a whole, agriculture was not the pre-occupation it became in Saxon and mediæval times. Hunting, fishing, herding, weaving, bee-keeping, metal work, carpentry, and, above all, fighting occupied most of the time and thought of a small population scattered wide over a land not yet drained and deforested. The 'trevs' or hamlets of the Celtic families consisted of light structures of timber, wattles, or mud, easily and frequently destroyed in tribal wars. In the West, at least, the population readily moved the site of its 'trevs' to get

fresh pasture and hunting ground, as the Welsh continued
to do until late in the Middle Ages.

'Such agriculture as there was,' says Vinogradoff, 'did
not make people strike deep roots into the soil.' This verdict, though certainly true of the West and of the Midlands, which the Celts left sparsely peopled and still under
forest, is hardly applicable, perhaps, (to certain wheat-
growing districts in the South and East.) Yet even in those
regions it is by no means proved that the Celts ever adopted
the open-field system of communal village agriculture and
the large nucleated township which was established by the
Anglo-Saxons when they, in their turn, occupied these
corn-growing districts. In most parts of the island, at any
rate, the tendency of the Celt was to scatter over the countryside in small family groups, continually subdividing,
each group with its own 'trev' standing in the middle of its
enclosed land, with the waste beyond.[5]

The most advanced regions of the Celtic civilization in
Britain lay in the South and South-East. There were the
best grainlands, the open pastures of the downs, the iron
mines and forges of the Sussex Weald, the Channel ports
and shipping (though London as yet counted for nothing),
the easiest communications with the Mediterranean traders and with the Celtic kinsmen overseas. Though there
was no town-life proper in the whole island, the largest
assemblies of huts were probably to be found near St. Albans and Colchester. Already 150 years before Christ,
south British tribes had a gold coinage of their own, imitated from the gold *stater* of the Kings of Macedon.[6] In the
last century before Christ the British Belgæ and other
southern tribes were in close political intercourse with their
brethren of Northern Gaul; some of them had even for a

[5] See note at end of chapter.

[6] Examples can be seen exhibited in the coin room of the
British Museum. The bronze shields, bronze and iron
weapons, and gold ornaments in the neighbouring hall and
in the iron-age room in the same Museum give some idea
of the skill and wealth of the Iberian and Celtic civilizations
in Britain.

few years acknowledged a King of the continental Belgæ as their suzerain. When, therefore, they learnt that the Romans were marching to subdue the north Gallic tribes, the Britons sent over ships and men who fought against Cæsar both by sea and land. It was one of the causes of his invasion of Britain.

Of Iberian and Celtic religion we know next to nothing save what little can be deduced from the fairy folk-lore of Celts in Christian times. Local gods and goddesses haunted particular springs, caves, mountains, forests and other natural objects, and easily became the local fairies and water-spirits of later times. The most detailed account of the old Celtic religion by a contemporary was written by Julius Cæsar. His imagination was stirred by the power of the organized caste of priests—the Druids—strong in Gaul and strongest in Britain; they had all education in their hands, they administered justice in the courts, and placed recalcitrant laymen under interdict. 'Persons thus excommunicated,' writes Caesar, 'are held impious and accursed; men will not meet or speak with them.' The power of the priesthood was distasteful to the Roman patrician, for Rome had not yet bowed her neck to the hierarchies from the East. 'All the Gauls,' he observes, 'are as a nation much given to superstition, and, therefore, persons afflicted by severe illness or involved in wars and danger either make human sacrifices or vow to do so, and use the Druids as their ministers in these ceremonies.' 'The Germans,' he adds, 'differ much from the Gauls in these customs. For they have no Druids to preside over their religion.' And if Cæsar had known the Anglo-Saxons and the Norsemen he might have said the same of them. The paganism of the Celts in France and Britain was a religion of fear and priest-craft as compared to the paganism of those other barbarian races destined to wrest from them the supremacy of the island.[7]

BOOKS FOR FURTHER READING: H. J. Mackinder, *Britain and the British Seas*; Donald Mackenzie, *Ancient Man in Britain*; Sir Cyril Fox, *Archæology of the Cambridge*

[7] *Cambridge Mediæval History*, Vol. II. Chap. XV.

Region, 1928, and *The Personality of Britain*, 1943; Vinogradoff, *Growth of the Manor*, Bk. I., Chapter I., and Bk. II., Chapter II.; Oman, *England before the Norman Conquest*, Chapters I.–II.; Quennell, *Everyday Life in Prehistoric Times*; Hippisley Cox, *The Green Roads of England*.

NOTE (See p. 27, above.): Celtic custom was probably one reason why the West of England has always been, from very early times, a land of enclosed fields and small hamlets. But much must also be allowed for the nature of the soil. For even the Nordic invaders did not establish the open-field system and the large nucleated township in districts not suited to agriculture on the large scale—not for instance on the moors of the North, or in the fruit gardens of Kent, or in districts that remained largely woodland. But the Saxons did establish the open-field and the large nucleated township in most of the East and Midlands. The question is—had the Celts the open-field system and the nucleated village in those eastern cornlands, afterwards taken over by the Saxons? Seebohm thought that they had, and Vinogradoff that they had not. There is no certain evidence. 'Air photography' of areas in Wiltshire and Hampshire produces results said to be unfavourable to Seebohm's hypothesis, and to indicate Celtic methods of enclosure and agriculture which the Romans left unaltered but the Saxon conquerors superseded. See O. G. S. Crawford, *Air-Survey and Archæology*.

CHAPTER TWO

Roman Britain

The Roman occupation intervened between the coming of the Celt and the coming of the Saxon, and delayed the latter for perhaps two hundred years. Celt, Saxon and Dane came over to slaughter or expel the inhabitants and settle in their place, but the Romans came to exploit and govern by right of superior civilization. In this they resembled the Europeans in Africa rather than the Pilgrim Fathers in America. Yet the natives of Britain were white men, capable of adopting Latin ways more fully than most Africans are capable of adopting the ways of Europe. Nor, on the other hand, had the Gauls and Britons an elaborate

civilization of their own, like the inhabitants of the Greek
and Oriental lands subject to the Roman sway. And, therefore, once the Roman conquerors had glutted their first
rage for plunder, their main effort was to induce their
Western subjects to assimilate Latin life in all its aspects.
Their success with the Gauls was permanent, and became
the starting point of modern European history. But in
Britain, after a great initial success, they had complete
ultimate failure. 'From the Romans who once ruled Britain,'
wrote Haverfield, the great student of the archæology
of the occupation, 'we Britons have inherited practically
nothing.'

In the end the Romans left behind them here just three
things of value: the first of these would have amused or
shocked Cæsar, Agricola and Hadrian, for it was Welsh
Christianity; the second was the Roman roads; the third, a
by-product of the second, was the traditional importance
of certain new city sites, especially that of London. But the
Latin life of the cities, the villas, the arts, the language
and the political organization of Rome vanished like a
dream. The greatest fact in the early history of the island
is a negative fact—that the Romans did not succeed in
permanently Latinizing Britain as they Latinized France.

Julius Cæsar won his place in the history of the world
by a double achievement—the political renovation of the
Roman Empire and its extension into northern Europe. He
planted the power of the Mediterranean peoples broad
and firm on the north side of the Alps, making Gaul a
Latin country for ever. And he showed how the outworn
machinery of the ancient world could be reconstructed on
new principles, by converting the provincial-minded Roman Republic, tossed about between a selfish aristocracy
and a debased city mob, into a disciplined and catholic-
minded Empire of the Civilized World, at once popular
and despotic. When his successors had rebuilt the Roman
State on these lines, its life was renewed for another five
hundred years in the West, and another fifteen hundred
in the Near East. The Cæsarean Empire became the link
between the ancient and modern world. It secured that

enough of the influence of Greece and Rome should survive to give some degree of common culture to the races composing the future Europe. It became the arena for the propagation of Christianity, which travelled to the four corners of civilization by the roads built and guarded by the Roman soldiers.

In order of time, Cæsar's work in Gaul was the prelude to his work for the Empire as a whole. And the subjugation of Gaul was only half accomplished when he found himself one day gazing across the Dover Straits. He surveyed the white cliffs like Napoleon, but with other thoughts in his head: for there was nothing to impede a visit to the island and nothing to prevent his safe return; the only question was whether it was worth his while to make the voyage, with more important work on hand.

His decision to invade Britain was not taken in the hope of setting up a Roman administration on the spot. He had neither the time nor the men to spare for that; his military position in Gaul, his political prospects in Italy were too precarious, for the rulers of the Republic loved him as little as the Senators of Carthage had loved Hannibal. But as leader of the opposition party, playing to the gallery in Rome, he had need of showy exploits; and he had need of tribute and slaves to enrich his partisans, pay his soldiers and fill his war-chest. An invasion of Britain might answer all these requirements. Besides, the tribes of North Gaul and South Britain were so closely allied that Gaul would be more submissive if its neighbour were constrained to pay tribute and to fear the mighty name of Rome. At least some first-hand knowledge of the politics and geography of the island was necessary for the would-be governors of Gaul.

[B.C. 55.] As a military undertaking his first expedition was a failure. He took too small a force, and scarcely moved ten miles inland from the Dover Straits. In the next year's invasion [B.C. 54.] on a larger scale, he won several battles, forded the Thames in the face of the enemy and penetrated into the Hertfordshire territories of Cassivelaunus, King of the Catuvellauni. That tribe was dom-

inant in southern Britain, and the jealousies caused by its
hegemony turned some of its rivals and subjects into allies
of the Roman invader, both in the time of Julius and a
hundred years later during the Claudian conquest. But
many of the Britons, including the men of Kent, put up a
stout fight against Cæsar, and though their undisciplined
infantry were useless against the 'legion's ordered line,'
the yellow-haired, athletic aristocracy of the Celts in their
scythed chariots clattered down the war-ways of the battle
like heroes of Homer, in a manner disconcerting even to
the veterans of the Tenth. The chariot, however, had seen
its day as a method of warfare; it had already been
abandoned in Celtic Gaul as well as in the Hellenized East,
and the British chiefs would have been more truly formidable if they had taught themselves to fight as cavalry. But
the island never had the luck to be defended by an
aristocracy trained to fight from the saddle, until the Norman conquest acclimatized the mediæval knight.

The expedition of 54 B.C., though not a failure like that
of the year before, was no great success. As Cicero complained to his cronies, the famous British gold was secured
in very inadequate quantities; the slaves were too ignorant
to fetch fancy prices in the market, and there had been
neither the time nor the means to carry off rebellious clans
wholesale to the auctioneer, as was Cæsar's practice in
Gaul. The expedition had no permanent results, except as
a memory on both sides of the Channel. The tribute soon
ceased to be paid. The rising of Vercingetorix, which
proved the real crisis of the war in Gaul, put an end to
Cæsar's further plans for Britain, if he had any. Then the
long Civil Wars, followed by the reorganization of the Empire under Augustus and Tiberius, gave the distant island
a hundred years of respite.

The conquest of Gaul by Julius Cæsar, more decidedly
than his invasions of Britain, had brought the South British
tribes into the orbit of Latin civilization. They were of the
same race and political group as the northern Gauls, and
the Gauls were now Roman subjects, many of them Roman

citizens. A peaceful penetration of the island resulted from the work of Cæsar, and prepared the way for the conquest under Claudius. The hundred most important years in the history of the world were not wholly a blank even in Britain. While Julius was being murdered and avenged, while the loves of Antony and Cleopatra were raising the question of the relations of East and West inside the Roman world, while Augustus was cannily constructing the Empire, while Christ was preaching and while Paul was being converted, far in the north Roman traders and colonists, working from the base of the Latinized province of Gaul, were establishing settlements in the interior of Britain and gaining influence at the courts of its tribal Kings.

Shakespeare's Cymbeline, unlike his Lear, was no myth. From 5 to 40 A.D. he reigned over the Catuvellauni, and so far increased their hegemony in the south of the island as to style himself on his silver coinage 'Rex Brittonum.' The use of the Roman language in his title is all of a piece with the good relations he cultivated with the Emperors Augustus and Tiberius. Just as Edward the Confessor prepared the way for the Norman Conquest by introducing Norman knights and clergy into England and making French fashionable at Court, so Cymbeline encouraged Roman traders and craftsmen to colonize the towns of Britain, and familiarized the leading tribesmen with the Latin language and civilization. Cymbeline moved his capital from Verulamium[1] near St. Albans to Camulodunum (Colchester) in the territory of the subjugated Trinovantes, whence his mint poured out gold coinage of the Roman type in great profusion.

To his reign, perhaps, belongs the origin of London as a city. Finds have been made in the river bed which suggest that the first edition of London Bridge may have been erected in timber before the Roman Conquest but during

---

[1] It is my general practice to use modern place-names as conveying more to the reader. But 'Verulamium' cannot be rendered 'St. Albans' without implying an identity of site which is remarkably not the case.

the age of Roman influence. It was perhaps during this transitional period that London began to exist at the bridge-head on the northern shore. There was certainly a place of some kind known as London at the time of the invasion under Claudius.

In any case the city that was to play so great a part first in English and then in world history, attained its original importance under the Roman rule. The name of London is Celtic, but it was not a great centre of Iberian or of Celtic civilization: in Cæsar's time and long afterwards, Middlesex was a forest, and much of future London a marsh.[2] But a bluff of hard ground afforded a good bridge-head where roads from the Kentish ports could cross the river and spread out again thence on their journeys north-ward and westward over the island. It was also the best landing-place for continental commerce coming up the estuary of the Thames. The bridge and port coincided in situation, and their geographic coincidence made the greatness of London.

The Romans, after they had conquered the island, made the fortune of London Bridge by concentrating upon it one-half of their great roads, from both north and south. And they made the fortune of London port by creating an extensive commerce with the Continent, which found in the long-neglected Thames the best means of entry. London was the point at which goods from Europe could be unshipped well inside the land, and sent to its most distant parts by roads planned not for the local needs of tribes but for the imperial needs of the province. The principal exports of Roman Britain, with which she pur-chased the luxuries of the world, were tin, skins, slaves, pearls and sometimes grain.

London became larger and richer under the Romans than she ever was again after their departure, until near

---

[2] The modern levels of London streets lie from five to twenty feet above the original London clay (or water). Town levels are always rising. Much of modern London was once a swamp or lake. On the difficult problems of London origins, see *London*, T. W. Page.

the Norman Conquest. The Roman walls enclosed an area corresponding very closely to the walls of the City in mediæval times, which were in fact only the Roman walls restored. In both periods London was a commercial, not a governmental centre. Officially she ranked lower in the Roman hierarchy than much smaller and less important towns.

It was under the Emperor Claudius, a century after Cæsar's exploring expeditions, that the actual conquest of the island took place. For many years it had been demanded and planned, as readers of Horace remember. As soon as there was an Emperor with a forward policy and leisure to carry it out, he was sure to annex those Celtic lands that lay beyond the Channel, and so round off his Gallic territories. Traders who had settled in Britain, courtiers and soldiers greedy for a fresh supply of slaves, lands and offices, were all agog for annexation. They were right in supposing it would not be very difficult. National resistance was out of the question among chiefs already half Romanized, and many of them bitterly resenting the domination of the Catuvellauni. A battle for the passage of the Thames estuary [A.D. 43.] and a march on Colchester sufficed to reduce the old empire of Cymbeline in the south-east of the island. Another year or two of fighting reduced the Belgæ of Wilts and Somerset, and the Durotriges of Dorset with their great earthwork fortresses. The Midlands, from Bucks to Warwickshire, were still forest land, too thinly peopled to resist. It was only when the legionaries found themselves on the edge of the Welsh mountains and the northern moors that the Romans, like every other successful invader of Britain, began to meet with serious difficulties. In 60 A.D. they were still struggling with the first stages of the Welsh problem; after coasting round the edge of the Snowdon massif, the legionaries were engaged, on the low-lying island of Anglesey, in the slaughter of the Druids and their fanatical followers, when news reached them that a great rebellion had broken out in their rear.

The rising of Boadicea is the exception that proves the rule of the easy submission of East and South to Roman influence. It was due to the exceptionally gross misconduct of the first exploiters of the conquest, who treated the Iceni and Trinovantes, by no means altogether unfriendly to Rome, much as the worser type of Englishman treated Bengal after Plassey, before the proper organization of the British raj had been undertaken by Clive and Hastings. The anger of the Iceni against wholesale confiscation and plunder was given dramatic intensity by the personal outrages inflicted on their Queen Boadicea and her family. The Celtic[3] fury was roused against Rome and the Romanizing Britons congregated in Colchester, Verulamium and London, where the patriots put many thousands of men and women to death with savage tortures and mutilations. The great number of these victims, although the traditional 70,000 be an exaggerated estimate, confirms other evidence that the Latinization of these cities had been in process before the conquest of seventeen short years back.

Returning from Anglesey by forced marches, the legionaries, as so often before, broke in a great battle the undisciplined and short-lived ardour of the Celtic onset. The late massacre was avenged with frightful severity on the Iceni of Norfolk, whose land did not recover for generations from the destruction then wrought. Boadicea took poison. The Roman system was re-established in south and east Britain, and ere long was marked with more justice towards the natives. The towns which the Iceni had destroyed were soon more flourishing than ever, especially London, growing yearly as the centre of a new system of North European commerce. The leading Britons of the rising generation, abandoning the habits of free warriors,

[3] Henceforth I use the word 'Celtic' in its usual popular sense to denote the admixture of Celtic and older Iberian. Boadicea, with her golden hair, was of the Celtic aristocracy in the stricter sense. Her real name was 'Boudicca,' but Cowper and Tennyson have familiarised the world with the more euphonious 'Boadicea.'

wore the toga with pride and learned to take delight in
Roman manners, language and art.

But there remained the problem of the North-West frontier. Until some effective system of military control had
been established over the Welsh mountains and the northern moors, warlike tribes would be continually descending
from those reservoirs of savagery to plunder the demilitarized inhabitants of city and villa in the plains below.

The Roman armies who for so many generations addressed themselves to this problem, were very different
from the warrior swarms of Celt, Saxon and Dane, very
different too from the feudal host of Norman times. A Roman
army was a highly drilled, long-service force, held together
under strict discipline all the year round and from year to
year, accustomed, when not fighting, to fatigue duty in
building roads, bridges and forts. Unlike the other invaders of Britain, the Romans did not achieve their conquests
by indiscriminate slaughter and destruction, nor by usher-
ing in a host of farmer immigrants, nor by the erection of
private castles. Their method of conquest was to make
military roads, planned on system for the whole island,
and to plant along them forts garrisoned by the regular
troops. It was thus that the legions were able, after a first
check, to do what the Saxons failed to do, and the castle-
building Norman Barons only did after long centuries,
namely, to subjugate and hold down the Welsh mountaineers. They could not Romanize the mountains as they
Romanized the eastern and southern plains, nor plant cities
at the foot of Snowdon and Plynlymmon. But by means of
roads and forts they had made an effective military occupation of Wales within five-and-thirty years of their
landing.

Devon and Cornwall they neglected, as an area too small
and isolated to be dangerous. Roman remains are scarce
beyond Exeter. But Somerset played an important part in
the new Britain. Within six years of the Claudian invasion,
the new Government was working the Mendip lead-mines.
And the waters of Aquæ Solis soon made Bath the centre

of fashion, luxury and leisure for Romano-British society, desperately resolved to reproduce under leaden skies the gay, lounging life of Imperial Rome.

But the real difficulty of the frontier problem, never wholly solved, lay in the North. Between Tyne and Humber lay the moorlands of heather and white grass that we know, varied in those days by vast forests of brushwood, birch and dwarf oak destined to disappear before the nibbling of sheep when the wool trade developed in a later England. In those desolate regions the savage Brigantes refused to listen to the voice of the Roman charmer, or to lay aside their native habits and warlike aspirations. Beyond them, in modern Scotland, lay the Caledonians, of Pictish and other race, partly Celtic; they were no more submissive than the Brigantes, and were yet more formidable from the remoteness and the physical character of their territory.

It was not till a century and a half had passed after the Claudian conquest that the Emperor Severus marked the final limit of the northern frontier by renovating [210 A.D.] the wall that Hadrian had erected [123 A.D.] from Solway to the mouth of the Tyne. Several times the Romans had tried to conquer Scotland; once under Tacitus' father-in-law Agricola, the great Governor of Britain, with his victory at the 'Mons Graupius' somewhere on the edge of the Highlands [84 A.D.]; once in the reign of Antoninus Pius [140 A.D.]; and once again under Severus himself. But the Romans failed in Scotland as repeatedly and hopelessly as the English Plantagenet Kings. Their failure was due not only to the frontal resistance of the Picts in their waterlogged straths and inaccessible mountains and forests, but to the frequent rebellions of the Brigantes in the rear. Until they abandoned Caledonia, the Romans' line of communication was too long, being exposed to the likelihood of attack all the way from the Humber northwards.

Some well-trenched camps and the ruins of Antoninus' turf wall from Forth to Clyde were all that the legions left behind them in Scotland—except indeed a greater sense of cohesion among the Pictish tribes, inspired by the common purpose of resisting and ruining the Roman Empire with all its walls and works. No attempt was made to add Ireland to the territory of the Cæsars.

The area of true Roman occupation was therefore confined almost exactly to modern England and Wales.[4] But this area was itself divided into two sharply contrasted regions, the Latinized South and East, the barbarian North and West.

North of Humber and Trent, west of Severn and Exe, Celto-Iberian tribalism survived in its more primitive form. This moorland half of Britain, where nearly all the garrison spent nearly all its time, was indeed the chief area of military occupation, but it was nothing more. It was patrolled by some 40,000 men, nearly a tenth of the total forces of the Empire. Their three bases were the great fortresses of York, Chester and Caerleon, each the headquarters of a legion. In Wales, the Pennines, Cumberland and Northumbria, the mail-clad infantry marched and countermarched along the roads they had made from mountain camp to mountain camp, through a sparse and savage population, either hostile or indifferent to their passage. Devon and Cornwall were an isolated pocket of Celtic tribalism. It was in the fruitful plains of the South-East that the Latinized Britons were concentrated, in a peaceful and civilian land, where the sight of a cohort on the march was

---

[4] Except, of course, that the wall of Hadrian and Severus ran along the northern bank of the Tyne, instead of along the crests of the Cheviot Hills. Impressed by the wild moors stretching away from the northern foot of the wall, visitors speak of it as running through a wilderness. In a sense this is true, but the course of the wall is accompanied on the south by the Tyne valley, a natural line of civilization where the modern towns and railway are found. The Cheviot tops, and indeed almost any other line across North England, would have been more difficult for purposes of supply. The Romans, while occupying the wall as their line, normally held a few forts north of it, but south of Cheviot; 'indeed,' says Haverfield, 'we may call Cheviot then (as now) the dividing line between north and south.'

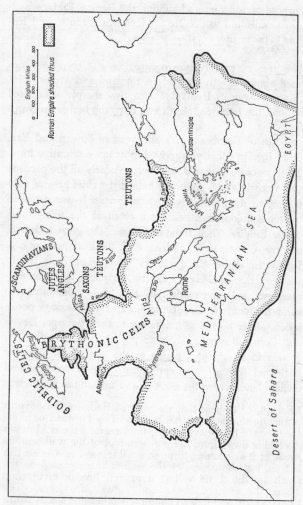

Map 2   The Roman Empire

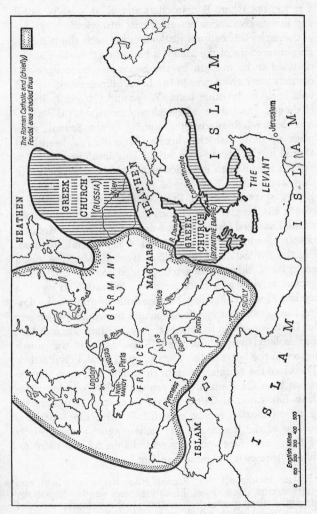

Map 3   Mediæval Christendom, about 1100 A.D.

The Roman Catholic and (chiefly)
Feudal area shaded thus

a rarity, but where Roman cities and villas were plentiful and Roman civilization powerful in its attraction.

Owing to this cultural distinction between the two geographic sections of the island, it happened that the districts destined to be overrun by the Saxon destroyer were the districts most given over to the Latin influences of city and villa life. On the other hand, Wales and Cornwall, Strathclyde and Lancashire, where alone independent Celtic life was destined to survive the coming of the Saxons, were precisely those districts wherein Celtic life had been least altered by the Roman occupation. This accident goes far to explain why Roman influence was permanent in no part of the island.

[SEE MAPS 2 AND 3.] But a second and more general reason can be given for Rome's failure to Latinize Britain as she Latinized Gaul. Britain was too far from the Mediterranean. Southern France is itself a Mediterranean land. But the civilization of the Italian city, the life of the forum and piazza, shivers when transplanted too far north. The ancient world was a Mediterranean civilization. It was the mediæval world that first became truly European, by losing the Levant and North Africa and by winning Germany for Christendom. In the ancient world, Britain was a distant and isolated outpost; in the Middle Ages, it was much nearer to the heart of the Christian and feudal civilization. Therefore the Norman work in the island had more permanence than the Roman. Not enough Italian or Mediterranean folk came to Celtic Britain to change the character of its civilization except superficially. But the superficial success of the Romans in the richest agricultural districts of South and East was very remarkable, all the more remarkable since it proved so transient.[5]

[5] By no means all the 'Roman' merchants, garrison and civil service came from Mediterranean lands. Especially after the first generation, many of the soldiers were of Celtic, Teutonic or other northern origin; in peace time perhaps 1000 to 1500 were paid off every year, but we do not know how many of them settled in the island after they had served their time. Nor is there evidence of any extensive immigration of civilians, though enough traders

The Mediterranean civilization, of which Rome had become the armed missionary, was based on city life. In that respect it differed from the Celtic civilization which it conquered and from the Saxon and feudal civilization that was destined to succeed it. The Roman Empire had grown out of a city state; it had annexed a number of other city states in the Mediterranean, and had planted new cities among the tribes of Gaul. The true life of the Empire lay in the hundreds of walled towns, linked up by military roads, that held together its otherwise unwieldy bulk. From each of these cities it strove to govern and transform the surrounding countryside. And so in south Britain the first thing the Romans did was to build cities.

Besides London and the greater municipalities there were many lesser towns like Silchester, which the Romans planned out in their rectangular fashion, and in most cases protected with stone walls. In these towns even the common workmen talked Latin and were educated enough to read and write it, as we know from the words they scribbled for their amusement on tile and potsherd as they worked, which modern archæologists have dug up and interpreted. It was a high civilization, much more elaborate than anything seen again for many centuries in England. But it was not a native product, sprung from the soil; it was the life of the great cosmopolitan Empire oversea, of which the more progressive among the island tribes were content for a while to become a part.

Beyond the city walls Roman civilization petered away by degrees, through regions of Romano-British 'villadom,' into regions of mere Celtic tribalism. The countryside was sprinkled with smart Roman villas, built of stone in the Italian style, adorned with mosaics, frescoes and baths. Attached to each villa was an estate, worked by slaves, or by *coloni* who were bound to the soil and to its proprietor under rules as harsh as those which bound the mediæval villein. If there was not liberty there was peace. So real was

must have come to teach the language and civilization of the Empire to large sections of the natives. Persons of foreign origin were chiefly gathered in the towns.

the *Pax Romana* in the demilitarized districts of the South-East that these country-houses were not fortified or even protected by a moat, like the mediæval castle and manor house. The only people trained to fight were the soldiers of the regular army: this was one reason why Romanized Britain fell so easy a prey to the invader when men could no longer count on the protection of the legions.

In some of our southern counties, villas are constantly being unearthed; in others they are seldom found. Celtic 'trevs' of the Roman period are occasionally dug up; the ground-plan of the hamlet and the form of the cottage are native, but the inhabitants used pottery and utensils of the Roman type. Celtic arts and crafts had been largely displaced by the prestige of the 'Samian' and other Italian wares, just as European models drive out the native arts of Asia and Africa to-day, not always to the true enrichment of the world. But there is no evidence what language or languages the rural Celts talked, nor how far if at all their land system and habits of life and agriculture had been altered by contact with Rome. To resolve such questions we have little to go upon, and high authorities like Haverfield and Vinogradoff have held more or less divergent views.

The area of agriculture and the area of land reclaimed from forest and fen were both extended in Roman times, at least in some districts, as for instance in Cambridgeshire. But even there the work was only begun; and the Midlands from Bucks to Warwickshire were still left in the main to the forest. The valleys of Thames and Trent, still waterlogged, contained no connected line of important towns and villages as in later days. The Roman did something for deforesting and draining, but the yeoman's work in these matters was left for the stalwart industry of Saxon and Danish townships, extended over a thousand years.[6]

[6] In discussing this matter, it is, however, dangerous to argue from the line of the known Roman roads, as though they indicate the line of cultivation and habitation. The Romans built their great roads from nodal point to nodal point, in order to link up the island regarded as a whole.

Nevertheless in those districts which were already re-claimed for the plough, Roman Britain raised enough grain to export considerably to the continent.

The government of Britain was far from being a rigid and uniform bureaucracy. For the Roman Empire, though at bottom a military despotism standing on the social basis of slavery, was in some respects very liberal. In accordance with its custom, the privileged municipalities in the island not only enjoyed self-government but had jurisdiction each over a rural area about as large as a modern county. There were five such governing cities: Verulamium, Colchester, Lincoln, Gloucester and York; mercantile London, though larger than any of these, had less official status.

The rest of civilized Britain was divided up into cantons, answering to Celtic tribal areas and bearing the tribal names. The cantonal administration was as far as possible centred on some Roman town not of municipal rank. It was characteristic of the Romans that instead of trying to stamp out native tribalism they used it as a means of government, while undermining its spirit by contact with their own more attractive civilization. Every inducement was offered to the Celtic chief to become Roman in dress, language and heart; on these conditions he could remain a Celtic chief in relation to his tribesmen, exercising his authority over them as a togaed Roman official. This policy, which might appear to an iron bureaucrat to be a dangerous concession to tribalism, became in fact the means of Romanizing the Celt with his own good will. The same cantonal system was established in Gaul; but whereas the cantonal names and areas survived the Frankish conquest of Gaul, they disappeared in the more destructive Saxon invasion of Britain.

Just as the Roman Empire, in contrast to some modern nationalist States, was easy-going in its dealings with racial custom in the annexed provinces, and merciless only when

Villages, villas and smaller cities were overlooked by the great road-builders and were served by smaller earth-roads not now specifically known as 'Roman.'

its political power was challenged—so in the sphere of religion, in contrast to the Christianity of the Dark and Middle Ages, the Empire put no shackles on philosophic speculation or on variety in religion, and struck only at those organizations like Druidism and the Christian Church which seemed to challenge its authority as a government. When it persecuted it was not from religious but from political motives. But the persecution of the Christians was not for that reason any less odious or less disastrous in its results, for the intermittent attacks made on the early Church by the Empire must have greatly helped to engender the persecuting spirit which the Church herself showed the moment that she got the upper hand, and which continued for fifteen hundred years to be the bane of Christendom. The persecution of Christians in Britain was probably on a small scale, for the Church there was on a small scale, but the story of St. Alban's martyrdom remains as the symbol of the fact.

Where the Empire detected no challenge to its authority, it embraced with open arms all local variations of polytheism, and attempted to identify the Celtic tribal deities and local nature-spirits with gods of its own Græco-Roman pantheon—itself an amalgamation made on similar principles. Zeus-Jupiter was not 'a jealous God,' and polytheism in all its various forms may almost be regarded as a single religion, whereas Judaism, Christianity and Mohammedanism are mutually exclusive. Although the Druidical priesthood had been suppressed as politically dangerous, the natives of Britain continued freely to worship their old deities, together with those of the Romans, while the polyglot army on the wall honoured all the gods of the far-flung Empire, but most of all the Roman gods, and strange Oriental cults like Mithraism. These latter had become important in the life of the Western Mediterranean, and undoubtedly prepared the way for the general acceptance of another mystic religion from the East.

Constantine made Christianity the official creed of the Empire a hundred years before the withdrawal of the legions from Britain; but even so the new cult does not

seem to have spread rapidly in the most distant of the
provinces, if we are to judge from the small quantity of
Christian remains unearthed in Romano-British sites. There
was, however, enough of it to survive among the Welsh
when every other Roman institution disappeared, because
after the departure of the Roman generals and officials,
the Christian missionaries, alone among the emissaries of
civilization, did not desert the Britons in their day of
trouble.

BOOKS FOR FURTHER READING: Haverfield, *The Roman
Occupation of Britain*, revised by G. Macdonald, 1924, and
Haverfield in *Cambridge Mediæval History*, I., Chapter
XIII. R. G. Collingwood, *Roman Britain*; Hume Brown,
History of Scotland, Chapter I. Roman chapters of works
of Oman, Cyril Fox, Vinogradoff, as above, pp. 28–29; R.
E. M. Wheeler, *Prehistoric and Roman Wales*, 1925; Col-
lingwood and Myres, *Roman Britain and the English Set-
tlements* (*Oxford History of England*, Vol. I.), 1936.

CHAPTER THREE

Beginning of the Nordic invasions. The Anglo-
Saxon Conquest

The settlement of the Nordic peoples in our island is the
governing event of British history. The various irruptions
of Anglo-Saxons and Jutes, of Danes and Norsemen form
a single chapter; it has its prelude in the first plundering
raids of Saxon pirates on the coast of Roman Britain well
before 300 A.D., and it ends about 1020 when Canute completed the Scandinavian conquest of England by reconciling on equal terms the kindred races of Saxon and Dane.
Between these dates the racial character of the inhabitants
of the country was fundamentally altered. It has since undergone slight continuous modification by the arrival of
Norman, Flemish, Huguenot, Hebrew, Irish and other immigrants. But the racial basis was fixed by the time of
Canute.

The Nordic invasions are more important than the Roman interlude, more important even than the Norman Con-

quest. The attempt of the Romans to Latinize the Celtic
civilization in Britain broke down because there were too
few Romans. And the attempt of the Norman-French aristocracy and clergy to Gallicize England, though it had
great and permanent consequences, was gradually abandoned in face of the facts of race, just as the attempt to
Anglicize Ireland has recently been abandoned for the
same cause. The Nordic conquest of England had larger
permanent results than any of these conquests, because it
was secured on a general displacement of Celtic by Nordic
peoples in the richest agricultural districts of the island.
The distinctive character of the modern English is Nordic
tempered by Welsh, not Welsh tempered by Nordic. In
Scotland the Celtic element is racially stronger, but in Scotland also the Nordic language and character have prevailed.

..Objection may be taken to the word 'Nordic,' as to all
terms invented in after times for historical purposes. But
to give a just conception of British history, a single word
must sometimes be employed to cover the German, the
Anglo-Saxon and the Scandinavian races. And to use the
word 'Teuton' or 'German' for this purpose is to give an
undue prominence to one part of the whole. The Teutons
or Germans whom the Romans knew and feared under
those names on the Rhine border and in Southern Europe,
were indeed of the same great stock and culture as the
Anglo-Saxons and Scandinavians, and a common term must
be employed for all three. But to employ for this purpose
the word 'Teuton' or 'German' suggests to the mind a people with the characteristics of the landward tribes who
were engaged in pushing down the barriers of the Roman
Empire to south and west—the Franks who conquered and
gave their name to Gaul; the Goths, Vandals and Lom-
bards who broke into Spain, the Balkans, Africa and Italy;
and the Germans who remained in the fatherland. But the
Anglo-Saxons and Scandinavians, with whom our story is
concerned, were the north-eastern and seafaring branches
of this great family, with definite attributes of their own.
Therefore to call the family as a whole by the name of

Teutons or Germans is misleading in its suggestions when we are speaking of the conquest of Britain.

The 'Nordic' race, then, had certain distinctive features which gave a family likeness to the innumerable and widely scattered tribes of Scandinavians, Anglo-Saxons, Franks and Teutons, who ranged, conquering and colonizing, from Ireland to Constantinople, from Greenland to the Desert of Sahara.

They had all originally come from the shores of the Baltic, though the ancestors of Franks, Goths and Vandals had wandered off west and south long before, in the course of the last millennium before Christ. All the kinsmen had much in common: allied languages; the religion of Thor and Woden after which most of the English and some of the German days of the week are called; a body of epic poetry celebrating common racial heroes, like Sigurd or Siegfried known from Iceland to Bavaria, and Beowulf who does in Denmark and Scandinavia deeds sung in an English poem; a common art for decorating weapons, jewellery and objects in daily use, with patterns of great beauty and richness, quite distinct from Græco-Roman art and rather less distinct from Celtic; and lastly, common customs of war and agriculture, varying considerably according to local conditions. There was much therefore to connect German, Anglo-Saxon and Scandinavian. But there is danger in the practice, once prevalent among historians, of applying to our Anglo-Saxon ancestors living on the North Sea and the Baltic in the Fifth Century, descriptions written by Cæsar and Tacitus of the German tribes on the Rhine four or five hundred years before. Modern archæology, armed with the spade, enables us to check this somewhat irrelevant literary evidence.

The Anglo-Saxons settled the greater part of Britain from the Forth to the borders of Cornwall, and the Jutes settled Kent and the Isle of Wight. Some modern scholars think of the Anglo-Saxons as being substantially one people, while others adhere to the distinction drawn by Bede between the Angles and the Saxons. In any case, at the time of their migration to Britain, Angles and Saxons were occupying parts of the coast of modern Denmark and Germany on both sides of the mouth of the Elbe, and the difference between them in language and customs was slight. The Jutes were a smaller tribe, kindred but distinct; they came to Britain either directly from their old home in Jutland, in northern Denmark, or, as some think, from their more recent settlements in Frisia and on the lower Rhine.[1]

Agriculture had been practised in the north-east of Europe ever since the later stone age. Many of the Anglo-Saxon invaders of Britain were farmers seeking richer ploughlands than the sandy dunes, heaths, marshes and forests of the north European shore. But many of them were deep-sea fishermen, seal-hunters and whalers, trained to hardihood in conflict with the storms, the sea-monsters and the pirates then common in the North Sea. Themselves pirates and plunderers when on the war-path by sea or land, they had a high sense of honour and much kindly good-nature in dealings with their own folk at home, as the fragments of their epic poetry testify. Fierce, courageous and loyal, they were accustomed to follow their chosen chiefs with great fidelity on marauding expeditions along all the coasts between Norway and Frisia.

Such were the migratory habits of these amphibious, restless folk in the first centuries after Christ; but we should not call them nomads, for wherever they settled they practised agriculture. The Anglo-Saxon form of government was autocratic Kingship, exercised by some member of a royal family supposed to be descended from the gods, although such autocracy was limited by the custom of the tribe, by the temper of the armed tribesmen, and by the personal qualities of the King himself. There was very little that was slavish in the Anglo-Saxon warrior. But the idea that our 'Teutonic' forefathers when they first came to England were in any formal sense a democracy appears to be erroneous. There were many grades of rank, wealth and freedom among them, and they were ruled by Kings.

[1] See Note (1) at end of chapter.

Pre-eminent among many lesser Kings who bore rule among our ancestors before their migration to England, was Offa, King of 'Angel,' regarded by the best modern authorities as an historical character, though much poetry and legend accumulated round his name. He waged war on the shores of the river Eider, now in Schleswig, but then the southern boundary of the territories of the Angles, against Teutonic tribes to the South. The fanciful may, by a somewhat forced construction, regard Offa's campaigns as the last war waged by the English against the Germans

Until a day more dark and drear,
And a more memorable year.

The Anglo-Saxons at the time of their coming to England had both Kingship and aristocracy. They were not 'farmer republicans.' The only possible basis for a primitive democracy is the strict tie of kinship and the bond of mutual aid to be rendered between all members of a wide clan, for unless he is so protected and supported the peasant falls into debt and thence into dependence or servitude. But even before the migration to Britain, tribalism was yielding to individualism, and kinship was being replaced by the personal relation of the warrior to his chief, which is the basis of aristocracy and feudalism. And this tendency was greatly increased when parts of the tribe migrated from the old continental home, under leaders who had engaged the personal service of warriors of different clans and sometimes of alien race. The English of England have always been singular for caring little about their cousins and ignoring their distant relatives: the very different practice of the Scot is partly due to the fact that he carries more Celtic blood in his veins.[2]

The naval and military organization of a group of migratory Anglo-Saxons, bound for the mouth of Ouse, Trent or Thames, was based not so much on kinship, as on the discipline of a ship's crew, and on the personal attachment of professional warriors to the chief who had organized the

[2] Chadwick, *Origin of English People,* Chap. XII.; Phillpotts, *Kindred and Clan,* pp. 205–276.

expedition. The solid farmers of the tribe may follow afterwards, with the women and children, in case the raid leads to a successful land-settlement. But the spear-head of the invasion is the chief and his followers. He himself wears the boar-shaped helmet and shirt of ring-mail, and wields the jewel-hilted sword of his ancestors, the work of Wayland Smith; he has presented a sword to the captain of each galley, and has given to every man in his train a round wooden shield and a long spear with ashwood shaft and iron head. He has fed them bountifully all winter with flesh, bread and strong drink at the 'ale-board' in his long timber hall, where they have praised him as their good lord, because like Beowulf he 'never slew his heart-fellows in drunkenness.' It is he who has undertaken to lead them this summer where good plunder and better lands are to be won by the shield wall.[3]

Hengist, the Jute, the traditional conqueror of Kent, may or may not partake in his person of the mythical. But at least he stands as the type of these great, forgotten makers of history, the men who in pursuit of their own hearty lusts for gain and for adventure—

[3] The poem of *Beowulf* describes the chief as constantly giving to his followers assembled round the 'ale-board,' not only spears, swords and shields but helmets and shirts or 'byrnies' of ring-mail—the 'hard war-net.' But *Beowulf* was written in an age well after the Conquest of Britain when armour was becoming more plentiful; also the poet would naturally tend to exaggerate the hero's wealth and munificence, like Homer describing the shield of Achilles or the hall of Alcinöus. The early Anglo-Saxon graveyards in England, of the actual period of the invasion, contain iron spear-heads and the iron bosses and handles of the round wooden shields; swords less often; helmets and byrnies practically never. Yet some of the invading chiefs must have worn helmets and byrnies, for these have been found in early treasure caches in the continental homes of the invaders. Doubtless they were too rare and valuable to be buried—for the Anglo-Saxon is practical as well as pious! Their axes were small and not very important weapons. The big battle-axe of Harold and his guard at Hastings was of later Viking origin.

Sharked up a list of lawless resolutes,
For food and diet, to some enterprise
That hath a stomach in't,

and with such help unwittingly founded England and all
that has since come of England in the tide of time. The
bones of these nameless chiefs are dug up to-day in 'early
Anglo-Saxon graveyards,' lying between the rusted shield-
boss and spear-head that expelled Rome from Britain and
drove the Celt into the West. Some of these great unknown
ones must have had what we should now call 'genius' as
'men of action.' For the true life story of a single one of
them, telling why he and his men decided to cross the sea,
where they landed, and in what manner they fought and
wrought and thought—for that how gladly would we give
whole libraries of later record!

But the past is inexorable in its silence. There are no
authentic chronicles of the Saxon Conquest. The Britons in
their refuge among the Welsh mountains relapsed into
Celtic barbarism, and if the priest Gildas wrote for them a
Book of Lamentations in Latin, it answers few of the purposes of history. The heathen Saxon invaders had indeed a
Runic alphabet; it would serve for a charm on a sword or a
name on a stone, but it was not used to take down annals,
or to transcribe the long-lost epics sung by the gleemen in
halls, of which more than one must have told the deeds of
some hero who came seeking Britain over deep water.

The historian has two points of light, and even those are
dim. He sees an orderly Romano-Celtic world late in the
Fourth Century, beginning to fall into chaos. Two hundred
years later he sees a Saxon-Celtic barbarism beginning to
emerge confusedly into the renewed twilight of history,
and he hears the marching chaunt of St. Augustine
and his monks bringing back with them the Latin alphabet and the custom of written record. Between these points
stretches a great darkness. The most important page in our
national annals is a blank. The chief names of this missing
period of history—Hengist, Vortigern, Cerdic, Arthur—may
be those of real or of imaginary men. All that archæology
and history together can do is to indicate—not the date,

leaders, landings and campaigns—but only the general character of the warfare that destroyed Roman Britain and
gave the land to the English.[4]

As early as the latter years of the Third Century, the Romans established a fleet specially charged to defend the
Gallic and British shores against the plundering raids of
Saxon pirates. The Empire was at the same time being
disturbed from within by the wars of its own rival Emperors and armies. In this game the legions quartered in
Britain often took a hand on behalf of their own chiefs. The
most singular of these pretenders was Carausius, the
warden against the Saxon raids, who from 286 to 293 A.D.
ruled the island as a sovereign and independent section
of the Empire, safe behind its own navy. Carausius has
been called 'the first sea-King of Britain.' After the reform
of the Empire by Diocletian and Constantine a few years
later, the reincorporated province of Roman Britain enjoyed a last golden age. An official known as 'the Count of
the Saxon shore' defended the coast from the Wash to
Portsmouth, by the aid of ten large fortresses, of which
Richborough in Kent was the chief, and a considerable
garrison withdrawn for this new purpose from the military
regions of the North-West. Each of the ten fortresses commanded a port, whence a fleet could issue to fight the in-

[4] The most fundamental points are in dispute. High
authorities differ as to whether the Hengist and Vortigern
story is true; whether Wessex was settled from the southern coast or from north of the Thames; whether there was
ever a Roman army of occupation in Britain again after
the 'withdrawal' of 407; when and how London fell;
whether the invasion of the north of England was at all
contemporaneous with that of the south. If anyone thinks
that I am too cautious in refusing either to accept or deny
so many well-known stories, let him read the last chapter of
Haverfield's *Roman Occupation of Britain*, entitled 'Saxon
England,' and the article by Ferdinand Lot at the beginning of *Mélanges d'histoire offerts à M. Charles Bémont*,
1913, besides the well-known passages of controversy by
Sir Henry Howorth, W. H. Stevenson, Chadwick, A. F.
Major, and Bury, *Later Roman Empire*, II. p. 201, etc.

vaders at sea. By this provision the civilized lowlands were rendered secure from Saxon attack for another half century. More villas appear to have been built and occupied in the island from 300 to 350 A.D. than at any other period; while British grain was sold on the Rhine and British cloth in the Levant. Whether or not these symptoms of prosperity imply that British society was in a less miserable economic condition than that into which the 'decurions' and 'coloni' of other provinces of the Empire had by this time fallen, we have no evidence.

In the last half of the Fourth Century the downfall began. As the spade of the archæologist gives proof, life and property then became insecure in the lowland area of Britain. Here and there villas were burnt or deserted, in the track of raiding bands of Picts and Brigantes from the North, or of the wild Irish tribesmen then known as 'Scots,' who swarmed in through the unromanized districts of the West. These local catastrophes were due to the great general cause: the heart of the Empire was weakening under attack nearer home; fewer and worse soldiers and civilians were coming from the continent to serve in Britain. As a consequence, a Celtic revival began, slow at first, but visible even before the final Saxon onrush destroyed the centres of Latin influence in the island. The civil and military connections with the Mediterranean became every year more shadowy, and the unromanized Celts from Wales, Caledonia and Ireland poured down over the land. Before Roman Silchester was abandoned under Saxon pressure, an 'Ogam stone' with a barbarous Celtic inscription had been set up in its streets, portentous to anyone who remembered what Silchester once had been.

In the course of the first thirty or forty years of the Fifth Century, though by what exact stages it is impossible to say, the Romanized Britons found themselves left to their own devices by an Empire that confessed itself unable any longer to help. It was only then that the Saxons became the chief instrument in the destruction of Roman Britain, begun in the previous century by the Celtic barbarians of North and West. We do not know whether or with what success the Saxons had renewed their raids between 350 and 400, but it is clear that at the opening of the new century they came over with increasing numbers and boldness. The state of the island pulverized by Picts and Scots, the breakdown of the true Roman regime, the conduct of the defence by Christian missionaries of a practical turn like St. Germanus in the place of regular Roman generals, —such things must often have been the theme of excited debate in log-built halls of the Anglo-Saxon chiefs, after the return from each successful plundering expedition. Why, the pirate-farmers began to ask each other, as they quaffed the mead, why should we take only what we can carry away? In these favourable new conditions the idea was mooted of wholesale immigration to these warm well-watered lands, rich in grain-fields and in pasture and in oak forests swarming with deer and swine.

As all evidence is wanting, we can only guess that the Saxon conquest was achieved by two distinct types of expedition. On the one hand, in view of the amount of fighting and destruction to be done, there must surely have been bands of warriors unencumbered by women and children, moving rapidly over the island by the rivers and roads, fighting the battles, storming the earth-work camps and stone-girt cities, burning the towns and villas, slaughtering and driving away the Romanized Britons, hurling back into the West the war-bands of rival barbarians from Caledonia and Ireland. But we must also picture to ourselves the shipping over of the families of the invaders, accompanied perhaps by the less war-like of the agricultural population, to take up new homes in the ground thus roughly cleared.

For the Anglo-Saxon conquest, like the Danish settlement in Alfred's day, had two aspects, and to omit either is to misunderstand the Nordic invasions of Britain. Like the Danes after them, the Anglo-Saxons were bloody-minded pirates, rejoicing to destroy a higher civilization than their own, and at the same time Pilgrim Fathers, come to settle on the land and till it themselves, not as mere exploiters and slave masters but as honest husbandmen. If they had not been barbarians they would not have destroyed Roman civilization; if they had not been Pilgrim Fathers their race would not in the end have replaced it by something better.

The rivers, deeper and more navigable than they are to-day, were the main routes by which the English first penetrated into the interior of the country henceforth to be called by their name.[5] The undecked galleys of shallow draught, in which they had so daringly crossed the North Sea, could be rowed far upstream into the very heart of the country, and then left under a guard in some island among the marshes or behind a palisade of stakes hastily cut from the forest. The rest of the disembarked war-band could then march across Britain with fire and sword. Such, as we know, was the method of the Danish invaders in the time of Alfred, and such probably was the method of the Anglo-Saxon invaders before them.

When once the Roman military system had collapsed, the Roman roads only served to hasten the pace of conquest and destruction. It was indeed by the side of rivers and not by the side of roads that the new race made its first settlements, as their earliest relics show, but the roads must greatly have assisted their wholesale conquest of the island.[6] One can see them, padding along the stone causeway, heavily laden with plunder but lightly burdened with the panoply of war. Laughing at their luck, they turn aside to sack a villa descried amid the trees. As the flames shoot up, the pampered cock pheasant, imported by the Roman

[5] For this statement we have the direct archæological evidence of the early Anglo-Saxon graveyards, which are nearly all situated either on some navigable stream or on a tributary leading directly from it. See Thurlow Leeds, *Archæology of the Anglo-Saxon Settlements*, pp. 17–19.

[6] Mr. Thurlow Leeds (*History*, July 1925) argues that the primæval Icknield Way (see Map 1., p. 22, above), which had been kept in use under the Romans, helped to draw the invaders along from the Wash to the upper Thames and so led to the foundation of Wessex from the North-East.

to adorn his terraces, frightened now by the shouting of
the barbarous seamen, scuttles off into the forest; he will
there become a wild bird of the chase, destined to play a
great part in the social history of the island through many
changing centuries.

We can say of these Saxon warriors, as they emerge for
the first time on the great stage of history, that they, like
their descendants, are 'a warlike but not a military people.' A spear and wooden shield apiece, with a few swords
among them, here and there a helmet, and perhaps one
mail shirt to every thousand men,[7] sufficed them to conquer the island. Yet the Latinized Britons should have
been able to pit against them the disciplined infantry, the
body-armour, the missile weapons and the cavalry of later
Roman warfare. We do not in fact know whether the defenders fought principally in the Roman or in the revived
Celtic fashion, when their half mythical King Arthur led
them to battle against the 'heathen swarming o'er the
Northern sea.' But in whatever manner the Britons fought
they were conquered by foot soldiers without the discipline of the barracks, without body armour or missile
weapons, but with prodigious energy and purpose. The
defenders had the further advantage of formidable camps
and steep earthworks crowned by stockades, very numerous all over Britain, besides the stone-walled Roman cities.
But one by one all obstacles went down before the half-
armed barbaric infantry landed from the long-ships.

We noticed in the last chapter, as a peculiarity of the
Roman system in its best days, that no class in the peaceful South and East of the island had been trained to self-
defence. The magnate of the villa, unlike the feudal lord
of later times, was not a fighting man; he had no fighting
train and no fortified mansion. Many of the cities indeed
were defended by magnificent stone walls, but their citizens were not accustomed to war like a burgher militia
in the Middle Ages. If the Roman world was more civilized
than the mediæval, it was proportionately more incapable

[7] See note, p. 52, above.

of local self-help if anything happened to the central government and to the regular army. Indeed, the feudal system gradually arose out of the welter of barbarian invasions, precisely to remedy this vital defect in the social organism.

The most recent historical theory of the Saxon Conquest is that the great work of destruction was accomplished, not by each small tribal band as it settled down in its own particular district, but by a 'host' of many bands acting together under a united military command. We know that the Danish marauders in Alfred's day were wont to sweep over the island in a composite 'host' obeying for awhile a single leader. The Danish analogy, though suggestive, is not direct evidence as to the size of the Anglo-Saxon bands and their relation with each other. But Gildas, the vague and tearful British historian of these disasters, writing about 540 A.D., rather more than a hundred years after the serious beginning of the conquest, appears to believe that destruction advanced rapidly across the centre of the island till it touched the Western sea at some point, and that the invaders then withdrew to some extent from the West, leaving blank ruin behind. If this actually occurred in the middle and latter part of the Fifth Century, it would explain why the Roman cities and villas of the Midlands and the Middle West were destroyed long before the English invaders took up their permanent abode in those parts. Antiquarian research has proved that Bath, for instance, lay in ruins, its fashionable pools choked up with thickets and inhabited by waterfowl, long before the Saxons settled there, and long before the date 577, which the doubtful authority of the Anglo-Saxon Chronicle gives for the final capture of Bath. All this is easy to understand if there was a destructive rush of the invading 'host' across the island at an early date, followed by partial withdrawal. The Midlands, sparsely peopled in Roman times, may have been left for awhile as no-man's land, a belt of destruction already lost to Latin civilization and not yet reclaimed by Saxondom. According to this theory the English 'host,' after its first great advance, retired from the West and dissolved

into its component parts, of which each proceeded to found
a Kingdom in the East of the island, and to busy itself
with the work of land settlement, married life and farming.

Such then is the theory of the advance and retreat of the
'host,' based on the Danish analogy, on the hysterical ex-
pressions of Gildas, and on the established fact of very
widely spread destruction at an early date. The theory
cannot be regarded as either proved or disproved. It en-
joys more favour at present than the older view enshrined
in the classic pages of Green, which was based on the
much later traditions of the Anglo-Saxon Chronicle.[8] This
theory ascribed the work of destruction, as well as that
of reconstruction, to isolated English bands, each working
by itself in its own area. Possibly there may be some truth
in both views. They are not mutually exclusive. During the
conquest of the island from the Forth to the Channel, there
was time and space for many different happenings. But it
is wise to confess that we do not know.

Whether the bands of invaders were small or great,
whether they acted separately or in concert, the destruction which they wrought was prodigious. The tradition of
the Welsh Christian remnant is summarized in the words
of Gildas the priest:—

Every colony is levelled to the ground by the stroke of the
battering ram. The inhabitants are slaughtered along with
the guardians of their churches, priests and people alike,
while the sword gleamed on every side, and the flames
crackled around. How horrible to behold in the midst of
the streets the tops of towers torn from their lofty hinges,
the stones of high walls, holy altars, mutilated corpses, all
covered with lurid clots of coagulated blood, as if they had
been crushed together in some ghastly winepress. . . . Of
the miserable remnant some flee to the hills, only to be
captured and slain in heaps: some, constrained by famine,

[8] The Anglo-Saxon Chronicle, begun at King Alfred's
order, is of course excellent authority for the Danish invasions and subsequent events with which its various
authors were contemporary, but is less good for the conquest four hundred years before. But its value has been
perhaps underestimated. See *The Rise of Wessex*, by T.
Dayzell Reed.

come in and surrender themselves to be slaves for ever to
the enemy. . . . Others wailing bitterly pass overseas.

The destruction of the Roman cities and villas was
wholesale and almost universal. The early Anglo-Saxons
were not city dwellers. They had no mercantile instincts
except for selling slaves overseas, and they lost their old
sea habits when they had won themselves good farm lands
in the interior. The most civilized of their desires was to
settle in large rural 'townships' and to till the soil on the
open-field system of village agriculture. That was to be the
sound basis of the new English civilization. Directed by
this instinct, they began at once to build for themselves log
houses grouped round the log hall of the lord. Split trunks
of forest timber, set vertically side by side, composed the
walls, for timber was there in plenty and they were no
slovens at work.[9] Such were the homes in which they had
lived beyond the sea, and they preferred the familiar
touch and smell of the walls of split oak to the nice villas
and town houses, fitted with every modern convenience,
which they might have occupied at their will as soon as
they had buried the corpses of the late owners.

We are told on the highest authority that 'no case is
known where Saxons dwelt in a Roman villa.'[10] Time and
spade may reveal some such cases, but they are scarcely
likely to be numerous. And as with the villas so with the
cities; the newcomers showed the same unwillingness to
live or to let anyone else live within the ramparts of stone.
In some cases indeed the sites had been rendered so important by natural advantages or by the convergence of
imperishable Roman roads, that they could not permanently be deserted. Chester, Bath and Canterbury were
reoccupied in the course of time; it is uncertain whether
London, Lincoln and York were ever completely abandoned or not, though it appears that they ceased for some

[9] It was only as timber became rather more scarce, that
houses began to be built of 'half-timber,'—a wooden 'fram-
ing' to be filled in with cheaper material. Baldwin Brown,
Arts in Early England, I., 26; II., 37–42.

[10] See note (2) at end of chapter, p. 72.

generations to be of any size or consequence. The junction of Roman roads and river passages ensured the ultimate greatness of London, Cambridge and various other places as soon as civilization began to make any recovery at all. There at least time and barbarism could not permanently obliterate the work of Rome.

But Silchester, Wroxeter, Verulamium and many other towns ceased for ever to be inhabited. St. Albans stands half a mile from the site of Verulamium, on the other side of the river; it is as though the old site had been purposely avoided. Villas and cities are constantly being dug up out of the ground, in places given over to tillage, pasture or moor. But for some centuries the Roman ruins must have stood, as familiar a sight as the roofless abbeys under the Stuart Kings, a useful stone quarry sometimes by day, but at night haunted in the imagination of the Saxon peasant by the angry ghosts of the races that his forefathers had destroyed. Fear lest the dead should rise shrouded in their togas, may have been one reason why so many sites were never reoccupied at all.

In the course of the Sixth Century, after the first and most savage flood of destruction had ebbed, and while the western half of England still remained in Celtic hands, however barbarously most of it may have been ravaged,—a chain of separate but contiguous Anglo-Saxon kingdoms grew up, stretching from Northumbrian Bernicia to Wessex. For centuries they were shifting their frontiers like a kaleidoscope, but the names and positions of certain shires in south-east England, such as Essex, Sussex and Kent, recall some of these very ancient States.

These early English Kingdoms were periodically at war with one another, and with the wild Welsh.[11] The Welsh too were forever at one another's throats. The Romano-Britons of the 'Arthurian' period had often been betrayed by the feuds and wickedness of their chiefs, if we are to

[11] Henceforward I begin to use freely the term 'Welsh,' the name given by the Saxons to the older races whom they drove into Strathclyde, Wales and the Devonian Peninsula.

believe Gildas. As Roman influence disappeared and Celtic tribalism revived, the intertribal warfare characteristic of the Celtic temperament revived with it, and according to Bede greatly assisted the Saxon Conquest.

The first result of that conquest was indeed to destroy the peace and unity of the old Roman province. Britain in the Fifth and Sixth Centuries must have been a fearsome chaos of warring tribes and kingdoms, while inside each of these loose political units, family carried on the bloodfeud against family, and was only sometimes persuaded to accept the 'weregild' compensation in open folk-moot, in hope of bringing the series of murders to an end. Public and private war was the rule rather than the exception. But in the chaos the deep foundations were being laid.

As fast as their conquests were made good, the Anglo-Saxons brought over increasing numbers of their own women and children. The tradition in Bede's time was that the whole 'nation of the Angles' had made the voyage, leaving empty the land whence they came. Their royal family, of which the chief figure in story and legend had been the heroic Offa I, migrated from the old Kingdom of 'Angel' in Schleswig and became the Kings of Mercia in England; the Danes poured in from what is now the Swedish mainland to occupy the parts of modern Denmark left unoccupied by the migration of the older inhabitants to the new 'Engle-land.' The shipping of many thousands of families from Southern Denmark to England was unique among the barbarian migrations of that period for the distance of sea traversed. When we remember that the emigrant ships in which they came over consisted of undecked galleys, we cannot withhold our admiration from these gallant women.

The colonizing energy of the English immigrants, combined with their savage destructiveness, altered the civilization and the racial stock far more than any other Nordic invasion of the period. Goth and Lombard in Italy, and Frank in Gaul had not destroyed the city life, the Christian religion or the Latinized speech of the conquered. But in Saxon England city life, Christian religion

EMERY WALKER LTD. SC.

Map 4   England of the Heptarchy

and Romano-Celtic language all disappeared, together
with the native tribal areas and the Roman administrative
boundaries; the sites of towns and villages were generally,

though not universally, changed, and their names are Saxon in perhaps nine cases out of ten. These things taken together imply a great alteration in racial stock, though the completeness of the racial change has sometimes been exaggerated.

It is, on the other hand, difficult to exaggerate the injury done to Romano-British civilization. It was crushed out between two barbarisms—invading Saxondom and the Celtic revival. For the lowland districts where it had flourished were exactly the districts swept by the besom of the Saxon destroyer. In the Welsh mountains and on the Cornish moors the civilized refugees, deprived of their cities and estates and surrounded by brother-Celts far less civilized than themselves, forgot in a generation or two the arts and traditions that had once enabled them to look down on the Saxon brute. The first result of the conquest was the loss of the crafts, science and learning of Rome; in the island as a whole there was a sharp diminution in the numbers of the population and in the acreage of cultivated land. Surviving Celt and incoming Saxon alike were rude barbarians. Yet because the Saxon now lived in the lowlands, he began to evolve a civilization of his own, which was very soon superior to that of the Welsh mountaineers. Geography inverted the course of history, making the Celt barbarous and the Saxon civilized.

The removal of the Welsh from the richest districts in the island was in part due to their own temper. They had submitted to the civilized Romans as to superior beings, but these Saxon savages could not be accepted as lords. Better to die fighting or escape across the sea to the new Brittany in Armorica of Gaul, or retire among the wild hills of Wales. The Welsh hated the Saxons so much that they would not even attempt to convert them to Christianity. For this neglect the Saxons of Bede's time afterwards reproached them, when the gospel had come from Rome and from Scotland but not from beyond Severn. The semi-nomadic habits of the dwellers in some at least of the Welsh 'trevs' made it easy for them to shift their ground and to get away from the detested Saxon conqueror. The attachment of the Welshman was less to the soil than to the clan, and the clan can move where it likes.

I have said that after the first wild onrush was checked, the border war between Welshman and Saxon went on as the normal condition of life. The chief events of this age-long war were the debouchment of the English of Wessex at the mouth of the Severn (traditionally after the victory at Deorham in Gloucestershire, 577 A.D.), and the debouchment of the English of Northumbria at the mouths of Mersey and Dee, after a victory near the ruins of Chester, 'the city of the legions,' in 613. The arrival of Saxondom on the Irish Channel at these two points left the Welsh of Strathclyde, Wales and the Devonian Peninsula as three isolated pockets of Celtic tribalism, cut off from each other and from the life of the plains.

Thus in a succession of advances covering several hundred years, the Saxons, or later on the Scandinavians in their place, conquered and settled Cheshire, Lancashire, Cumberland and Westmoreland, the Severn valley, Somerset, and finally Devon, where the Saxon settlement was not completed till the Ninth or Tenth Century. But all the time the Saxons were getting more civilized and the Welsh more accustomed to them as neighbours. Long before the English advance had ended, both sides were Christian. Therefore, in these more westerly districts Celtic race and custom survived to a larger extent. But it was only in Cornwall and the unconquered Welsh mountains that language and civilization remained predominantly Celtic.

It is not possible to define accurately the proportion of Welsh to Nordic blood in any district. But it can be laid down as a general rule, good for both north and south of the island, that as we move from east to west we pass by successive stages from the Nordic to the Welsh. There are, however, exceptions to this rule: pockets of Welsh were left behind in the East, as in parts of the fen-country and of Hertfordshire; and the Norsemen afterwards made settlements on the extreme west coast, as in South Wales and

North Lancashire, where the Vikings in their long-ships turned the rear of the Welsh from the sea.[12]

In Wessex and Mercia, though the language was changed, there were many more Welsh left alive than in the older Saxon settlements further to the east. In Wessex, which by that time included Dorset and Somerset, we find the laws of the Saxon King Ine in 693 acknowledging the rights of a separate class called Welshmen, sometimes as holders of land and military servants of the crown. But even in Kent and East Anglia some racial elements of the former population must have been transmitted through the women. It is not possible to suppose that the Jutish and Anglo-Saxon firstcomers would at once have brought over so many women of their own that they never mingled with the captive Welshwomen, the Andromaches of the conquered race.

The whole question of the number of Welsh spared by the conquerors is indeed very uncertain. The traces of Celtic in the language that was spoken in Saxon England are negligible, being confined to about half a dozen words. That proves much against Welsh survival. But it does not prove everything, for Celtic Ireland speaks English to-day; and if that be attributed to schools and the printing-press we must remember that the population of South-West Scotland, who were to a large extent Celtic in blood, adopted the English language in the depth of the Middle Ages at a time when even the Scots were unlearned folk.

---

[12] Such a case is the Lake district. Its place-names are chiefly Norse, occasionally Celtic, but never early Anglo-Saxon. Chiefly between 900 and 1000, the Vikings came up the Solway and the estuaries of the Furness region, and thence settled the dales of Lakeland, being the first to clear and drain the valley bottoms and plant the still existing farms. The old Celtic tribes of the district had lived halfway up the fellside, on flat places of the moorland; their traces are often found where no one would live to-day. They were not exterminated; indeed, sheep on the fells used to be counted in Celtic numerals till quite modern times, so presumably the Norse farmers kept them as shepherd thralls. W. G. Collingwood's *Lake District History*, 1925.

Another strong argument against extensive Welsh survival is the Nordic character of the place names in England. Some of the natural features, indeed, seem to have kept a Saxon variant of their old names,—as 'coombe' for valley, and Bredon and Avon for certain hills and streams. Some even of the early Anglo-Saxon names for districts, like Kent and perhaps 'Lindsey,' recall the Celtic past. But names of villages and homesteads are very seldom pre-Saxon, outside the regular Welsh areas; and this fact is most significant of the completeness of the disturbance and resettlement effected by the Nordic conquerors. Yet even here we must be on our guard; an Anglo-Saxon termination may conceal a Celtic root, as in *Trump*ington and *Mad*ingley; and purely Saxon names like Walton, Wallington and Walworth, and the Norse Birkby, are believed to mean the home of the Welsh or Britons.

Unlike the German and Scandinavian, the English is a mixed race though mainly Nordic—whatever the exact proportion may be. The Celtic and pre-Celtic blood, which probably flows to some extent in the veins of everyone who to-day claims English parentage, may have influenced the English temper. On the other hand, the difference discernible between modern English and modern German or Scandinavian might also be accounted for by the long centuries of residence in the very peculiar climate of Britain, and in the social and political security of an island that was well defended against invasion after 1066. But we still like to dream that English poetry owes something to wild Celtic fancy wedded to the deep feeling and good sense of the Nordic races. Shakespeare came from a shire that was close to the old Severn valley borderland of Welsh and Saxon conflict. All such speculations are fancy, in some indeterminate relation to fact.

The Celt remained with diminished lustre, but the Roman passed away out of the story of Britain. As has been said above, he left behind him three things as permanent legacies—the traditional site of London, the Roman roads and Welsh Christianity. .

It is a moot point whether or not, during the fiercest
time of the Saxon Conquest, London was ever completely
abandoned. If, as is possible, it was at one time quite deserted, its re-establishment as a Saxon town on a more
modest scale followed very soon, for by the time of Bede
(700 A.D.) it was again spoken of as an important centre
of commerce, as commerce was accounted in those barbarous times. We may fairly regard the Romans as the
founders of London. The concentration of their road system at that point in the navigable Thames, made London's
commercial revival certain, for the Romans, when they left
England, did not take their roads away with them.

The importance of the Roman roads after their makers
had gone, lay in this: no one made any more hard roads in
the island until the turnpike movement of the Eighteenth
Century. Throughout the Dark Ages and in early mediæval times, these stone highways still traversed an island
otherwise relapsed to disunion and barbarism. The Roman
roads greatly increased the speed of the Saxon, Danish
and Norman Conquests, and aided, both in peace and in
war, the slow work of Saxon and Norman Kings in uniting
England as one State and making the English nation.
Thanks to the Roman legacy, Britain had better national
highways under the Saxon heptarchy than in Stuart times,
though in the later period there were more by-roads. The
imperial stone causeways, often elevated some feet above
the ground, ran from sea to sea, generally keeping to
higher land, but where needful marching majestically over
bog and through forest. If the bridges soon fell in from neglect, the paved fords remained. For centuries wild tribes
who only knew the name of Cæsar as a myth, trod his
gigantic highways and gave them the fantastic names of
Watling Street, Ermine Street and the Foss Way. Gradually the stones subsided and men were too careless and
ignorant to replace them. Next, the road was used as a
quarry, when the mediæval Englishman, having somewhat
exhausted his timber, began to build for himself dwelling-
houses of stone. From driving roads they declined into
pack-horse tracks, finally disappearing for the most part in

moor or ploughland. Stretches of them have been repaired and modernized, and the motor car now shoots along the path of the legions. But other stretches,—and those the best beloved,—are reserved for the Briton or Saxon who still fares on foot; they are to be traced as green lanes, starting up out of nowhere and ending in nothing, going for miles straight as a die through the magical old English countryside.

The third legacy of the Romans was Welsh Christianity. Their latest importation into Britain survived all their older and more characteristic institutions. There are but few traces of Christianity in the Romano-British world revealed by the spade of the archæologist, and this makes all the more remarkable its survival as the only relic of that civilization among the Welsh. One reason was this: when the military and political system of the Cæsars departed from Britain, it never returned; but missionaries of the Christian religion kept coming back from the Latinized continent to encourage the Welsh during the dark period after the Northumbrian wall was broken, when the Picts and Scots were attacking from north and west, and the Saxons from south and east. Deserted by the rest of the civilized world, the Welsh were not forgotten by the missionaries. Such a one was Saint Germanus, the traditional hero of the 'Hallelujah victory' that he won over an army of combined Picts and Saxons in 430. The story tells how the Saint, formerly a distinguished soldier of Rome in Gaul, having come to Britain on a mission to put down Pelagian heretics, returned to his old trade, took command of the multitude of frightened Britons and led them to victory over the dreaded heathen invader. It may indeed be an exaggerated clerical account of a transaction that is otherwise totally lost to our knowledge, but it is highly characteristic of that period,—symbolic even. The Christian clergy, men of affairs and education when such qualities were becoming rare, stood in the gap whence the Roman soldier and governor were in retreat. In the day of trouble the Christian faith got a hold over the Welsh, which had not belonged to it as the official religion of later Roman

rule in Britain. We shall see the same process repeated
when the Saxons, newly Christianized, in their turn pass
under the hammer of the heathen Danes and Norsemen.
'Give peace in our time, O Lord,' 'because there is none
other that fighteth for us but only Thou, O God,' has a
curious sound in the modern English liturgy; it seems to
speak of the Christian God as the only ally, but not a very
formidable safeguard in a world all gone wrong. But to a
Welshman dispossessed by the Saxons in the Fifth Century, or a Saxon dispossessed by the Danes in the Ninth,
it would have appeared a very just statement of the case.[13]

In these circumstances, the Welsh of the Fifth and
Sixth Centuries came to regard Christianity as their dis-
tinguishing mark which, together with their love of bardic
music and poetry, enabled them to feel superior to the
Saxon savages who were exterminating them from the
plains and confining them to the hills and moorlands of
'wild Wales.' The old Welsh bard's prophecy about the
ancient races, once lords of Britain, thus describes their
fate:—

Their God they shall praise,
Their language they shall keep,
Their land they shall lose except wild Wales.

A similar development of Celtic Christianity took place
in the remote peninsula of West Wales or Cornwall. On its
tin-bearing moorlands and beside its woody streams running down to coves of the rocks, a race of local saints unknown to the rest of Christendom lived their lives and
left their names to the villages of Cornwall, memorials of
those stirring times when British civilization perished and
British Christianity found creative vigour under the ribs of
death. The lost history of the romantic age of Cornwall
must have been largely maritime, for it was closely connected with the history and religion of Armorica on the
Gallic shore opposite. Thither the Britons of the island fled
from the Saxon invader, in such numbers that Armorica of

[13] How old the words actually are is uncertain,—possibly
not older in fact than the Eleventh Century.

the Romanized Gauls became 'Brittany' of the Celtic revival, never to be fully absorbed in the life of Latin France,
not even in the era of the French Revolution when the
'Bretons' held out so fiercely against the great changes that
the rest of France had ordained.

BOOKS FOR FURTHER READING: Professor Chadwick, *Origin of the English Nation*; Haverfield, *Roman Occupation*,
last chapter; Leeds, *Archæology of Anglo-Saxon Settlements*; Baldwin Brown, *Art in Early England*; *Cam. Med.
Hist.*, I., pp. 380–91; Professor Chambers, *Widsith, a
Study in Old English Heroic Legend*; R. H. Hodgkin, A
History of the Anglo-Saxons, 1935; *Introduction to the Survey of English Place Names*, Place Name Society, Vol. I.,
1925; Myres on *The English Settlements*, in the first vol. of
the *Oxford Hist. of England*, 1936.

NOTES AT END OF CHAPTER 3: (1) For the origin of the
Anglo-Saxons and Jutes see Chadwick, *Origin of the English Nation*; *Cam. Med. Hist.*, I., pp. 384–85; Cyril Fox,
Cambridge Region, pp. 238, 284–86, 296; Leeds, *Archæology of Anglo-Saxon Settlements*, and Chambers' *Widsith*,
pp. 237–47.

(2) Haverfield, *Roman Occupation* (1924), p. 274.
Haverfield's statement that 'no case is known where Saxons
dwelt in a Roman villa,' is not contradicted, though it may
be qualified by Cyril Fox, *Cambridge Region*, pp. 282–83.
Mr. Fox there says: 'There is evidence of the superim-
position of Anglo-Saxon settlements on Roman sites in the
Cambridge Region. Apart from Cambridge itself, Roman
houses at Litlington, Bartlow, Wymondley (H) and
Stansted (E) are sited in or immediately adjacent to the
Anglo-Saxon nucleus. But this is not necessarily to be regarded as evidence of continuity; it may be merely a result
of the operation of economic laws.'

CHAPTER FOUR

Mediterranean Influence Again. The Return of Christianity

Primitive societies, if they are ever to move on towards
knowledge, wealth and ordered freedom, are obliged to
travel in the first instance not along the path of democratic
equality, but along the path of aristocracy, Kingship and

priesthood. The heathen clan or tribe may be relatively equalitarian, and poverty may be more or less equally distributed among its members, but it can never move forward in mass order towards higher civilization and the freedom of the individual. When men collectively are very poor some few must be made rich if there is to be any accumulation of wealth for civilized purposes. When men collectively are very ignorant, progress is only possible through the endowment of an educated few. In such a world, organization can only begin through personal ascendancy and can only be rendered permanent through privilege. Education and spiritual religion are, in those primitive times, inextricably bound up with superstition and the ascendancy of the priest over the layman, as Bede's History so innocently and charmingly demonstrates on every page. In our own democratic and partially scientific age these conditions of progress in the past may seem strange to some, but they are a large part of the secret of early English history. The greatest student of those times has written:—

If we describe several centuries as feudal, then feudalism will appear to us as a natural and even a necessary stage in our history: that is to say, if we would have the England of the sixteenth century arise out of the England of the eighth without passing through a period of feudalism, we must suppose many immense and fundamental changes in the nature of man and his surroundings. If we use the term in this wide sense, then (the barbarian conquests being given us as an unalterable fact) feudalism means civilization, the separation of employment, the division of labour, the possibility of national defence, the possibility of art, science, literature and learned leisure; the cathedral, the scriptorium, the library are as truly the work of feudalism as the baronial castle. When, therefore, we speak, as we shall have to speak, of forces which make for the subjection of the peasantry to seignorial justice and which substitute the manor with its villeins for the free village, we shall—so at least it seems to us—be speaking, not of abnormal forces, not of retrogression, not of disease, but in the main of normal and healthy growth. Far from us indeed is the cheerful optimism which refuses to see that the process of civilization is often a cruel process; but the England of the eleventh century is nearer to the England

of the nineteenth than is the England of the seventh—
nearer by just four hundred years.

So Maitland wrote thirty years ago, and the chapters of
this book which endeavour to sketch the Anglo-Saxon and
Norman periods must be to a large extent a comment on
this 'deep speech' of his. Kingship, feudalism and ecclesias-
ticism grew together as harmonious parts of a general movement. King, thegn and Bishop, though often rivals, in the
main fostered one another's power. All three were at once
the exploiters and the saviours of an otherwise helpless
society. The period during and after the Danish invasions
will offer the best ground for describing the growth of
feudalism and Kingship, the origins of which we have already noticed in the period of the Saxon Conquest. In the
present chapter, covering the years between that conquest
and the coming of the Vikings, we must attempt the difficult task of appreciating the change of religion as the first
great step forward of the English people on the path of
civilized life.

The Christian conquest of the island was the return of Mediterranean civilization in a new form, and with a new message. At the Kentish ports, through which the legions had
come and gone, landed Augustine of Rome and Theodore
of Tarsus; they established here a hierarchy imitated from
the officialdom of the defunct Roman Empire, and the English Kings in turn borrowed, from this new civil service of
the Church, forms and policies fitted to the needs of the
infant State. Christianity meant, also, the return of learning
to the island, and the beginning among the barbarians of a
political and legal civilization based on the arts of reading
and writing in the practicable Latin alphabet.[1]

[1] It is with the arrival of the Christians in Saxondom that
we begin to get *written* laws, chronicles and poems. One
source, however, the historian loses,—the weapons and
ornaments which the heathen Saxons buried with their
dead, but which Christian custom omitted. 'Graveyards,' all-
important for the heathen period, are of much less service
in the Christian epoch. Fortunately, we have literary
evidence instead.

Christianity spoke also of strange matters, totally foreign to the Nordic mind, and in great part foreign to the mind of ancient Rome: it taught charity, humility, self-discipline, a concern about spiritual things, an active and uneasy conscience, an emphasis on the distinction between soul and body to the disparagement of the latter, a great fear and a great hope about the next life perpetually governing action in this one, the submission of the freeman to the priest,—partly as being the wiser man of the two, partly from superstitious awe,—great stress on dogma and consequently, as a strange corollary to the religion of brotherhood, the novel religious duty of persecuting every heathen and every heretic. Like Kingship and feudalism, mediæval religion was not an unmixed blessing. But the play of these forces upon the old easy-going Nordic character produced after a thousand years the Englishmen of Tudor times, and, without disrespect to our more distant ancestry, we may confess that they thought of more things in the Mermaid Tavern than in those Saxon mead-halls where Widsith, the minstrel, 'his word-hoard unlocked.'

The worship of Odin and Thor, the religion common to primitive Anglo-Saxon and Scandinavian, was pre-eminently a layman's religion, a warrior's religion, a religion of high-hearted gentlemen not overburdened with brains or troubled about their own souls. Its grand old mythology inculcated or reflected the virtues of the race—manliness, generosity, loyalty in service and in friendship, and a certain rough honesty. The social standards of the modern English schoolboy come nearest to it, as the most elementary expression of the racial character. The Danes had a word for acts of cowardice, desertion or dishonourableness of any kind—'nidings vœrk,'—as distinct from the ordinary breaches of the law, and more terribly punished by public opinion. It was worse to be a 'niding' than a man-slayer. The liar, too, is rather despised than honoured. The Nordic race would not have found its hero in Jacob or even in Odysseus of the many wiles—in spite of many similarities between the society described in Homer and in *Beowulf* respectively. The favourite heroes of the northern warrior world, like Njal of Iceland on the eve of the coming thither of Christianity, are praised by their neighbours because they 'never lie.'

At the time of the first contact of the Odin worshippers with Christianity, the sacrifice of slaves and captives, common to all primitive religions, had not completely died out on the continent, though there is no evidence of it in Saxon England. The sacrifice of cattle or horses was very common, accompanied by sacred feasting and drinking, which, in accordance with Pope Gregory's advice, were converted into Church feasts and 'Church ales.'

The Nordic religion was not a religion of dread, or of magic formularies to propitiate hostile powers. Instead of covering its temples with frescoes of the tortures of the damned, it taught people not to be afraid of death. Its ideal was the fellowship of the hero with the gods, not merely in feasting and victory, but in danger and defeat. For the gods, too, are in the hands of fate, and the Scandinavian vision of the twilight of the gods that was to end the world showed the heroes dying valiantly in the last hopeless fight against the forces of chaos—loyal and fearless to the last. It is an incomplete but not an ignoble religion. It contains those elements of character which it was the special mission of the Nordic peoples to add to modern civilization and to Christianity itself.

But, when all is said, the old Saxon and Danish faith was a religion of barbarism with no elements in itself of further progress, and the spontaneous conversion of its adherents to Christianity seemed a confession of this fact. The old religion was merely a traditional expression of racial character, not an outside force at work upon that character. It did little for learning or art. It did not preach humility, charity, or anything else that was difficult. It did not foster religious ardour in any form. And it was not intolerant; no missionary is recorded to have suffered martyrdom while converting the Anglo-Saxons. English heathenism had no defences, good or bad, against the Christian attack. Its scattered priesthood had no corporate consciousness, no privileged position. Coifi, the high priest of Odin in the

Yorkshire region, when Paulinus first came preaching to Edwin of Northumbria, declared that he got nothing out of the service of his gods, not even the first place at the King's court, and forthwith rode at the head of the people to overthrow the shrine of which he was the keeper.

Bede also reports another and nobler speech in favour of adopting Christianity, delivered by one of King Edwin's thegns at the same Witan:

The present life of man upon earth, O king, seems to me, in comparison with that time which is unknown to us, like to the swift flight of a sparrow through the house wherein you sit at supper in winter, with your Ealdormen and thegns, while the fire blazes in the midst and the hall is warmed, but the wintry storms of rain or snow are raging abroad. The sparrow, flying in at one door and immediately out at another, whilst he is within, is safe from the wintry tempest; but, after a short space of fair weather, he immediately vanishes out of your sight, passing from winter into winter again. So this life of man appears for a little while, but of what is to follow or what went before we know nothing at all. If, therefore, this new doctrine tells us something more certain, it seems justly to deserve to be followed. *life after death*

The Christian missionaries had, indeed, an immense advantage in bringing a clear-cut cosmogony and definite doctrines about heaven and hell, how to attain the one and avoid the other. In contrast with these precise dogmas, the old religion only presented a vague and poetical version of popular superstitions about the next life. These are exemplified by the Icelandic story in *Burnt Njal,* where the newly slain warrior, Gunnar, is overheard by his son, Hogni, singing of his last fight from inside his burial cairn.

Now those two, Skarphedinn and Hogni, were out of doors one evening by Gunnar's cairn on the south side. The moon and stars were shining clear and bright, but every now and then the clouds drove over them. Then, all at once, they thought they saw the cairn standing open, and, lo! Gunnar had turned himself in the cairn and looked at the moon. They thought they saw four lights burning in the cairn, and none of them threw a shadow. They saw that Gunnar was merry, and he wore a joyful face. He sang a song, and so loud, that it might have been heard though they had been further off:

He that lavished rings in largesse,
When the fight's red rain-drops fell,
Bright of face, with heart-strings hardy,
Hogni's father met his fate;
Then his brow with helmet shrouding,
Bearing battle-shield, he spake,
'I will die the prop of battle,
Sooner die than yield an inch,
Yes, sooner die than yield an inch.'

After that the cairn was shut up again.

It may be taken as the swan-song of that fine old heathen society, for a few years later the Christian missionaries came to Iceland, one of the last strongholds of Nordic heathendom, and the best men of the island, including Njal the truth-teller, promised them backing.

Anglo-Saxon heathendom perished four hundred years before Scandinavian. From geographic causes England lay in the path of Christian influence long before it reached Denmark, Norway or Iceland. The English Woden was overthrown in the Seventh Century by a vigorous encircling movement from North and South at once, the religion of Columba and Aidan coming from Scotland, the religion of Gregory and Augustine coming from Rome. It might, indeed, have been expected that the attack would be launched from the West, but the Welsh Christians still hated the Saxon intruder too much to try to save his soul.

Nevertheless, the Welsh had indirectly assisted in the conversion of England, for St. Patrick was a Romanized Briton. Probably the lower Severn was the scene of his early home, whence raiding Scots of Ireland had carried him captive in the opening years of the Fifth Century. His subsequent conversion of Ireland (432–61) started Christianity on the long circuit by which it returned to Northern England. Columba carried it from Ireland to Western Scotland (563), and from Scotland it converted Northumbria through the mission of Aidan (635), a generation after the landing of Augustine in Kent (597).

Though the Irish Christianity of Columba and Aidan became a rival to the Roman Christianity of Gregory and Augustine, Patrick had not intended to found a Church hostile to Rome. Bearing a Roman name,—Patricius,—he was a citizen of the old Empire, as proud of his Roman rights as St. Paul himself. He studied in Gaul, and held his commission thence from a Church which already regarded the Bishop of Rome as an important adviser on doubtful religious questions, though not as lord paramount. Patrick, though not very learned himself, brought to Ireland the inestimable gift of the Latin language of which the Celtic genius soon made such good scholarly use in profane as well as sacred letters. He did not, like Cyril, the Apostle of the Slavs, set out to found a separate Christian civilization for the race he converted. He desired to make Ireland a part of Roman Christianity and civilization, at a moment when the Roman Empire in the West had scarcely yet breathed its last and was completely identified in the minds of men with the Christian religion. The acceptance of Christianity in Ireland, as later in England, was in part due to the admiration felt by the barbarians for the Empire even in its fall, and for all things appertaining to Rome, very much as Christianity is accepted by African tribes to-day as representing Europe.

Nevertheless, the Church which Patrick caused to triumph in Ireland developed after his death in a direction away from Rome. The fall of the Empire in the West, the extirpation of Latin institutions in the neighbouring island of Britain, and the barbarian conquests in France and Italy for awhile isolated Ireland from Mediterranean influence, and gave opportunity for the rise of a native Celtic Church and civilization. The fact that the barbarian inroads did not reach Ireland till the coming of the Vikings in the Ninth Century, gave time for the efflorescence of the artistic, imaginative and literary life of early Irish Christianity.

But, though Irish Christianity flourished in the midst of Irish society, it did not transmute it as Anglo-Saxon Christianity transmuted Anglo-Saxon society. The social structure in Ireland offered no platform on which it was possible to erect a hierarchy of the Roman order, still less a parish system. Till the Vikings came there were no cities. Till Strongbow came there was no feudalism. The Irish were organized in a number of hostile and warring tribes, each tribe held together by the tie of kinship and each governed by its chief, over whom the 'High King' at Tara was suzerain rather than sovereign. Irish Christianity was perforce tribal. It was not parochial, nor in the Roman sense episcopal, though there was a plethora of insignificant Bishops, mostly without sees. Its real life was monastic. The normal Irish monastery was connected with a single tribe, and acknowledged no ecclesiastical superior capable of controlling its Abbot.

Celtic monasticism did not represent the conventual ideal of St. Benedict. It was a congregation of hermits planted in some remote spot, often on a rocky mountain or island. Each lived in his own beehive hut of wattle, clay and turf; but the huts had been collected together for mutual intercourse and security in a fortified village or *kraal*, under the command of an Abbot. The monks had many-sided activities, for they were hermits, scholars, artists, warriors and missionaries. The individual monk would sometimes go out into the world to preach, to compose tribal feuds or lead tribal wars; sometimes he would copy and illuminate manuscripts in the monastery; sometimes he would depart in search of a more complete seclusion, like St. Cuthbert when he left the company of his brother monks at remote Lindisfarne for the still deeper solitude of the Farne Islands.[2]

This Irish monasticism, both in its original home, and in its mission lands of Scotland and Northumbria, produced a rich crop of saints. The stories of their lives, many of them preserved by Bede, are singularly attractive. The freshness and the light of dawn glimmer in the legends of Aidan and

[2] St. Cuthbert submitted to Rome in 664, but the traditions of Scoto-Irish Christianity remained potent in his life; nor were these traditions quite dead even in Bede—who was, therefore, eminently suited to write 'The Ecclesiastical History of the English People.'

of Cuthbert. To this form of monasticism we owe not only the Book of Kells but the manuscript art of Lindisfarne, wherein Celtic and Saxon native ornamentation were blended in perfect harmony with Christian traditions from southern lands. The Irish monks also revived a knowledge of classical secular literature, which had almost died out in Western Europe. While Pope Gregory the Great was reproving a Gallic Bishop for studying Latin grammar and poetry, the Irish Christians were busy saving it for the world in their remote corner where the Papal censure was unheard. Thence they carried it to the England of Benedict Biscop and Bede, where it greatly fructified; finally, in the days of Charlemagne, it was taken back across the sea by Alcuin to begin its reconquest of the illiterate continent.

Scotland, England and Europe owe a great debt to the Irish churchmen. Yet they did little to civilize and nothing to organize the people of their own island, whose tribalism continued as before. The merits and limitations of the Celtic Church were closely connected; the breadth of freedom and individual choice implied a looseness of organization which left the Church little power when the first golden impulse had spent its force.

Such was the Christianity which invaded heathen Scotland from Ulster. The most effective of these missions was that of 563 under St. Columba,—warrior, statesman and hermit,—the greatest and most typical abbot of the Irish monastic ideal. On the small island of Iona off the West coast of Scotland he founded his cluster of beehive huts, whence the missionary monks swarmed over Northern Britain, and whither they returned periodically for repose, common counsel and solitary meditation.

In Columba's day the future Scotland[3] was already di-

[3] The division between England and Scotland, though adumbrated in Roman times, see note, p. 38 above, was in abeyance during the Dark Ages. Saxon Northumbria overlapped the Cheviot border on the East, and Celtic Strathclyde overlapped it on the West. Scotland had even less pretension to internal unity than England.

vided between Saxon and Celt. The Saxon had established
himself in the south-eastern corner of the lowlands; this
rich district, afterwards known as Lothian, was then the
northern part of the Kingdom of Northumbria, which at its
greatest extent stretched from the Humber to the Firth of
Forth. King Edwin of Northumbria was fortifying his
'Edwin's Burg' on the famous rock, as the northernmost
stronghold of Saxondom in the island. All the north and
west, and most of the centre of the future Scotland was
still Celtic; yet it was destined in the long run to adopt
the Saxon tongue and civilization, perhaps without great
racial change. The history of Scotland is largely the history
of that process of Anglicizing the Celt. Had it not been for
the early settlement of the Anglo-Saxons in the south-
eastern lowlands, Scotland would have remained a Celtic
and tribal country, and its future history and relations to
England might have borne more resemblance to the story
of Ireland or of Wales.

In the days of King Edwin, the Saxons of Northumbria
were still hostile intruders in Scotland, constantly at war
with the Celtic world in the upper Tweed as well as farther
north. And the Celtic world was constantly at war within
itself. Apart from the innumerable tribal divisions and
feuds, there were three main Celtic races—the Picts of
North Scotland and of Galloway, probably most of them
Goidelic Celts; the Britannic Celts of Strathclyde; and the
latest comers, the Scots, from Ireland, settled in Dalriada,
modern Argyllshire. The Scots from oversea were destined
to give their name but not their civilization to the whole
land. The history of these early times, no less than the
settlement of Protestant Ulster in James I's reign and the
Irish immigration into Clydeside in recent times, reminds
us that the connection between West Scotland and North-
East Ireland is a constant factor in history.

Columba, himself an Irish Scot, gained great influence
over his fellow Scots of Dalriada, and over the Picts of the
North. The Britons of Strathclyde were more gradually
brought under the influence of the new religion. At the

Map 5 Scotland and Northumbria in the Dark Ages

opening of the Seventh Century the Christianity of Iona had a firm hold on many at least of the Chiefs and tribes of Celtic Scotland. But the Saxons of Northumbria still vacillated, according to the chances of battle or the personal beliefs of their Kings, between the worship of Woden and the Roman form of Christianity preached to them by Paulinus, one of Augustine's men. Before describing the conversion of Northumbria by Scoto-Irish Christianity, we must turn our attention to Augustine's mission in southern England, the other wing of the Christian invasion of the island.

Gregory the Great, the first of the great Popes, was the true founder of the mediæval Papacy. In 590 he received into his charge the defenceless and impoverished Bishopric of Rome, surrounded by triumphant barbarians amid the ruins of a fallen world. In a dozen years he had raised it up in the imagination of mankind as the heir to the defunct Empire of the West.

The change of European leadership from lay to clerical hands was reflected in the personal story of Gregory's life. Having begun his career as a wealthy Roman patrician, he employed his high administrative talents as Prefect of the City for awhile. Then he suddenly abandoned his social privileges and political duties to live as a humble monk on the Cælian Hill. Promoted thence to be Bishop of Rome, he exerted on behalf of the Church the genius of a Cæsar and the organizing care of an Augustus. His letters of advice to the Churches of Western Europe on every religious, political and social interest of the day, were accepted not indeed as having legal power but as having an unique moral authority. If the Papacy was, as Hobbes called it, 'no other than the ghost of the deceased Roman Empire, sitting crowned upon the grave thereof,' it was a living ghost and not a phantasm. Since the governing power of the Empire had perished in the West, a ghostly authority was welcomed by distant Kings, Bishops, monks and peoples, as giving some hope of progress, concord and righteous impartiality in a world of chaotic violence. This new conception of old Rome was about to take a strong hold of Anglo-Saxon England.

Augustine was no more than the worthy instrument of Gregory the Great. The impulse for the conversion of the 'Angles' into 'angels' came from Gregory in person. And, when Augustine and his fellow-missioners turned in despair back from their dangerous journey, he sent them on again with admonition and encouragement.

[597.] When Augustine landed in Thanet the Kingdom of Kent was evidently not unprepared to receive the gospel. It was the most civilized of the English States and had the closest connections with Christian France. The wife of King Ethelbert of Kent was herself a Christian Frank. Owing to the absence of deep attachment to the pagan religion which we have noticed above as characteristic of the Nordic world of that day, the Kings were often persuaded by their Christian wives to adopt the religion of the more civilized part of mankind, and their subjects seldom resisted the change.

Augustine did not convert England. He converted Kent, founded the see of Canterbury, and made it the solid base for the subsequent spread of Roman Christianity over the island. Outside Kent progress was at first slow. Augustine's claim to supremacy over all Christians in Britain by virtue of his Roman commission, was rejected by the Welsh clergy at a conference near the mouth of Severn where both parties lost their temper. Nearer home, the missionaries were, after some years, expelled from London, whose citizens now reappear in the page of history in a position partially independent of the small Saxon Kingdoms on either side of the lower Thames. The continued paganism of London was a chief reason why effect was never given to Gregory's plan to make London, and not Canterbury, the Metropolitan See.

The first striking success of Roman Christianity outside Kent was Paulinus' conversion of the great King Edwin of Northumbria, again through the agency of a Christian

wife.[4] [627.] As Edwin was ruling from the Humber to the
Forth, and had vassal Kings in other parts of the island, it
seemed for a moment that England was already half won
for Christ.

But the missionaries had as yet no deep hold on opinion
outside the Royal Court, and the fortunes of religion were
for a generation to come subject to the wager of battle, and
to the whims or deaths of rival Princes. For thirty critical
years Northumbria was fighting to preserve its supremacy
in the island from the rising power of Mercia, and these
political wars affected the issue between Christ and Woden. Woden was favoured by King Penda of Mercia, while
the champions of the Cross were Kings Edwin and Oswald
of Northumbria, who both lost their lives fighting against
him. Yet the ultimate triumph of Mercia did not prevent
the triumph of Christianity.[5] The struggle was not a war
of religion. Penda did not persecute Christianity and
passed no such laws against its practices as the Christians
subsequently passed against the cult of Woden. 'King
Penda,' writes Bede, 'did not forbid the preaching of the
Word even among his people, the Mercians, if any were
willing to hear it. But, on the contrary, he hated and despised those whom he perceived to be without works of
faith, when they had once received the faith of Christ,
saying that they were contemptible who scorned to obey
their God, in whom they believed.'

Penda's allies against Northumbria were the Christian
Welsh under their King Cadwallon, savage mountaineers
who revenged the wrongs of their race on the Northum-

[4] See p. 77, above.

[5] 633 Heathfield; Penda defeats and kills Edwin. 634
Heavenfield; Oswald defeats and kills Welsh Cadwallon,
ally of Penda. 642 Maserfield; Penda defeats and kills Oswald. 655 Oswald's brother, Oswy, defeats and kills Penda.
659 Wulthere of Mercia throws off the Northumbrian yoke,
but Christianizes Mercia.

It must be remembered that Mercia gets less than justice done to its importance and power in the history of
Bede the Northumbrian, and in the Anglo-Saxon Chronicle
instituted by Alfred King of Wessex.

brian Christians with a cruelty far exceeding that of the heathens of Mercia against their brother Saxons. Yet the fact that Penda sought Welsh allies at all implies that the barrier between the two races was becoming less impenetrable. It was during this period that Mercia extended Saxon rule and Saxon colonization into the Magasaetas, the lands beyond Severn, subsequently bounded to the West by King Offa's Dyke.

[SEE MAP 4.] The political outcome of these wars was the decline of Northumbria and the rise of Mercia. In the course of the Seventh Century Mercia not only annexed the smaller Saxon States of Hwicce, Lindsey and Middle Anglia, but claimed lordship over East Anglia and Essex and began to thrust Wessex to the south of the Thames, struggling to wrest from her the Chiltern district. The smaller Saxon Kingdoms were being swallowed up, and the battle for their reversion lay between Wessex and Mercia. Although the independence of Northumbria as a separate Kingdom was maintained until the coming of the Vikings, she retired from the struggle for political supremacy, but retained the leadership in art, letters and religion throughout the period of Cuthbert and Bede. Not only the Lindisfarne gospels, but the Cross at Bewcastle and the 'Franks casket' in the British Museum testify to the prolonged vigour of Northumbrian art, when the South European tradition of representing the human form had enriched the beautiful scroll and design work of Celtic and Saxon native art.

It is remarkable that until the middle of the Seventh Century, power in Saxon England had lain in the North, which never again claimed the leadership until the industrial revolution made coal and iron more valuable than cornfields. Archæological evidence suggests that the Anglo-Saxons were slow though sure in developing the agricultural wealth of the South; and until they had done so it was always possible for the warriors of the northern moorlands to establish an ephemeral supremacy. London, too, though in a measure independent of the neighbouring kingdoms, was yet of small account. It was only after the coming of the Danes that the City of London stepped into her destined place as the leader of England, the principal seat of wealth and power though not of Royalty.

The religious consequences of the wars against Penda had been the disappearance of Paulinus' Roman Christianity from Northumbria, and its replacement by the mission of Aidan from Iona at the invitation of King Oswald in 635. Aidan founded the monastery of Melrose whence the Lothians were evangelized, and the monastery of Lindisfarne on Holy Island, a site chosen in obvious imitation of Iona. At Lindisfarne, Aidan was Abbot and Bishop in one. The ascetic yet cheerful life of these ardent, lovable, unworldly apostles of the moorland, who tramped the heather all day to preach by the burnside at evening, won the hearts of the men of the North. Indeed, Christianity had never, since its earliest years, appeared in a more attractive guise.

Until the Seventh Century was more than half spent, the monks of the Church of Iona did quite as much as the men of Canterbury to convert the English race. They reconverted relapsed Northumbria and Essex, and evangelized Mercia. Some Irish hermits established their huts as far south as still heathen Sussex. But want of organization rendered the durability of their work doubtful, so soon as the zeal of their successors should decline. Already in Bede's time the historian noted how great was the falling-off in the spirit of Northumbrian religion, how lax the life of the monasteries had become, how much less the clergy were respected than in the days of Aidan and his first disciples. But by that time the organization of Rome had triumphed throughout England, and good organization can survive periodic lapses of zeal.

The success of the Iona mission on English soil revived the disputes between the Celtic and Roman Churches, which Augustine and the Welsh had defined without solving at their abortive conference on the banks of Severn. So long as the Celtic Church had remained in Celtic territory, Rome could afford to overlook its remote existence. But when rivalry began for the possession of Saxon England, the issue could no longer be evaded. The men of Iona, like the Welsh, had a date for Easter different from the Roman; and their priest-monks shaved from ear to ear across the front of the head—possibly a reminiscence of Druidism—instead of making a round tonsure on the crown. These trivialities were the ostensible subjects of dispute and anathema. But behind lay far more important differences of spirit and organization, which in that epoch were involved in the question of submission to Rome.

Again the decisive event was brought about by a woman. The wife of Oswy King of Northumbria undermined her husband's faith in the orthodoxy of the Church of Iona, whose champion he had been ever since the death of his brother Oswald. Oswy summoned the Synod of Whitby[6] in 664, and gave his own judgment in favour of the claims of Rome as the inheritor of Peter's commission. The men of Iona, rejected in the house of their Northumbrian friends, could no longer maintain the struggle in England. Some, like St. Cuthbert, accepted the new order of things, others retired back into the Celtic wilderness. In the course of generations, Scotland, Wales and Ireland gradually came into line with the rest of Western Europe.

It cannot be denied that the decision of Whitby contained the seeds of all the trouble with Rome, down the ages to come. But men must live in and for their own epoch. The early adhesion of all the English Kingdoms to the Roman system of religion gave a great impetus to the movement towards racial unity, kingly and feudal power, systematic administration, legislation and taxation, and territorial as against tribal politics. The English, as we have seen, were already moving away from tribalism much more rapidly than the Celts; the choice at Whitby may have been prompted in part by a desire to get away from Celtic and tribal things, and to imitate the superior organization of the Frankish Kingdom, where the Roman municipal sys-

---

[6] The name Whitby, like other place-names ending in 'by,' is Danish, and therefore of later date. But the Synod which met at the monastery of Saxon 'Streanaeshalch' is always called by the more familiar Danish name of the place.

tem had not been extinguished by the barbarian invaders. The new Roman hierarchy would be a substitute for Roman bureaucracy and for municipal life which the Anglo-Saxons in their wilder days had destroyed, and were beginning dimly to regret.

A greater centralization and unity of system and purpose in ecclesiastical affairs throughout all the English Kingdoms led the way towards political unity under a single King. The administration of the Church became the model for the administration of the State. Methods and habits of mind based on discipline, system and the work of scribes were engendered in the life of the Church and spread thence to the secular world. And since the Churchmen, being the only learned men, were the chief advisers of the Crown and its first Secretariate, the new Roman ideas passed all the more easily from the sphere of the Church into the sphere of the State. Kingship gained new allies—men as skilled to serve with brain and pen, as the thegns with muscle and sword. Kingship gained also a new sanctity and a higher claim on the loyalty of the subject, through hallowing by the Church and by clerical theories of sovereignty drawn from recollections of the Roman law. It was only after the Norman Conquest and the days of Hildebrand, that Church and King became rivals as well as allies.

Christian leaders of the new type, by becoming statesmen and great prelates, did England yeoman's service. But the change put them in no small danger of becoming hard-faced officials, territorialists greedy above all things of lands and power for the Church. The old spirit of the Iona mission—humble, ascetic and full of brotherly love—had one last impersonation in Cuthbert of Lindisfarne, a convert to the Whitby decisions.

The man who organized the new hierarchy and brought all monastic and episcopal England under the dominion of Canterbury, was Theodore of Tarsus, Archbishop from 669–90. The first remarkable man among the successors of Augustine, he stands out as perhaps the greatest Prince of the Church in all English history. His career is the chief example of the value to England of her close relation to

the Papacy of that day, which supplied the northern island
with the best that the Mediterranean civilization still had
to give. At a time when France and Germany were sunk in
barbarous ignorance, the Pope sent us Theodore, a Greek
of Tarsus in Asia Minor, who brought with him the African
Hadrian as his lieutenant. Both men were adepts in the
best Greek and Latin scholarship of Italy and the Levant.
With the help of the Englishman, Benedict Biscop, they
brought over from the Mediterranean a good store of books,
the indispensable but all too rare equipment of learning.
Canterbury became a school not only of Latin but of Greek.
The new influences from southern lands, combining with
the liberal traditions of Celtic scholarship in the north of
England, produced the school of Bede at Jarrow, and the
library at York where Alcuin studied. Thence religious and
secular learning migrated back to the continent and taught
Latin literature to the Empire of Charlemagne, when the
Danish invasions for a while extinguished the lamp of learn-
ing in the monasteries and libraries of Northumbria.

The intellectual life of Bede (673–735) covered the
whole of the limited range of the learning of the Dark
Ages. But we moderns value him most as the 'father of
English history.' The first in the long roll of mediæval
chroniclers of our island, he told the tale of the Church of
Iona in England and its rival of Canterbury, writing at a
place and time in which the memory of both was still alive.
He could not be unfair to the memory of Aidan and his
disciples, deeply as he deplored their unorthodoxy, for he
was a Northumbrian well knowing how and by whom his
own people had been converted. His feelings towards the
schismatics of Wales were much less tender.

The spread of the Roman influence over the island from
Canterbury carried with it Church music, till then mainly
confined to Kent. The Saxons took to it kindly and it
greatly strengthened the hold of Christianity on the people.
The triumph of Rome meant also the growth of ecclesiastical architecture. Aidan's 'Scottish' successors had been
content with timber walls and roofs of reed even for their

cathedral on Lindisfarne. But after Whitby the builders of
the new regime aspired to give to their churches something
of the grandeur and permanence of Rome. The roofless
shells of Roman cities and villas with which England was
then so thickly sprinkled, afforded ready-hewn quarries of
squared stone, and were not without influence as models to
the church builders of the Seventh and Eighth Centuries,
who had also their memories of crypts and basilicas seen on
pilgrimage in Italy or in Merovingian Gaul. After the era of
Charlemagne, the influence of the romanesque Rhenish
and German architecture became strong in the England
that recovered from the Danish invasions. Most of the
Saxon churches, including all the largest, were eventually
pulled down to make way for Norman or Plantagenet successors. But this should not blind us to the fact that stone
churches were being multiplied in Saxon England at a
time when the laity still built their halls and cottages of
wood.[7]

The organization of the English Church was begun in
669 by Theodore of Tarsus as a man of sixty-eight, and was
carried on by him for twenty years of vigorous old age.
There was much opposition, and he beat it down. The
essence of the reform was Theodore's creation of a sufficient number of Bishoprics, not of the roving missionary
type of the Celtic Church, but with definite and mutually
exclusive territorial sees, all subject to Canterbury. The
monasteries were also subjected to the general ecclesiastical system; they continued indeed to grow in wealth and
numbers, but they were no longer independent and no

[7] Most of the parish churches were still of timber at the
time of the Norman Conquest, but some were already of
stone. Wing church, in Bucks, remains as an example of
a rural church built of stone on a large scale in Saxon
times; with its crypt it is an obvious imitation of Italian or
Frankish models. So was the great Hexham Abbey, built
by Wilfrid in the Seventh Century, in stone taken from the
ruined Roman cities of the neighbouring wall of Hadrian;
the crypt still remains intact. At Brixworth, in Northampton-
shire, the bricks from some neighbouring Roman ruin have
been used by Anglo-Saxon builders.

longer the sole agencies of the Church, as they had almost become in Celtic Christianity.

After Theodore's day, as a result of his preparation of the ground on episcopal lines, the parish system began slowly to grow out of the soil, first in one township, then in another. Before the Norman Conquest most of the island was supplied with parish churches and parish priests, men who were not monks, and who in Saxon times were often married.

Just as in the mundane sphere the great work of Anglo-Saxon and Dane was to multiply townships in clearings made at the expense of the forest, so in the ecclesiastical sphere the work of the same pre-Norman period was to map out England in parishes, each with an endowed priest and a place of worship. The two movements together laid the foundations of the rural England we know. The parishes were often identical in area with the townships, in districts where the township was itself a large aggregate. But in North and West England we often find a number of townships in one parish, because the townships were mere hamlets or single farms.

The chief agents in the creation of the parish system were the Bishops and the thegns. The Bishops, no longer merely monastic in their outlook, encouraged the growth of the secular, that is the non-monastic, clergy, who were more subject than the monks to episcopal authority, and were spread abroad in direct and continual contact with the laity. The thegn or local magnate gave the land or endowment. In the first instance the priest was often the private chaplain attached to the thegn's hall, but in the course of time his successor became the parson of the parish. The heirs of the original lay benefactor naturally claimed control over his nomination, but the Bishop was effectively his commanding officer.

A very large proportion of the sites of the parish churches of rural England are of Saxon origin, though not much of the Saxon building has survived the active piety of subsequent generations. The essential life of Saxon England was village life, and the parish church and the graveyard around it became the centre of the village for most purposes, mundane as well as spiritual. As the worship of Woden and Thor gradually died out, or was suppressed as devil-worship by the intolerant laws dictated by the victorious clergy, the whole population found its dearest associations in life and in death gathered round the parish church.

The growth of the power and influence of the Church, spiritual and progressive on one side, was feudal and aristocratic on the other. But it is only modern thought that speaks of the two aspects as distinct. It was one and the same movement, and contemporaries saw nothing incongruous. Ecclesiastical dues enforced by heavy penalties, the tithe or tenth of the gross produce of the soil, were necessary to build up the mediæval Church, with its art, architecture, leisure, learning and civilization. Yet these dues were a burden on the farmer, and helped to reduce many freemen to poverty and serfage.

Anglo-Saxon Kings, first of Mercia and Wessex, then of all England, at the instigation of their favourite prelates and to save their own souls, endowed Bishoprics and monasteries with a vast proportion of the soil. It was the clergy who first taught the Kings how to alienate lands and royal jurisdiction by written charters, for the benefit of feudal magnates both lay and clerical. It was the clergy who taught Anglo-Saxon proprietors how to make written wills, and wills often enriched the Church. The Church, in elaborating the legal and learned aspects of daily life, was thereby promoting the feudal system based on territorialism, the sharp distinction of classes, and the increasingly unequal distribution of wealth and freedom. 'Richly endowed churches mean a subjected peasantry,' writes Maitland. At the time of Domesday the 'four minsters, Worcester, Evesham, Pershore and Westminster, were lords of seven-twelfths of Worcestershire.'

In Anglo-Saxon times, both before and after the Danish invasions, it is impossible always to distinguish clearly between Church and State. Not only did Bishops and clergy

compose the principal part of the King's civil service, as
remained the case throughout the Middle Ages, but before
the Norman Conquest there were no separate Church
Courts. The Bishop sat side by side with the Ealdorman or
sheriff on the bench of the Shire Court, where spiritual and
secular laws were indifferently administered. Those laws
of the Anglo-Saxon Kings which the clergy first reduced
to writing from popular oral tradition, are an example of
this state of things. Written in the Anglo-Saxon language,
but in the Latin alphabet of the clerical scribes, the laws
have a dual character. They are, in part, a schedule of
tribal custom, particularly as regards the price to be paid
for injury to life and limb in the frequent barbarous quarrels
of a primitive people: 'If one man slays another, 100 shillings wergeld,' 'if a bone is laid bare, three shillings,' 'if an
ear is struck off, twelve shillings.' But the laws also register
the high claims and privileges of the Church and her new
jurisdiction over sin. All were enforced together in the
Shire Court, at once a temporal and an ecclesiastical tribunal.[8]

[8] See Attenborough, *Laws of the Earliest English Kings,*
1922. A few quotations from the laws of Ine of Wessex
(*circa* 690) will illustrate various points:—
'A child shall be baptised within 30 days. If this is not
done the parent shall pay 30 shillings compensation. If,
however, it dies without being baptised, he shall pay as
compensation all he possesses.'
'If a slave works on Sunday by his lord's command, he
shall become free. . . . If, however, a freeman works on
that day, except by his lord's command, he shall be reduced to slavery.' This law and others show that the
Church had not set its face against slavery as such. 'Church
dues shall be rendered at Martinmas. If anyone fails to do
so he shall forfeit 60 shillings and render 12 times the
Church dues.'
'If anyone steals without the cognizance of his wife and
children he shall pay a fine of 60 shillings. If, however, he
steals with the cognizance of all his household they shall
all go into slavery.' 'If a thief be taken [in the act] he shall
die the death, or his life shall be redeemed by the payment
of wergeld.'
'If anyone slays a foreigner [a man not of Wessex] the

The political influence of the Church was inextricably involved with the religious awe in which it was held by Kings and people. When we read in the Anglo-Saxon Chronicle of powerful rulers of Mercia and Wessex abandoning their thrones to end their days as monks or as pilgrims to Rome, we cannot wonder at the vast alienation of land to the monasteries, or at the predominance in the courts of Offa of Mercia and Egbert of Wessex of the only class who knew how to read and write, who alone understood the administrative systems of the great Frankish monarchy oversea, and who, moreover, were the only people capable of instructing the King and his thegns in the formularies necessary to avoid eternal torment and attain eternal bliss.

Yet the Anglo-Saxon world was by no means entirely given over to the cultural and ethical ideas of Mediterranean Christianity. The new religion was to some extent affected by the temper of its latest converts, the gallant thegns of the North, nurtured on heroic poetry and legend. In the 'Dream of the Rood' the Christian poet, probably a Northumbrian of the Eighth Century, has thus blended the two strains:—

Stripped himself then the young hero,
that was God Almighty,
strong and brave:
he mounted the high cross
courageously in the sight of many,
when he wanted to set mankind free.
I trembled when the hero embraced me.
I dared not bend to the earth.

King shall have two-thirds of the wergeld and his son and relatives one-third.' 'The wergeld of a Welsh taxpayer is 120 shillings.' The ordinary punishments are death, slavery, scourging and fine—not imprisonment. Elaborate rules are laid down for sanctuary in a church.

In the contemporary laws of King Wihtred of Kent we read 'Men living in illicit unions shall turn to a righteous life repenting of their sins, or they shall be excluded from the communion of the Church.'

The written portions of Anglo-Saxon law which have come down to us are but fragments of the various 'customs' that governed proceedings in the courts of that day.

The majority of the high-hearted Nordic warriors, though generally respectful to the clergy, had not forgotten their ancestors, and were moved by much the same ideals of conduct as before. Anglo-Saxon poetry, like much mediæval and modern poetry, is sincerely Christian in form when religion is specifically mentioned, but is pagan in tradition and pure human in feeling. Only a few fragments of the wonderful Saxon epics have come down to us, and there is no reason to suppose these fragments were the best. The longest of them, the poem of *Beowulf*, though the matter of the tale is as childish as the tales told by Odysseus in the hall of Alcinöus, has something of Homer's dignity of feeling and of style.

The principal virtues praised in the Saxon epics were the loyalty of the warrior to his lord, the readiness of men to meet death in battle, the courage, courtesy and magnanimity of the lord himself. For it is the poetry of the hall, sung before Kings and thegns. The typical hero of these poems is a man unrestrained by tribal custom or religious observance, a man to whom the love of adventure is the breath of life, generous but passionate—Achilles or Hector but scarcely Odysseus. In many respects the life resembles that of Homer's day. Each was a free Heroic Age, wherein the warrior chief played his part unshackled. Even when Christianity and territorial feudalism were beginning to lay new restraints on the individual, Anglo-Saxon society had in it much that was disordered, fierce, noble and tragic. Here is a piece of it, taken from the Anglo-Saxon Chronicle, which gives a living picture of South England during the years when Offa was reigning over the Midlands:

[755.] This year Cynewulf and the West Saxon witan deprived his kinsman Sigebert of his kingdom, except Hampshire, for his unjust doings. And Hampshire he held, until he slew the ealdorman who longest abode by him. And then Cynewulf drove him into Andred [the weald], and he abode there until a swineherd stabbed him at Privets flood, and avenged the ealdorman.

[786.] And King Cynewulf fought very many battles against the Welsh [on the Somerset border in Devon]; and after he had held the kingdom about one and thirty years he purposed to expel an etheling, who was named Cyneard: and Cyneard was Sigebert's brother. And the etheling learned that the King, with a small band, was gone to Merton [in Surrey] to visit a woman; and he there beset him and surrounded the chamber on every side, before the men who were with the King discovered him. And, when the King perceived this he went to the door and there manfully defended himself, until he beheld the etheling, and then he rushed out upon him and sorely wounded him; and they all continued fighting against the King until they had slain him. And, upon this, the King's thegns, having discovered the affray by the woman's cries, each, as he was ready, and with his utmost speed ran to the spot. And the etheling offered money and life to each of them, and not one of them would accept it; but they continued fighting until they all fell, except one, a British hostage, and he was sorely wounded.

Then, upon the morrow, the King's thegns whom he had left behind him, heard that the King was slain. Then rode they thither. And, at the town wherein the King lay slain, they found the etheling and those within had closed the gates against them; but they went then forward. And the etheling offered them their own choice of land and money if they would grant him the kingdom, and showed them that their kinsmen were with him, men who would not desert him. And they then said that no kinsman was dearer to them than their lord, and that they never would follow his murderer. And they, in turn, bade their kinsmen that they should go away from the etheling in safety. But the kinsmen said that the same had been bidden to those who before had been with the King, and that they themselves would now pay no more attention to such offers.

The etheling was killed in the fight that followed, and all his men with him, because they chose death rather than show themselves less noble than the King's men the day before. In this incident we see how the ethics of Anglo-Saxon heroic poetry might be translated very accurately into terms of every-day life.

BOOKS FOR FURTHER READING: Baldwin Brown, *Arts in Early England,* Vols. I. and II.; Professor Bury, *Life of St. Patrick*; Mrs. Green, *The Irish State to* 1014; *Cam. Med. Hist.*, Vol. II., Chaps. VIII. B, XVI. B., XVII. and Vol. III., Chap. XIX.; Chadwick, *The Heroic Age*; W. P. Ker, *English Literature, Mediæval,* Chap. II.; Professor Chambers, *Widsith,* as before, especially Chap. VII.; R. H.

Hodgkin, *A History of the Anglo-Saxons,* 1935; F. M. Stenton, *Anglo-Saxon England,* 1943.

CHAPTER FIVE

The Second Nordic Invasion. Viking Settlement and Influence

Thus far had the first Nordic settlers in Britain advanced on the path of civilization and national unity when the second wave of Nordic invasion broke upon them in their turn. The heathen Danes and Norsemen destroyed for awhile the higher civilization of the island collected in its monasteries, and for awhile increased its disunion by establishing the Danelaw over against the areas ruled by Saxon and Celt. Yet before a hundred years were out, the Scandinavian invasions were seen to have greatly strengthened the forces of progress. For the Vikings were of a stock kindred to the Saxon, but even more full of energy, hardihood and independence of character, and with no less aptitude for poetry and learning. They brought back to the island those seafaring habits which the Saxons had lost in their sojourn on up-country farms, and it was due to them that a vigorous town life revived in England for the first time since the departure of the Romans. Had it not been for the Scandinavian blood infused into our race by the catastrophes of the Ninth Century, less would have been heard in days to come of British maritime and commercial enterprise.

The deficiencies of the Anglo-Saxons, prior to this stern process of reinvigoration, were indeed many and great. They had so much forgotten their sea-craft that when Alfred sought to make a navy he sent for Frisian mercenaries. The Saxons had never developed town life, except to a slight extent in London. Their great economic service to Britain was their work as pioneer farmers and lumbermen, living in large townships or in isolated homesteads and 'dens' in the clearings they made in the forest. But the men of the township had little concern with what went on beyond the waste surrounding their lands, and regarded with suspicion every 'foreigner' from beyond it. 'If a man from afar or a foreigner,' say the dooms of Kent and Wessex, 'fares through the wood off the highway and neither hollas nor blows a horn, he shall be counted a thief and may be slain or put to ransom.'

Kings and Bishops were striving to create a national or at least a provincial patriotism, but with very limited success. Northumbria was isolated, decadent, torn by feuds which were to leave her an easy prey to the Dane. Mercia had held the leadership in the glorious reign of Offa II (757–96), whose descent was traced through twelve generations to that Offa I, hero of many a tale and ballad, who had reigned over Angel, the old racial home in Schleswig four centuries back. But Egbert of Wessex had broken Mercia's power at Ellandune (825), and established instead the supremacy of his own Kingdom. But Egbert was no more King of all the English than Offa before him. These successive 'bretwaldas' of the pre-Danish Heptarchy,—Edwin of Northumbria, Penda and Offa of Mercia, Egbert of Wessex,—had only the shadow of empire in Britain. Their supremacy depended on prestige which a single stricken field could make or mar. Machinery was lacking for the permanent subjugation of distant provinces. The victors of the hour had no garrisoned forts and no standing army in the vassal States. The King's personal following of thegns, however devoted, was not large; the 'fyrd' could only be called out for a few weeks, and the Saxon farmers had no desire to colonize other Saxon Kingdoms as conquerors, though they were still busy invading and settling new lands in Welsh territory beyond Exe and Severn.[1]

In the hour of serious foreign invasion the English King-

[1] The Magasaete and Wreocensaete (dwellers near the Wrekin) were early English settlements on the Wye and higher Severn valleys, in constant conflict with the Welsh. Their territory was delimited by Offa's Dyke, *circa* 784. See Map 5, p. 83, above. The thegns of Wessex were in no less constant conflict with the Welsh of the Devonian border, which the Saxons were constantly thrusting back and back till it reached the present boundary of Cornwall.

doms proved able to lay aside their feuds and help one another against the Vikings, more at any rate than the tribes of Ireland in like case. Nevertheless they fell one after the other without having evolved any coherent plan of national defence. The desire to be united in one State only came into being as a later consequence of the Danish wars, after Northumbria and Mercia had been destroyed by the heathen flood. Out of the stress of the same conflict arose new feudal and civic institutions which made Egbert's descendants more truly Kings of England than the founder of their line had ever aspired to be.

The course of history would have been very different had not the royal family of Wessex provided a long succession of able warriors and statesmen, including Alfred the Great. In the absence of elaborate institutions the affairs of a primitive society depend on the personal accident of the quality of its Kings. The richest and most populous part of old agricultural England—East Anglia—had failed in the race for leadership because it had no prince of the calibre of Edwin of Northumbria, Penda of Mercia or Alfred of Wessex. The Danes soon found how safe it was to land on the shores of helpless East Anglia and thence to overrun decadent Northumbria and declining Mercia. Wessex, the State that lay furthest removed from the landing bases of the invaders, happened at that time to have more resisting power than any other of the kingdoms, thanks to Alfred and his brothers, and it was apparently owing to this accident of historical geography that the Vikings just failed to complete their conquest of England.

Would things have been very different in the end, or very much worse, if the Scandinavians had extended their power up to the borders of Cornwall and Wales in the Ninth Century, as they did in the Eleventh under Canute? The question is not easy to answer, if we assume that once the Danes were established in England they would in any case, like the conquerors of Normandy, have soon abandoned Woden for Christ. But the might-have-beens of history are only the shadows attending on the triumphant event. The event decreed that the work of reconstructing civilization after the Danish raids, and reconciling the two branches of the Nordic race in England, should fall in the first instance to Alfred the Great and his progeny.

Although 'Viking' means 'warrior' and not 'creek-man,' the Vikings were men of the creeks. Denmark[2] was a land of sandy flats through which crept tortuous channels of the sea. Norway was a land of fiords—precipitous gorges in the mountain plateau, carrying the tide into the heart of the hills, in some places for a hundred miles. Here and there along the winding course of these fiords, a plot of fertile ground between the precipice and the estuary left room for cornfields and a group of wooden chalets. Hard by, a steep slope bore the dark forest down to the water's edge, inviting the lumberman and the shipbuilder. Above, on ledges of the fellside, among sounding streams and waterfalls, the cattle lowed on the summer pastures. High over all, the barren mountain ranges, the breeding ground of Norse legend and poetry, rose up towards glacier and snow-field, dividing the settlements on the fiords one from another each as a puny kingdom, delaying for centuries the political union of Norway, and thrusting the hardy inhabitants out to sea to seek food and fortune there.

Fur-traders, whalers, fishermen, merchants, pirates, yet all the while assiduous tillers of the soil, the Scandinavians had always been an amphibious people. Ever since they had occupied their present homeland at some undefinable date in the stone age, the sea had been their road from settlement to settlement and their only communication with the outer world. But till the end of the Eighth Century the area of their piracy had been chiefly confined to the shores of the Baltic. They had been content to prey on one another and on their nearest neighbours. It was only

[2] So called because Scandinavian Danes had settled in the districts left empty by the Angles who had gone to England. See p. 63, above.

in the age of Charlemagne that they began to cross the ocean and attack the Christian lands of the West.[3]

Why, it is often asked, were they suddenly inspired to go so far afield in such numbers?

Several answers have been given, each containing perhaps some element of truth. Famine, following a bad harvest in those inhospitable climes, sometimes drove whole settlements to seek new lands. There were three classes among the Scandinavians—thrall, carl and earl. Polygamy, practised chiefly among the earls, produced a superfluity of landless young men, unwilling to be starvelings or dependents; in love with war and adventure, though not above trade by the way; proud of their swords and ring-shirts, of their red cloaks, gold ornaments and long yellow hair—for the Vikings were dandies rather than slovens, save when one of them felt the 'baresark' fury upon him. Such were the raw materials of the Viking movement. It is also pointed out that in the last thirty years of the Eighth Century Charlemagne and his mailed Frankish horsemen approached the southern border of Denmark, on the cruel crusade which offered the Saxons of Germany the choice between baptism and death. The Danes gave asylum to the Saxon patriots and were naturally alarmed at Charlemagne's proceedings in their neighbourhood. Some have

[3] Their amphibious habits they carried with them to their overseas settlements. See Burnt Njal for Iceland, and the Orkney Saga, where we read of Sweyn—'He had so great a drinking-hall that there was not another so great in all the Orkneys. Sweyn had in the spring hard work, and made them lay down very much seed, and looked much after it himself, but when that toil was ended he fared away every spring on a Viking voyage, and harried about the Southern Islands and Iceland and came home after midsummer. That he called Spring-Viking.' He then reaped his crops and ended the year with an Autumn-Viking. A strenuous and varied life!

The Viking has fared well in modern English fiction. Kipling's Joyous Venture in Puck of Pook's Hill has caught his historical character with rare felicity, and the first story in John Buchan's Path of the King is a fine piece of historical imagination.

thought that the armed and threatening approach of the Christian warrior world aroused the Danish worshippers of Woden to raid the monasteries of the British Isles. But those early raiders came from Norway rather than Denmark, and the Scandinavians had no sense of political unity as a nation. Neither were they religious fanatics. They were savage robbers in an age of universal savagery, and they had what others had not—a noble joy in maritime adventure and exploration. It is probable that peaceful Scandinavian traders had visited England before the age of the Viking raids, but the evidence about them is so slight that nothing of importance can be deduced.

Many definable causes may have contributed to the Viking invasions, but the wind bloweth where it listeth and there is an element of chance in the rise and decline of great movements. The outburst of energy that carried the secluded inhabitants of the creeks to Constantinople and Greenland, that founded Normandy, the English Danelaw and the Irish towns, may have been due to the mere force of example and fashion, the cumulative power of a ball once set rolling by the casual success of a few adventurers.

At any rate, in the closing years of the Eighth Century, while Offa of Mercia was still alive, occurred the first recorded Viking raid in Western Europe. Three long-ships, with perhaps a couple of hundred rascals on board, landed somewhere on the peaceful coast of Wessex, killed the King's reeve who came to demand their business, and put to sea again before they could be caught. No more Vikings were seen in those parts for long years to come, but there followed in quick succession a series of similar raids on the coasts of Northumbria, Scotland, Ireland and Wales. The water-thieves plundered the monasteries temptingly situated, after the manner of the Celtic Church, on islands and capes peculiarly exposed to attack from the sea. Lindisfarne, Iona and many shrines of less name were robbed of their treasures, and the monks were either massacred or carried off to be bartered as slaves on the continent. The ill-guarded wealth of the shrines would fully account for these proceedings without our being forced to attribute to the pirates a fanatical hatred of Christianity provoked by Charlemagne's Saxon crusade. Nor was the gross cruelty of these raids anything exceptional. Even while they were in process the Anglo-Saxons were dealing out the same measure to one another. 'This year,' says the Chronicle for 796, 'Kenulf, King of the Mercians, laid waste Kent as far as the marshes, and took Pren, their king, and led him to Mercia and let his eyes be picked out and his hands cut off.'

These attacks on the monasteries of the British coastline seem to have been the beginning of the Viking movement. We can imagine the next stage with likelihood enough, if we shift the scene to Norway and Denmark. The successful raiders have returned, loaded with gold and gems. Along every fiord and estuary rumours run that the churches of the west are paved with gold, that there are no warships in the western seas, and that a new way has been found to get rich quick with a little lively adventure. It is added that some of the ploughlands out west seem richer even than those of Stavanger. The needy Earls' sons talk over the tidings at the ale-board and look round for leaders and followers.

Slowly, during the fifty years or more before the movement reached its height, all Norway and Denmark awoke to the truth that there was no sea-power to protect the British Islands or the famous Carolingian Empire; that the Anglo-Saxons and Franks were land-lubbers, and that the Irish for all their missions and colonizings used mere coracles and canoes. The world lay exposed to the sea power of the Vikings, a prey for their greed and a playground for their love of joyous adventure. Soon the young man who had not been out a-Viking was chaffed at the ale-board and scorned by the maidens, some of whom accompanied their men folk oversea and fought fully armed in the shield ring. As with the simple Swiss peasants after the easy victories of Morat and Nanci, war and plunder abroad became the chief national industry, absorbing the best energies of the rising generation. The last and most

EMERY WALKER LTD. SC.

Map 6   Viking Routes

important stage was reached when permanent immigration and land settlement oversea took the place of plundering raids.

The Scandinavians had always been traders as well as pirates in their dealings with one another in home waters, and so they remained in the larger field of foreign enterprise now open to them. They combined the pride of the merchant with the very different pride of the warrior, as few people have done. In a tomb in the Hebrides a pair of scales has been found buried in a Viking chief's tomb, alongside his sword and battle-axe. Their first thought when they founded a colony in England or Ireland was to build fortified towns and to open markets. By land or sea they were prepared to trade with the newcomer or to cut his throat according to circumstances or the humour of the hour. Such indeed, for centuries to come, was the custom of sailors from every port of mediæval Europe, not excluding Chaucer's Shipman and some of the Elizabethan heroes. But the Vikings put an energy all their own into the practice both of piracy and trade, adding thereto great military qualities on land, unusual with Jack ashore.

As the Ninth Century wore on, a large part of the whole Scandinavian people had been a-Viking to the most various parts of the world. They carved their runes on the stone lion of the Piræus that now keeps guard before the Arsenal at Venice. They were known to avenge in the streets of Constantinople blood feuds begun among themselves in Dublin. Their far journeys brought them wealth, civilization and the knowledge of cities and men. The Saxon peasant, who regarded them as outer barbarians, was ignorant and provincial compared to them. Their Eddic poetry was succeeded by no less splendid prose Sagas, historical novels recording with extraordinary realism the romance of their heroic life.

There were three routes of Scandinavian activity in the Viking era. First there was the Eastern route, followed mainly by the Swedes, who penetrated the heart of the Slav territories, to Novgorod and Kiev; at Kiev they founded the original Russian State, and sailed thence down the Dnieper and crossed the Black Sea to annoy the walls of Constantinople itself.

The other two routes lay to the West. There was the route followed mainly by the Norsemen or men of Norway, which we may call the Outer Line. It led to the most adventurous sea-voyages, to the settlement of Iceland and Greenland and the discovery of North America. It led to the Orkneys, Caithness, Ross, Galloway and Dumfries, where large Scandinavian colonies brought the first Nordic element into the life of Highland and South-Western Scotland. The Isle of Man was occupied as the Malta of the new maritime power in the Irish Sea, which had become a Scandinavian lake. By this Outer Line important colonies of Norsemen were planted in Cumberland, Westmoreland, Lancashire, Cheshire, and on the coast of South Wales.

Ireland was for a while overrun, and Dublin, Cork, Limerick, Wicklow and Waterford were founded as Danish towns, the beginning of Irish city life.

Thirdly, there was the Inner Line, mainly followed by the Danes from Denmark. By that way attacks were delivered on the north coast of Europe and the east and south coasts of England. That way went the largest hosts of Viking immigrants, in the days of Alfred of Wessex, seeking to win wide lands to plough and to rule. These great armies, composed of bands enlisted under many allied kinglets, learnt to obey a single war chief so long as the season's campaign lasted. The 'host' passed freely from France to England and back again, according as the resistance was stronger or weaker first on one side of the Channel, then on the other. Their mighty and protracted operations ended in the creation of two Danelaws, each of the first importance in history. The smaller one, which they carved out of the Frankish Kingdom, was named after them Normandy; the larger Danelaw consisted of all eastern England between Thames and Tyne. Finally the Norse settlers in Lancashire and Cumberland joined hands across England with the Danish settlers from Yorkshire, so that at this point the Scandinavian race predominated from sea to sea.[4]

The Viking followers of the Outer and Inner Lines often crossed each other's path. Danes and Norsemen were found together in Normandy, in South Ireland and in North England, and both indifferently penetrated into Spain, the Mediterranean and the Levant. All this amazing exploration, which touched the coast of North America five hundred years before Columbus, this habitual and almost daily defiance of the storms of Cape Wrath and the Hebrides, was conducted in open long-ships, propelled by oars in the hands of the free warriors themselves, aided, when the wind served, by a single sail of striped colours and costly material. Over the low waist of the brightly-painted ship hung the line of round shields, yellow and

[4] See p. 67, above, and note.

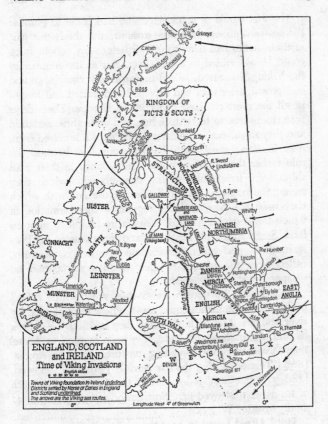

Map 7

black alternately, while the high dragon-prow broke the billows in front, a terror to Christian men who saw it coming. The courage and sea-craft of sailors who could venture in such ships on such voyages has never been surpassed in maritime history. They often paid toll for their daring. Alfred's Wessex was saved once by the drowning of a 'host', when a storm piled up 120 Danish galleys against the cliffs of Swanage. [877.]

The first bands of marauders who had come to plunder the seaward abbeys had little armour, and the better part of their tactics had been to sail off before any serious force could be assembled to catch them. But as the number of the Vikings increased, so did their military knowledge and equipment, after they had travelled and traded and fought in all the most civilized countries of Europe. Their fleets rose from three to forty, to a hundred or to three hundred and fifty ships, each ship carrying perhaps a hundred men. And in these great hosts body-armour had become the rule rather than the exception. The Vikings in their mail shirts were irresistible for the strength with which they swung the long two-handed battle-axe, the skill with which they used the bow, and the regular wedge formation in which the disciplined ships' crews were taught to fight on land. Siege craft with mangonel and mine was an art they learned to perfection. Meanwhile the Saxon peasants, called from the plough in their woollen shirts, had no weapon but shield and spear.

In mobility the odds were no less great. Until Alfred built a fleet, the Danes could move where they pleased by river and sea. And on land, when they had left the galleys behind a garrisoned stockade, they soon learned to 'horse' themselves from the breeding pastures of East Anglia. [866.] Thence, during the five terrible years that followed, [866–71.] the 'host' rode through the length and breadth of England, destroyed first Northumbria, then Mercia, and finally invaded Wessex.

Until Alfred learnt to beat them at their own game, the strategy of the Danes lay in surprise attacks delivered on distant and unexpected points. It was impossible for the 'fyrd' of English farmers on their slow feet to catch up with these galloping warriors, or to fight armoured men if they ever got near them. It is even doubtful how often the 'fyrd' or *levée-en-masse* of this primitive character was called out in Alfred's day. A dozen years after the first 'horsing' of the Danes, we read that Alfred with his forces 'rode' in pursuit of them. [877.] To hunt down and fight the invaders, Alfred was driven more and more to rely on his mounted and armoured thegns and their vassals, the class that specialized in war. When war becomes serious, it necessarily becomes professional, and requires changes that re-act upon the whole social system. The Danish wars meant another advance on the road to feudalism in England.

Thus both sides became mounted infantry, but not yet cavalry. Although Dane and Saxon rode to the battle-field, and fled or pursued on horseback, they had not acquired the art of fighting from the saddle. But those Vikings who had become the ruling classes in Normandy learnt the value of shock-tactics on horseback from the Frankish knights who opposed them on the banks of the Seine. In the fullness of time the Franco-Viking cavalry returned under William to the conquest of the Anglo-Danish infantry at Hastings.

Alfred the Great is naturally to be compared to Charlemagne, after whom it is possible that he modelled many of his doings. Each was the champion of Christ against the heathen, of the new feudal Kingship against chaos. Each had many-sided talents as warrior, administrator and scholar, suited to an epoch before professional men abound, when a King can himself teach, govern and lead his subjects in peace and in war. If Alfred's lot was cast in narrower geographic limits than the Napoleonic arena of Charlemagne's activities, his work has lasted longer. He and his sons made England one for ever. The memory of Charlemagne does not suffice to unite Germany and France.

[871.] By temperament a scholar, and of ailing health, Alfred was forced into the field in early youth to lead the grimmest warfare of that terrible epoch. But harsh experience schooled without souring his gentle qualities. At the age of twenty-two he was second-in-command in the campaign of Ashdown and the eight other 'folk-fights' when Wessex was striving desperately to thrust the Danish host off the chalk ridges south of Thames; England north of the river had already submitted to the Danes. The young man at once won the confidence of the army, and when in the middle of that year of battles his elder brother died, he was chosen king by the Witan. His nephews were passed over, for minors were excluded by custom and necessity in days when a King's first business was to lead the folk to war.

[878.] Seven years later came the crisis of his life. The Danes, secure in the possession of North, Midlands and East, at last overran Wessex by an unexpected raid at mid-winter. Alfred's subjects began to fly oversea. He himself with a small army of Somerset warriors held out in the island fastnesses of the Parret fenland. Fifty miles beyond lay the Cornwall of that day, where the Welsh enemies of Wessex were often in league with the Dane. On so narrow a thread hung the cause of English independence. But the Saxon thegns who had recently colonized Devon stood strongly for Alfred, and destroyed a Danish force that had been landed in his rear. Such was the confidence inspired by his leadership even in this desperate hour, that the thegns of conquered Wilts and Hampshire answered once more to his summons and rode to rejoin his banner. The battle of Ethandune reversed the whole situation, and the Danish leader, Guthrum, accepted terms, known as the Treaty of Wedmore, whereby he and his followers underwent baptism and agreed to retire into the 'Danelaw,' leaving Wessex free.

Having found the resistance of South England stiffer than they had hoped, many of the 'host' transferred their operations to France. A few years later Alfred extracted from Guthrum a still more advantageous treaty defining the southern frontier of the Danelaw; it was to run along Watling Street and the Lea river from its source, leaving London to the English King.

[878–900.] Such was the political geography for the remainder of Alfred's reign. The Danes, on the way to become Christian, were settled as acknowledged masters of North-Eastern England. All Saxon territory to south of them was united under Alfred. If his descendants should conquer the Danelaw, they would be the first Kings of

England, for Mercia, East Anglia and Northumbria had disappeared from the list of sovereign states.

Only the wreck of old Northumbria—Bernicia beyond Tyne—had not been conquered by the Vikings. This Saxon district between Tyne and Cheviot assumed the name of Northumberland and dragged on for many centuries a precarious existence between England and Scotland. But Saxondom between the Cheviots and the Forth, which now first began to be called Lothian, became increasingly involved in Scottish history, because the Danelaw cut it off from the main current of Saxon history to the south. At the same time the Norse invaders of the western sea cut the connections between the Scots of Ireland and the Scots of Scotland. In these ways the Viking invasions drove Scotland in upon herself, and hammered her warring tribes into something a little more like union. It was in the Viking epoch that Kenneth MacAlpine became King of the united Picts and Scots. [844–60.] He moved the relics of St. Columba and the centre of Scottish religion from Iona, with its backward glance over the sea at Ireland, to Dunkeld in the heart of his united kingdom.

After the Christening of Guthrum and the fixing of the limits of the Danelaw, Alfred's life entered a new and happier phase that lasted till his death. His position in southern England was relatively secure; the tide of events flowed with him now; he was regarded by all Saxons, both within and without the Danelaw, as their sole champion even the christened Danes, constantly increasing in number, felt reverence for this English Charlemagne. There were indeed more Viking invasions from over sea, but the Danes of the Danelaw backed the newcomers half-heartedly, for they themselves were now settled men with farms and wives, fearing reprisal since they now had lands of their own to be raided. And Alfred, copying Danish methods, had rebuilt London as a walled and garrisoned town, held by English burghers, whose duty it was to defend it against attack; the chief gate of England was locked against the Danes. [878–900.]

In the intervals of these later and less terrible wars, Alfred enjoyed whole years of respite in which he could indulge in tasks very near to his heart. He began English prose literature by translating Bede's Latin into Anglo-Saxon, and by translating and compiling handbooks of theology, history and geography for his subjects' use; and he initiated the keeping of the Anglo-Saxon Chronicle, the first historical record ever composed in English. He fetched over foreign scholars, and welcomed learned refugees from Mercia and the North, in the hope of repairing, in Wessex at least, the desperate ravages of the Danish raids, which had swept away the libraries and learned men of the earlier England, and had left a clergy who no longer understood the Latin of the mass they sang. Alfred, moreover, founded the first 'public schools' for teaching letters to the sons of noblemen and thegns, extending for the first time the gifts of learning to some of the higher laity, so as to fit them for the tasks of modern administration.

The revival of letters and religion was slow and artificial, the gift of an industrious king to an ignorant clergy and people. It was no longer the glad, confident morning of Cuthbert, Bede and Alcuin. Learning had indeed received a terrible blow in the sack of the Northumbrian and Mercian monasteries, but at least Alfred had set recovery afoot, and the new growth of city life due to the Danes would in the end do more for the higher civilization than monasticism at its best.

During the last twenty years of his reign, Alfred strengthened the institutions of Wessex both in peace and war. He created a fleet. He made an available army system, and put permanent garrisons into earthwork forts of the Danish type. He set up a sound administration worked through the shire and its officers. It was all very primitive, but better than anything there had been before in England. [EDWARD ELDER, 900–24.] Thus armed, his son, Edward the Elder, and his daughter, the lady Ethelfleda of Mercia, proceeded after his death to the reconquest of the Danelaw, which Edward's son and successor, Athelstan, completed. [ATHELSTAN, 924–40.]

The Danes of the Danelaw had shown themselves deficient in political unity as soon as they settled down upon the land. A number of rival settlements, each under a ruler styled King or Earl according to fancy, had less cohesion than the English of the remodelled Kingdom of Wessex. The Vikings had been apt to unite for offensive warfare under temporary war chiefs, but the oneness of the 'host' that had trampled England under foot was not reflected in the political arrangements of the Danelaw, which therefore fell before the returning wave of Saxondom.

Edward the Elder and Athelstan are the first whom we can justly describe as Kings of England. [EDGAR, 959–75.] Edward's grandson Edgar, in a prosperous and peaceful reign, was clearly recognized as such. The Danelaw, after absorbing the other English kingdoms, had itself been absorbed by Wessex. Only Celtic Wales and Celtic Scotland were still independent, and even their kings and princes sometimes acknowledged a vague supremacy in Athelstan and Edgar, who for their part regarded themselves as 'Emperors of Britain.'

A new unity had grown out of the cleaving and sundering of the Danish conquests. So long as the Viking battle-axe was crashing through the skulls of monks, and the English were nailing to their church-doors skins flayed off their Danish enemies, the hatred between Anglo-Saxon and Scandinavian was profound.[5] But it was not permanent. In days before the printing-press, the memory of inter-racial wrongs and atrocities was not artificially fostered. Green earth forgets—when the school-master and the historian are not on the scene. And these two Nordic races were of kindred stock, with many instincts and customs in common. After the Danes had accepted baptism, it was easy to merge them with the English under the rule of the House of Wessex, for they had not come over to found a Scandinavian Empire, but to seek good farm lands. So

[5] There is no doubt about the Danes' skins. See H. St. George Gray's paper in the *Saga Book of the Viking Club*, Vol. V., anno 1906–7. It is only one of many reminders of the barbarism of heathen and Christian alike in that age.

far were they from enslaving their neighbours, that their Danelaw contained many freemen and no slaves, in sharp contrast to Wessex. Settled down prosperously in their new quarters, under their own Danish laws and Danish earls and lawmen, they could tolerate the light rule of English Kings.

There was now only one King, but for generations to come there was a rich variety of customs and 'laws' in the land. The Common Law—that is the law common to all England—was built up in Plantagenet times by the professional lawyers of the King's courts; but in Anglo-Saxon times there was no such body of men and no body of case law for the whole nation. Certain written laws were sometimes issued by the King with the help of his Bishops, perhaps for the guidance of all courts. But every Shire or Hundred Court and every court of private jurisdiction might also have its own customary local laws. The Danes clung strongly to their own, and the region of the 'Dane law' had its name thence.

Law, like many other good things, received a stimulus from the coming of the Danes. The very word 'law' is Danish, and has survived its rivals, the Anglo-Saxon word 'doom' and the Latin word 'lex.' The Scandinavians, when not on the Viking war-path, were a litigious people and loved to gather in the 'thing' to hear legal argument. They had no professional lawyers, but many of their farmer-warriors, like Njal the truth-teller, were learned in folk custom and its intricate judicial procedure. A Danish town in England often had, as its principal officers, twelve hereditary 'law men.' The Danes introduced the habit of making committees among the freemen in court, which perhaps made England favourable ground for the future growth of the jury system out of a Frankish custom introduced later by the Normans. In the laws of Ethelred the Unready we read 'that a gemot be held in every wapontake, and the twelve senior thegns go out, and the reeve with them and swear on the halidoom that is given into their hand that they will accuse no innocent man nor conceal any guilty one.' This is Danish, and very near to a mediæval jury of presentment, though not its direct original.

The conception of justice in the Anglo-Danish period shows traces of three different origins. First the old idea, common to Saxon and Scandinavian, was the 'wergeld' or money compensation for a wrong, to be paid to the injured party or his kin to prevent feud, a conception once covering almost the whole field of justice, but on the wane as the power of the courts became stronger and the feeling of the clan weaker; slowly, throughout the late Saxon period, 'slaying' loses much of its character as a blood-feud between families and becomes increasingly an affair between the community and the murderer.[6] Secondly, there was the new doctrine of the Church that wrong-doing had the further aspect of sin or moral wrong, to be expiated by penance. And thirdly there is the peculiarly Scandinavian view, found in Anglo-Danish laws, that certain acts such as cowardly flight or desertion of one's chief were dishonourable—'nidings værk'—to be punished as deeds unworthy of the free warrior. From the time of Alfred onwards, we find special penalties and special reprobation attached to the crime of treason to the King or to a man's lord; the growth of the law of treason and petty treason is due, in part, to the increase in the power of the Crown and of the feudal lord, partly to the influence of Roman law coming in through the clergy, and partly to the strong ethical feeling of the whole Nordic race, expressed alike in Anglo-Saxon and Scandinavian literature, of horror of the man who betrays or deserts his chief.

[6] How slowly the law got the strength to replace the blood-feud and to bring the accused into court otherwise than by the force of arms of the aggrieved party, we are reminded by Alfred's laws, e.g. 'If anyone chances to meet his enemy, not having known him to be at home, and if he will give up his weapons, he shall be detained 30 days and his kinsmen informed. If he will not give up his weapons, then he may be attacked.' 'A man may fight on behalf of his lord if his lord is attacked, without becoming liable to blood-feud.' The laws of Edmund and of Canute show that the blood-feud was still a custom even in their day.

The Danelaw, during its brief period of independence as a confederation of Scandinavian communities, had been organized round the life of its towns. The Roman walls of Chester were repaired first by a Viking chief, and the commercial life of Chester and York was revived by Scandinavian enterprise. Roads were scarce but rivers were deep, and commerce was borne in barges to the wharves of inland towns. The famous 'five boroughs' of the Danes—Lincoln, Stamford, Leicester, Derby and Nottingham—served both as military garrisons and as trading centres. Each was protected by a palisaded mound and ditch; each had its own 'law men,' its own army and its own sovereign 'Jarl' or Earl. From the borough, the Earl and his army ruled a wide surrounding district. There is something analogous to Roman practice in the political importance of the Danish town, though it was purely Scandinavian in origin.

When Edward the Elder and his sister Ethelfleda of the Mercians set about conquering the Danelaw, they did it by imitating and taking over the Danish borough system. Alfred had set the example in London and elsewhere in Wessex, and his son and daughter spread the net of fortified English 'burhs' up the Severn valley and across the Midlands. They repaired the stone walls of ruined Roman cities, or piled up new earthworks round tactical points unguarded before. In each fortress they planted a permanent English garrison holding lands on burgage tenure, with the duty of defending the place. As fast as they conquered the Danelaw, they divided it into shires like those of Saxon Wessex; but each of the new shires was moulded round the administrative centre of some Danish borough, and its boundaries were probably those of the Danish military district attached thereto. Such is the origin of the shires of the east midlands—Lincoln, Derby, Nottingham, Leicester, Northampton, Huntingdon, Cambridge, Bedford. An ealdorman, with a shire-reeve beside him to represent King and people, answered to the King for one or more of the old shires of Wessex, or of the new shires of recovered Mercia. But a Danish Earl answered to the English King for each shire of the annexed Danelaw.

The new English Kingdom was thus equipped with a garrison system and with organs of administration which had been wanting to the shadowy empires ruled over by Offa and Egbert.[7] And so the familiar shape of modern England, with its famous shires and towns, comes out line by line under our eyes, as we watch the clouds drifting and lifting over the chaos of the Anglo-Danish wars. So much we can see even from far off, but if we could watch the Tenth Century map at closer quarters, we should see no less clearly one country village after another grow modestly into being along the newly drained river valleys and across the slowly diminishing area of forest.

Although the boroughs had been formed in the first instance to meet the military and administrative needs of both sides in the Danish wars, they soon took on a commercial character. The Danes were indefatigable traders, faring across the sea and claiming on their return to be 'thegn-right worthy' in their honourable character of overseas merchants, all the more if some of the goods they brought back had been won by hard knocks rather than by hard bargaining. The Saxons caught up some at least of their commercial ideas and habits. The special peace of the King protected the borough and all within it. And, when Edward the Elder published a law that all buying and selling must take place in a market-town before the town reeve, he aided the concentration of business in the new boroughs. The citizens were at once warriors, traders, and farmers of the adjoining lands. In days to come, their milder descendants might find it enough to be traders and farmers only, when the mounted Norman knight took over the fighting part of their business and retired proudly into his stone donjon overlooking the town. And when, after many centuries, specialization had been carried one step further, the citizens ceased to till the soil and confined themselves altogether to crafts and commerce.

Such, in one of its aspects, was the origin and development of the English town. But no English town has the

[7] See p. 100, above.

same history as any other. And some of the larger stone-walled cities, particularly London, never completely submitted to the feudal world outside, but preserved down the ages an adequate military control of their own defence.

BOOKS FOR FURTHER READING: Gjerset, *History of the Norwegian People*, Vol. I.; W. G. Collingwood, *Scandinavian Britain* (S.P.C.K., 1908); Beatrice Lees, *Alfred* (Heroes of the Nations Series); Oman, *Art of War in Middle Ages*; *Cam. Med. Hist.*, Vol III., Chap. XIII., XIV., XX.; R. H. Hodgkin, *A History of the Anglo-Saxons*, 1935; F. M. Stenton, *Anglo-Saxon England*, 1943.

CHAPTER SIX

Life in Later Saxon England. Feudalism Encroaching. Canute and the Nordic Maritime Empire.

War, invasion and bloodshed were normal conditions of life in Saxon England. Nor did the advantages of our island position begin to appear before the strong Norman Kings and their following had taken hold. So long as the sea was the highroad assistant to every invader, 'England bound in with the triumphant sea' was bound a helpless victim, and her ill-defended charms were as well known to the warrior races of Northern Europe as were Italy's to those of the South.

Nevertheless the slayers and marauders could not be everywhere in the island at once. The habitations of man were more secluded then than now, surrounded by marshland and forest; there were no maps to reveal their whereabouts and few roads to guide the spoiler to his prey. A story is told of times much more recent than the Danish raids, how Scottish moss-troopers failed for a whole day in their search for so important a place as Brinkburn Priory, amid the wooded dells of Coquet, until it was betrayed at the last moment by the sound of its own bells on the evening air. It is likely that, when the Danish 'host' was riding through a countryside, people in quiet parishes were chary of ringing their bells.

An Anglo-Saxon lived in some respects an enviable life,

so long as he could avoid being 'hewed amain with swords mill-sharp'—the ending of most folk in his favorite poems. We too seldom ask ourselves what his life was like, because, while the life of the later Middle Ages and even of Roman antiquity presents itself to the eye and the imagination through the work of masonry, the Saxon period has vanished from the landscape; most preconquest churches have been rebuilt, and the wooden chalets and halls where life was spent have left neither trace nor tradition, unless it be in the architecture of some of our fine old English barns. But those halls were great places in their day. Lowland Switzerland can still show us how noble and spacious a wooden structure can be, when it is the natural product of a native art tradition, with no limit to the building material on the spot, save the labour of cutting it down. The log halls of Saxon thegn and Danish jarl were decorated with carving and paint both outside and in, and hung with burnished armour, though the smoke eddying under the rafters in search of the hole in the roof diminished the sense of luxury. The thegn and his family were resplendent in cloaks of many colours. Articles of daily use were fantastically carved by native craftsmen. The art of the English jeweller was very fine, as the 'Alfred jewel' and others still remain to prove.

It was seldom that the thegn or his followers possessed any books, unless he were an assiduous courtier of King Alfred. But the bards every evening chanted their epics through the smoke drifts of the hall to an audience that loved noble and resonant language far more than their descendants of to-day. The form and colour of things seen and the sound of fine words were a greater part of the pleasures of life in that simple age than in our own more intellectual world.

Saxon and Dane each came of a thirsty race, and many an acre of barley went to fill the ale-horn. 'Yuletide' feastings, common to the earliest traditions of both races, and rehallowed as 'Christ Mass' by the Church, were as merry in the thegn's wooden hall as afterwards in the stone donjon of his Norman supplanter.

But in the main, life was an out-door affair for rich and poor, a constant hand-to-hand struggle of a hardy folk with untamed nature. In the intervals of peace, when neither public war nor private blood-feud was disturbing the district, the thegn and his personal retainers laboured at spearing and netting the wolves and foxes, and keeping down the deer, hares, rabbits and wild fowl, if the crops were to be saved and the larders well stocked with meat. Hunting was always a pleasure, but it was not then a sport. It was a duty, which, like the sterner duty of war, devolved more and more on the thegn and his attendants, as functions became more specialized. But every freeman could still hunt on his own land, and it is probable that many serfs and thralls suffered no rebuke in taking game off the limitless waste; some were employed for no other purpose. It was still a hard struggle for man collectively to make head against the forest and its denizens. The King of England did not yet 'love the tall stags as if he were their father' nor had the harsh code of the Royal Forest yet been imported from Normandy. Landlords were not yet tempted to strain their authority on behalf of game preservation, for the game could still preserve itself only too well. For ages still to come, a large proportion of the people's food consisted of wild game of all sorts, and the half-wild herds of swine in the forest. If Englishmen had been forced in the Tenth Century, as their more numerous descendants were for awhile in the Nineteenth, to live chiefly on such grain as they could grow in the island, those primitive agriculturists would have been hard put to it to live at all.

What a place it must have been, that virgin woodland wilderness of all England, ever encroached on by innumerable peasant clearings, but still harbouring God's plenty of all manner of beautiful birds and beasts, and still rioting in a vast wealth of trees and flowers,—treasures which modern man, careless of his best inheritance, has abolished and is still abolishing, as fast as new tools and methods of destruction can be invented, though even now the mere wrecks of old England still make a demi-paradise of the less inhabited parts of the island. We conjure up the memory of what we have lost in speaking of Robin Hood's Sherwood or Shakespeare's Arden, but it was older than Robin Hood and vaster than Arden. It was the land not merely of the outlaw and the poet but of the whole Anglo-Danish people. Had some of them at least the eyes to see the beauty in the midst of which they went about their daily tasks? When Chaucer and the late mediæval ballad-makers at last found a tongue for the race, the first use to which they put it has recorded their joy in the birds and flowers, the woods and meadows. In Tudor times the pop-ular songs of the day give the impression that the whole people has gone a-maying. Did not some such response to nature's loveliness move dimly in the hearts of the Saxon pioneers, when primrose, or bluebell rushed out over the sward of the clearing they had made in the tall trees?

In certain respects the conditions of pioneer life in the shires of Saxon England and the Danelaw were not unlike those of North America and Australia in the Nineteenth Century,—the lumberman with his axe, the log shanty in the clearing, the draught oxen, the horses to ride to the nearest farm five miles across the wilderness, the weapon ever laid close to hand beside the axe and the plough, the rough word and ready blow, and the good comradeship of the frontiersmen. And in Saxon England, as in later Amer-ica, there were also the larger, older and more settled townships, constantly catching up and assimilating the pio-neers who had first started human life in some deep 'den' of the woodlands. Every one of the sleepy, leisurely gar-denlike villages of rural England was once a pioneer settle-ment, an outpost of man planted and battled for in the midst of nature's primæval realm.[1]

The work of colonization and deforestation in later Saxon England was carried on under feudal leadership. 'We wonder not,' wrote King Alfred, 'that men should work in timber-felling and in carrying and building, for a man

---

[1] The termination 'den' so common in our village names often denoted a swineherds' woodland colony of some mother village, which stood some considerable distance away in the better cleared country.

hopes that if he has built a cottage on laenland of his lord, with his lord's help, he may be allowed to lie there awhile, and hunt and fowl and fish, and occupy the laenland as he likes, until through his lord's grace he may perhaps some day obtain book-land and permanent inheritance.' The feudal lord was to the Anglo-Saxon pioneer what the State was to his remote descendant in America and Australia. In those early times 'the State' in the modern sense scarcely existed. A man looked to his lord for military protection, for justice or something more in court, and often for economic help as well; in return the lord restricted his freedom, became a large sharer in the profits of his labour, or claimed much of that labour for himself.

In the Anglo-Danish period the King's thegn, who is also the peasants' lord, is pre-eminently the armed warrior with helmet and chain shirt falling below the hips, the mounted infantryman in heavy armour on whom the King relies in case of invasion. The thegn devotes his life to hunting and war, and to the service of his own overlord,— the King it may be, or else some Bishop or Abbot, or some greater thegn than himself. Personal loyalty rather than abstract patriotism inspires his service, and it is not always the King to whom the personal loyalty is most felt or exclusively owed. In succession to the Saxon thegn, the Norman knight, still more completely armed and trained to fight from the saddle, will stand just one step higher above his neighbours as a specialist in war, and therefore feudalism as a social system will reach its climax after the Norman Conquest. It will decline with the advent of longbow and gunpowder. For feudalism, though a system of law and land tenure, really depends for its spirit on the military superiority of an aristocracy in arms.

After the breakdown of the tribal and clan organization, and before the rise of the State, feudalism was the only method by which a helpless population could be protected, war efficiently conducted, colonization pushed forward, or agriculture carried on with increased profits. For it was a process of differentiating the functions of warrior and husbandman. The Anglo-Saxon ploughman was not only an unskilled but an unwilling soldier. He disliked being called out every few months. He wanted to be left alone in Cowstead or Nettleden to till the soil in which he had taken such strong root. He had forgotten the warlike desires of his ancestor who helped to sack the Roman villa hard by. His lord, the thegn in the high hall of the township, should protect him in local troubles; and the King and the assembled thegns should protect him in the day of national danger. The thegn, for his part, ceased to handle the plough and spent his time in war and talking about war, in hunting and talking about hunting, and in doing rough justice among his neighbours according to traditional law and custom. Already we have the embryo of the future squire and Justice of the Peace, except that the Anglo-Saxon prototype of the squire is pre-eminently a soldier.

So the ploughman ceased more and more to be a warrior, and the warrior ceased to be a ploughman. Differentiation of function led away from equality—away from liberty even. But it led to settled order, to civilization, to wealth, and finally in the course of centuries to a much fuller liberty for the individual than the freeman of a savage tribe can possibly enjoy.

Meanwhile the conditions of life were harsh enough on the lower classes of husbandman, the thralls and serfs whose labour was in different degrees required to support the thegns and the clergy in their specialized functions. There exists a dialogue of about the year 1000, which gives us, with a pathetic realism, a single glance behind the scenes of the national stage:—

'What sayest thou, ploughman? How dost thou do thy work?'

'O, my lord, hard do I work. I go out at daybreak driving the oxen to field, and I yoke them to the plough. Nor is it ever so hard winter, that I dare loiter at home, for fear of my lord; but the oxen yoked, and ploughshare and coulter fastened to the plough, every day must I plough a full acre, or more.'

'Hast thou any comrade?'

'I have a boy driving the oxen with an iron goad, who also is hoarse with cold and shouting.'

'What more dost thou in the day?'

'Verily then I do more. I must fill the bin of the oxen with hay and water them and carry out the dung. Ha! Ha! hard work it is hard work it is, because I am not free.'

The shepherd in his turn answers:

'In the first of the morning I drive my sheep to their pasture and stand over them, in heat and in cold, with my dogs, lest the wolves swallow them up. And I lead them back to their folds and milk them twice a day; and their folds I move; and I make cheese and butter, and I am true to my Lord.'

The oxherd says:

'When the ploughman unyokes the oxen, I lead them to pasture and all night I stand over them waking against thieves,'

for cattle-lifting was then a great part of life, not merely on the Scottish and Welsh borderlands as in later years, but in all the unquiet island.[2]

The peasants of this dialogue were evidently doing customary services upon their lord's home farm or domain land, under more or less servile conditions. In the Tenth and Eleventh Centuries there were many grades of servile and semi-servile tenure, varying according to the local circumstances, and according to Danish, Welsh or Saxon custom. There were 'geneats,' 'cottars,' 'geburs,' shepherds, bee-keepers (for honey was the only sugar), swineherds, and many others, each owing to the lord so many days' work a year for such and such purposes, or so much rent in kind. In the Danelaw the proportion of small freeholders was largest and the number of actual slaves a minimum, while in the Western and more Celtic shires the opposite was the case. In the districts where the incoming Danes settled, they tended to break up the encroachments of feudalism, lay and clerical, and to favour freedom; but the effect of their raids and ransomings on the other parts of England was to hasten the degradation of the peasant,

[2] The later English custom of leaving sheep and oxen to graze without a herd or watcher present, was remarked on in Tudor times by foreigner visitors as a custom peculiar to England. It argued a high degree of safety from robbers as well as wolves, that was only very gradually attained.

who 'bowed his head' for bread or protection to the thegn or the abbey, or was ruined and sold up owing to the burning of his farm by the Vikings, or the intolerable burden of the Danegeld. Thus when the Norman came he found the North and East freer than the South and West.

Taking the country as a whole, in spite of much local variation, there was a tendency in these later Saxon centuries towards the growth of a large class or classes of semi-free peasants, into which the slave or thrall rose, and the freeman sank. This important double process will come clearly to light after the Conquest, when the French feudal lawyers will give a definiteness and universality to this half-servile class under the title of 'villeinage.'

In the Anglo-Danish times it was laid down as a rule of law and police that 'every man must have a lord,' to be answerable in court for his misdoings. Only thus could the peace of the united English Kingdom be maintained, now that the old clans and kinships, long decadent, were ceasing altogether to function in the sphere of justice and police. Since a man's relations were no longer answerable for him, his lord must answer for him instead.

The lord, whether thegn or prelate, performed in each locality many of the functions, judicial, military and economic, performed by the clan in more primitive societies, and by the State in the modern world. The new Kings of all England could keep only a very rough and ready control over the general body of their thegns, for purposes of national defence and for little else. For local purposes they were fain to grant away rights of justice and administration which they had not the machinery to exercise from the centre, making them over to powerful local magnates, lay or clerical. It was only after the Norman Conquest and the growth of a more elaborate civilization, that the Plantagenet Kings gradually assumed administrative and judicial control over the localities, and formed the modern idea of the nation and the modern machinery of the State.

Saxon times witnessed the growth of feudal power, and witnessed also the growth of Kingship not as its enemy, but as its ally. The battle between the Crown and the centrif-

ugal tendencies of feudalism was postponed till after the
Norman Conquest. In the days when the Kings of Wessex
became Kings of all England, greatly as the prestige of the
Crown was thereby increased, the very extension of the
boundaries of their realm compelled them to decentralize,
leaving more power to local magnates. The shire machinery
was the King's chief organ of administration. So long as the
realm had been confined to the manageable area of old
Wessex, a single magnate had answered to the King for
each single shire. But with the formation of the new enlarged Kingdom, this machinery was compromised to meet
the new facts. Edward the Elder and his sons, and even
Canute himself, were fain to allow powerful subjects to be
Ealdormen or Earls of two, three, finally half-a-dozen or
more shires each.[3]

United England, just because it was united, came to be
administered in four, six or eight 'Earldoms,' as these large
divisions were called.[4] To some extent they carried on the
submerged life of the former political divisions of the island
—Wessex, Northumbria, Mercia, East Anglia,—and thereby
the more Danish districts were not in effect subjected to
the direct rule of Wessex. Government by Earldoms,
though feudal in form, had analogies to Home Rule in
modern Empires too large and too little homogeneous for
united administration. William the Conqueror, as we shall
see, was destined to give the death blow in England to
this centrifugal tendency, which continued for many cen-

[3] A subordinate officer administered each single shire, under the Earl who ruled the group of shires. This shire
officer became known as 'shire-reeve,' later 'sheriff.' He
served in a dual capacity, primarily as the representative
of the King's interest, but for some purposes as officer and
agent of the Earl (W. A. Morris in *E.H.R.*, 1916). After
the Norman Conquest the Earl (except in a few shires)
disappeared, the Bishop retired with his spiritual cases to
the new Church Courts; the Sheriff was, therefore, left as
sole ruler of the shire for the King, and as agent of the
King's orders only. The 'Hundred,' called in Danelaw the
'Wapentake,' was a territorial division of the shire.

[4] See Map 8, p. 152, below.

turies longer to divide mediæval Germany and France into great feudal provinces.

Such was the triumph of political feudalism in the newly formed Anglo-Danish Kingdom. And there was the same feudal tendency in the sphere of justice at the expense of the communal or public courts.

In the communal courts of Shire and Hundred, the law of the district—whether Danelaw, law of Mercia or of Wessex, or some obscurer provincial custom—was administered by the freemen suitors of the court as judges, presided over by the Ealdorman, Shire-reeve or Hundred-reeve on behalf of the King. There was as yet no 'common law' of all England, no Courts of King's Bench or Common Pleas, no Judges of Eyre or of Assize. These local communal courts were the Royal Courts, the courts of the land, so far as the King and the country as a whole can be said to have had courts at all.

But in the same period feudal justice was encroaching upon the communal courts. From the time of Edgar onwards, we find the King perpetually alienating the rights of the Crown, and particularly the power and jurisdiction of the Hundred Courts, to abbeys and feudal magnates. Whole districts are put under the judicial control of monks or Bishops, Earls or thegns, by grants of *sac and soc, infangthef* and *hamsocne*.[5] And with the judicial powers, the judicial revenues also—the valuable fees and fines of the courts—pass from the King to the private landowners whom he most fears or favours.

Private justice was encroaching on public justice. Was this reaction or progress? It was deplorable that the King should not be strong enough to enforce public justice through public courts. But if in fact he was not strong enough, it was better that justice should be administered somehow and by someone, than that thieving, manslaying and cattle-lifting should pass unpunished. Very possibly the change was often popular at the time it was made, if

---

[5] *Sac and soc*=the right to hold a court; *infangthef*=the right to try and to hang a thief taken on one's land; *hamsocne*=house-breaking, or the right to try cases of it.

men got better and quicker justice from their strong neighbour lord or abbot than from their distant King or his weak
'reeve' in the Hundred Court. But we cannot at this distance of time tell whether the lay and clerical beneficiaries
of the grants of *sac and soc* were really the best people
to hold the courts, or only the strongest and most cunning
to seize the envied privilege. In any case it was to be the
great merit of the Norman and Plantagenet Kings that they
devised machinery by which the Crown was able gradually to reverse this Anglo-Danish alienation of royal rights,
and to bring back public justice into public hands. That is
one of the chief reasons why the name and office of King
has been popular in England.

The latter half of the Tenth Century, between the first
and second period of the Danish wars, witnessed an important crisis in religious history. The Danish invasions in
the time of Alfred, so destructive to the monastic centres of
Christian enthusiasm and learning, had completed the
decadence of conventual and clerical life which Bede had
noted in his own time. The burning of the great Northumbrian and fenland monasteries disorganized Christianity
north of the Thames, and many districts were subjected to
heathen jarls and 'hosts.' Even in Wessex it was long before Alfred's efforts to stimulate learning and religion led
to any widespread movement among the clergy. The reconquest of the Danelaw and the partial conversion of the
Danes were principally due to the Christian laity, the vigorous Kings of the House of Wessex and their thegnhood.
There is no evidence that Alfred, Edward and Athelstan
owed as much to clerical advisers as the Kings before and
after their time.

Until the middle years of the Tenth Century the monasteries remained sunk in one of those ever recurring
lapses by which human nature has always avenged itself
upon the demands of asceticism. The monastic endowments
were enjoyed by married clerks, many of whom lived in
their own homes with large households and in considerable
luxury. Monasticism had almost ceased to exist in any real

sense; it had certainly ceased to exert any great influence upon the island. Whether the growing movement for the foundation of parish churches and parish priests would have been able to make good in mediæval England if there had been no monastic revival, may be an interesting subject for speculation and controversy, but is not a question that history can attempt to answer.

The fact is that monasticism revived. A new spirit came over from the French Abbeys of Cluny and Fleury; this 'Cluniac' movement was one of the many offshoots of the great Benedictine rule. Under this inspiration certain reforming Abbots and Bishops, of whom Dunstan was one of the most effective, but by no means the most intolerant, re-enforced the conventual discipline and the ascetic ideal in many English convents, sometimes not without blows and turmoil. At the same time King Edgar (959–75) and his successors were persuaded to rebuild and re-endow the fenland monasteries such as Ely and Peterborough, and to enrich the monks of the new movement everywhere with vast territorial and judicial power over their neighbours.[6]

Under this new impulse English religion moved forward towards the more extended claims of the Church in the days of Hildebrand, Pope Gregory VII [1073–85.], whose ideals were to a large extent imposed upon England by her Norman Conquerors. In the end the movement enforced celibacy even on the parish priests, increased the international character of the Church under the Papal headship, and led to the full development of the doctrine of transubstantiation, the great importance attached to the worship of the Virgin Mary, and many other characteristic religious movements of the later Middle Ages. The monastery in fact was destined to be the principal breeding

[6] The fenland monasteries did much for the draining and colonization of the fen country. The grants of *sac and soc*, judicial in their most obvious aspect, were connected with another side of territorial feudalism, the aid given to reclaiming and colonizing waste land, by feudal lords, lay and clerical.

ground whence religious idea and practice emanated for centuries to come, and to hold a great place in the economic and social life of feudal England.

Few would have prophesied such a future for monasticism when Dunstan [924–88.] was a boy. He himself took a leading part in the revival as the youthful Abbot of Glastonbury, and remained a sympathetic but less active friend to the movement when he became Primate. The stories of his clerical intolerance in this and other matters which once gave him his chief historical reputation are untrue. The son of a thegn of Somerset, Dunstan had a Celtic excitability of religious temperament remarkably blended with the cool and just judgment of a statesman. He was for many years the most influential of the advisers of the Crown. His power at Court was one of the many signs of the revival of the Church and was fully justified by the use he made of it. The disasters of the Kingdom began again when Ethelred the 'Redeless' ceased to enjoy the 'rede' or counsel of Dunstan.

The new feudalism made little distinction for its own purposes between cleric and lay. Thegns and prelates were alike lords holding lands of the King, and owing him service in war and peace. The revival of ascetic religion stimulated piety and fashion to reward the worthy monks who had thus forsworn the world afresh—with land, jurisdiction and treasure! By the time of the Norman Conquest, shires like Worcester, Wilts and Dorset were as much owned and governed by churchmen as by barons and knights. The monks took to forging charters of the lands they claimed— the clerical method of 'estate jumping' to match the drawn sword of the baron.

The civil jurisdiction and temporal power of churchmen, not resented in those days, was sowing the seed of future evil on the grand scale. But the lavish monastic endowments prepared the way also for the architectural glories of the later Middle Ages. And all the while the parish churches were rising, in village after village, and the impact of Christianity on the Nordic character was at work, unseen. Doubters may perhaps wonder whether the

Church would have survived the rough feudal centuries if she had not herself acquired the feudal power that so sorely compromised her ideals.

During most of the Tenth Century the Viking movement was in abeyance. Emigration from the Baltic lands fell off, and the Scandinavian colonists spent their time in building up towns, farms and institutions in the lands which their fathers had won with the battle-axe. It was due to this ebb in the tide of invasion that Alfred's children had been able to effect a nominal reconquest of the Danelaw, on condition of leaving its Scandinavian character untouched. The era of Edgar and Dunstan followed as a brief period of peace and prosperity. And then, during the reign of the incompetent Ethelred the Redeless, the storm broke once more. [978–1016.]

[988.] The Vikings were again on the war-path, and this time, under Sweyn Forkbeard, King of Denmark, they made South England the special object of their attack. Normandy and the English Danelaw, being under Scandinavian rule, they naturally spared, while their cousins in Yorkshire and East Anglia equally naturally did nothing to thwart them or to help the decadent Saxon King to save his Wessex. The unity of Saxon and Dane in the island was still incomplete, and the weakness of the new Kingdom of England stood revealed. The Danelaw has been called 'the rock on which the old English Nationality foundered.' Ethelred was indeed a weak and foolish King and his reign was one long disaster, but there were other than personal and accidental causes for the collapse of England before the renewed Danish invasions.

[988–1016.] In the long wars that ensued before Canute won the throne, there are two features of special interest, —the Danegeld and the part played by the city of London.

Danegeld had been levied and paid in Alfred's day, but in those primitive times the Danes had more often preferred to enrich themselves by direct plunder of place and person. Both sides were now rather more civilized, and the ransom in gold of the whole country became the more usual method of the latter-day Vikings. Nor does there seem to have been so much Danish demand for estates and land-settlement as in the time of Alfred. Many of the victors were content with enriching themselves out of the Danegeld, and spending the wealth so gained on houses and estates in Scandinavia. Historians are astonished at the sums paid to them in Danegeld, far exceeding what the same tax afterwards rendered to the Norman and Plantagenet exchequer, and out of all proportion to the rateable value of the land. No doubt the relative peace of the Tenth Century had enabled English thegns and churchmen to amass treasure and personal property of all kinds, especially the exquisite work of the English gold and silver smiths, which now went into the Danish melting-pot, as the plate and jewels of Renaissance England paid for the wars of Charles and Cromwell. Some of the vast ransom remained in England, being spent there by the freehanded and pleasure-loving Vikings, but much of it crossed the seas.

The sums extorted from the peasantry were ruinous, and hastened the decline of the freeholder into the serf. The Danegeld holds indeed a great place in our social, financial and administrative history. Direct taxation began in this ignominious form. Under the weak Ethelred it was the normal way of buying off the Danes. Under the strong Canute it became a war tax for the defence of the realm. Under William the Conqueror its levy was regarded as so important a source of revenue that the first great inquisition into landed property was made with this end in view. Domesday Book was originally drawn up for the purpose of teaching the State how to levy Danegeld. The collection of this great national burden, originally entrusted to the township, passed into the hands of the lord of the manor. First Canute, and then still more definitely the Norman Kings, preferred to deal with a single man rather than with the local community, thereby subjecting each village more than ever to its lord. For the lord became the tax-farmer. And the man who answered financially for the land tended to become in the eyes of the

State the owner of the land and the lord of all who lived on it.

The other remarkable feature of the renewed Danish wars is the part played by London. The city magnificently fulfilled the hopes entertained by Alfred a hundred years before, when he fortified and colonized London as the guardian of England's gate against the Danes. In Ethelred's reign her citizens were the heart of English resistance, far more than the inept and cowardly King. When at last he died, [APRIL 1016.] two years after his fierce Danish rival, Sweyn Forkbeard, there followed a brief struggle for the throne of England between the two young heroes, Edmund Ironside son of Ethelred and Canute son of Sweyn. London was Edmund's rock of strength. But his death a few months later [NOV. 1016.] ended the war; and the Saxon Witan, bowing to the necessities of the case, chose Canute as King. The proximity of the Danelaw on the flank of the contest in South England made the choice of the Danish candidate natural, and after Edmund's death inevitable. Owing to the qualities latent in the young Canute, it proved also fortunate beyond expectation.

The elective character of the English monarchy comes out more clearly at this epoch than at any other before or after. Canute, Harold and William the Conqueror had none of them a valid legal title to the throne, save the choice of the Witan, or acknowledgment by the individual magnates of the realm. But such choice was enough to give legality to the results of conquest or the wishes of the nation. The Witan was not the origin of the later English Parliament, which grew up out of Anglo-Norman institutions. Nor was the Witan a popular or representative body. It was a haphazard assembly of Bishops, Earls, royal officials and other magnates, who by no means always proved themselves as 'wise' as their name suggests. When once a new King was on the throne their power of controlling him depended on character and circumstance, rather than on any 'law of the constitution,' for none such existed. But they had by custom the right to fill the throne vacated by death, and at the end of the Saxon period that power was being exercised with an extraordinary free-dom: not merely the order of succession but the royal family itself was on more than one occasion changed. The idea of a divine right of succession lodged in an individual and not capable of alteration by any human authority was, so far as English history is concerned, an invention of James I's over-busy brain.

The part played in the later Danish wars by London as an almost independent military and political power, is the more remarkable because her municipal rights were, nom-inally, meagre in the extreme. There was no Mayor or Alderman, and the port-reeve was a royal official. Instead of the democratic 'wards' of later London history, we find the City area divided into 'sokes' or private jurisdictions granted by the King to lay and clerical magnates. Munici-pal self-government was still in the future. As yet even the freedom-loving Danish towns were ruled by hereditary 'lawmen,' and the other market towns and 'burhs' of Eng-land, scarcely yet distinguishable from rural villages or royal forts, were subject each to its lord, whether King or thegn, or, as often was the case, to a number of thegns.

But the real power, wealth and independence of the port of London, alone of English cities, had far outrun her municipal status in the eye of law. The fact that Win-chester rather than London was regarded as the official capital of the peripatetic monarchy gave to the great port on the Thames a measure of real political independence, and an attitude of external criticism towards the royal power; that spirit, kept in bounds by genuine loyalty and patriotism, continued to inspire London down the cen-turies until it culminated in the great doings of the Stuart epoch. Very different is the history of Paris, the dwelling-place of the Kings of France.[7]

The accession of Canute, though so stoutly contested by

[7] The Saxon Kings had palaces inside the London walls and sometimes resided in them. The action of Edward the Confessor in building his palace *outside* the walls, at Westminster, had immense unforeseen consequences in the history of London and of England. See p. 154, below.

the Londoners, was a blessing for them in disguise. Commerce between his English and Baltic dominions grew very large, when piracy was put down on the North Sea and the ports on both sides were opened to mutual trade. The Danish merchants became the leading citizens in London, as they had long been in York and the towns of the Danelaw. In the Eleventh Century the Danish 'lithsmen' and 'butsecarles' of London took the lead in transmarine trade, in the naval defence of the island, and in disputes over the succession to the throne. Many of them at first were heathen, but St. Clement Danes and dedications of City churches to St. Olaf tell the tale of their conversion. 'Men of the Emperor,' from Cologne and elsewhere, were also settled in London with their own trading establishments. London regained the place she had first acquired under the Romans as the chief emporium of North European commerce.

[1016–36.] Canute, the son of Sweyn Forkbeard the old Viking, became an Emperor on the model of Charlemagne, and a King of England following in the footsteps of Alfred along the path of reconciliation and renewal. Having won Kingship over the English by force of arms, he put them on a real equality with the Danes, and was loved by all his subjects alike. His father had been a heathen more often and more genuinely than a Christian, and the boys had been brought up in the worship of Woden; yet Canute died in the odour of sanctity, a high favourite with monastic chroniclers. For he became a great benefactor of abbeys, and his laws enjoined the more rigorous payment of tithe and Church dues, the observance of Sunday and the final suppression of the heathenism that lingered in parts of the Danelaw and still more among the new-comer Danes, whom he himself had led from oversea. The very ancient song that has given so pleasant a picture of Canute to many generations of Englishmen, shows how completely he obliterated in the imagination of men the record of his Viking youth:

Merry sungen the monkës; in Ely
When Cnut King rowed thereby.
Row, cnichts, near the land
And hear we these monkës sing.

The monks of Ely would have sung a less merry tune if
they had seen him coming as a boy in his father's war-
boat along the channels of the fen. But the age of the
Vikings was over at last; Canute, King of Denmark, Norway, England and the Hebrides, had transmuted all that
terrible energy into a beneficent Empire of the Nordic
maritime peoples.

The more famous legend of his rebuke to preposterous
courtiers by the seashore, though also very ancient, would
more fitly have been attached to some wise King of lands
nearer the sun, surrounded by his satraps and eunuchs.
The hard-bitten housecarls and Vikings and Saxon thegns
who guarded Canute had very different ideas of speech
and service from those of Oriental hyperbole and servitude.
Indeed it would be hard to find a local habitation for
the story, because, in lands where courtiers flatter so
grossly, the tide does not rise so fast or so far.

For the first few years after 1016 Canute was a foreign
conqueror in England, holding his throne by the sword.
But in 1020, after his return from a happy expedition oversea to secure his succession to the Danish throne, he
adopted in England the policy of reconciling the two races
on a basis of equality, and he began his famous alliance
with the Church. In many vital respects his policy differed
from that of the Norman who conquered England fifty
years later. The Danish 'host' who had won the throne
for Canute was paid off in Danegeld instead of in confiscated estates. Anglo-Saxon and Danish were in equal
favour as languages in the garth of the King's House at
Winchester, and Canute issued a collection of Anglo-Saxon
laws. The Church in Canute's reign was governed chiefly
by Anglo-Saxon churchmen, whom Canute took into high
favour as civil servants at his Court; thence he promoted
them to Bishoprics. Under his patronage churchmen from
England went over to Norway and Denmark, and played

an important part there in the prolonged struggle between Christian and pagan. There is no doubt that whereas William the Conqueror found the French clergy abler and better trained than the Saxon, Canute found the Saxon clergy less badly trained than the Scandinavian. But the whole attitude of the two Conquerors towards the leaders of the conquered English was as different as possible. Not only in the Church, but in the State and the army the Saxon thegns were trusted and used by the Danish King. The great Earldom of Wessex was governed by his favourite Saxon, Godwin, who now first rose to fame.

After he had paid off the 'host' and the fleet that conquered England, Canute kept a navy of forty ships and a small standing army of 'housecarls.' The 'housecarls' were a bodyguard of heavily-armoured, professional, mounted-infantry, drawing the King's pay, and bound together in a military guild of which Canute himself was a member. It was at once a 'cash nexus,' and a brotherhood of honour and of personal service. The element of feudal land-tenure was wanting, for although some housecarls obtained estates in England they did not owe their service as housecarls on account of their lands. At first entirely Scandinavian, the force soon included many Saxons. Essentially Viking in origin and Anglo-Danish in development, the housecarls perished with Harold at Hastings. The Norman conquerors did not revive the force, for under their more purely feudal system England was organized with land-tenure as the key to civil and military institutions.

The supersession of Canute's work by the Norman Conquest within a generation of his death makes it very difficult to estimate either its importance or its excellence. If he had lived till sixty instead of dying at forty [1036.], he might have left a more permanent mark on the world's affairs. He was a great ruler of men, and he was on the way to found a Nordic Empire astride of the North Sea, with Scandinavia for one pillar and England for the other. Sea-power would have been its cement and its master-spirit. If he had succeeded he would have changed the history of the world. But the material difficulties of distance were too great for the rude appliances of that age. In the Eleventh Century it was as difficult to hold together an Empire astride of the North Sea, as it was difficult in the Eighteenth Century to hold together an Empire astride of the Atlantic. Indeed the connection between Denmark, Norway, the Hebrides and England was purely personal; they were each of them ruled by the same energetic man, but there was no Imperial machinery and no feeling of common patriotism. England herself had to be governed in four great Earldoms, and Norway was still very far from being a real political unit.

[1042–66.] Canute's incapable Danish successors soon dissipated the loose confederation. Edward the Confessor, the restored Saxon monarch of independent England, looked no longer towards Scandinavia but towards French Normandy, and prepared the way for the Norman Conquest. Scandinavia and England, after being closely associated in hatred and in friendship for several centuries, drifted far apart, when England was drawn by the Normans into the orbit of France. Instead of remaining a maritime and Nordic State in touch with Scandinavia and only slightly connected with the main body of Europe, England became for many generations almost a part of French feudal civilization, engrossed either in her own island interests or in the continental ambitions of her French-speaking Kings. It is generally assumed that this change was quite inevitable and that on the whole more was gained than lost thereby. It may well be so. But the fact that Canute attempted a very different orientation for England is of profound interest, and though his Empire broke up, it was not without permanent effect, for it reinforced the Scandinavian and trading elements in the English nation.

BOOKS FOR FURTHER READING: Gjerset and Collingwood, as for last chapter; Larson, *Canute*, in Heroes of the Nations Series; Vinogradoff, *English Society in the Eleventh Century*; *Cam. Med. Hist.*, Vol. III., Chapter XV.; F. M. Stenton, *Anglo-Saxon England*, 1943.

CHAPTER SEVEN

The Norman Conquest up to Hastings. 1042–66

From the time of Alfred to the time of Canute, the influences that refashioned Britain had come from Scandinavia; for the next hundred years, dating from the accession of Edward the Confessor [1042.], they were to come from Normandy. The same is true in a less degree of European history as a whole.

The Norman aristocracy, Scandinavian by origin, retained all the Viking energy in colonization and in war, but had become converts to Latin culture. For that or other reasons the Normans were distinguished by a quality which the Scandinavians at home and in England lacked, the instinct for political unity and administrative consolidation. That instinct was the most valuable of the Conqueror's many gifts to England.

It was the Normans who turned back from Europe the tide of Scandinavian influence. [SEE MAP 8.] The province which their Viking ancestors had carved out of France as another 'Danelaw,' became the citadel whence the language, arms and manners of French feudalism sallied forth to the conquest of the world, more particularly of Naples, Sicily and the British Isles. Britain, not yet capable of becoming as in Shakespeare's day 'a world by itself,' had oscillated for two hundred years between Scandinavia and continental Europe. Her position was at length rudely determined for her by the French-speaking Norman Duke. The battle of Hastings was not only a great English but a great European event. For, with Britain closed to Scandinavia and opened to France, the Vikings were locked up in their fiords, and ceased to threaten or attract Christendom. The mounted spearmen who conquered at Hastings imposed their 'chivalric' ideals and feudal relationships on the northern world, where the memory of Viking and thegn grew dim in the twilight of the past. Latin speech, literature and religion reigned unchallenged, until many centuries later the secession of Britain upon new lines of her own again redressed the balance of North and South.

Yet we must not too closely identify Norman with Latin civilization. The culture that the Normans imported into England was indeed Franco-Italian,—the culture of Tail-lefer, the French minstrel, and of Lanfranc and Anselm, the Italian Churchmen. But the monarchy brought over by the Normans was the monarchy of their own strong Dukes, not of the weak French Kings at Paris.

The Norman State was unique, and requires to be specially studied by searchers after the origins of things English. First founded by Danes and Norsemen, it had come to differ very widely from the districts similarly planted by the Vikings in Britain. It differed also from the rest of France. In Normandy the majority of the inhabitants were French peasants in origin and character, their backs patiently bent to the tillage of the soil. But the Scandi-navian minority included the fishermen and the merchants of the estuaries along the coast, and the feudal aristocracy of the land; these grandchildren of the fiord still had their faces turned seaward with unabated ancestral love of roving and adventure, although they had adopted the speech, religion and customs of the French.

The jarl, in becoming a feudal baron, had learnt the new continental methods of war from the French enemies and allies whom he had met upon the Seine: instead of fighting on foot with the battle-axe of his fathers, he fought from the saddle with the spear and sword, and made his position in the country safe by piling up a high circular mound with a wooden fortress on the top, whence he could the more safely rule his peasants and defy his foes. Now heavily armed cavalry and private castles are the final flower of fully developed feudal society, and neither of them existed in England before the Normans brought them across the Channel.[1]

[1] The mound castles of England are Norman (see Baldwin Brown, I. 106–10). The Saxons and Danes made earth-work enclosures to protect towns and royal forts, but not

Duke
baron
knight

Norman feudalism had become strictly territorial, after the French model. The barons of the province owed military service to the Duke on account of the lands they held from him, and not, as many thegns in England still owed service, on account of personal or national obligation. The barons were bound to ride under the Duke's banner in his constant wars against Anjou, Maine or Brittany; each led his quota of five, ten or thirty knights due from his barony, the quota being always, for purposes of military convenience, assessed in units of five knights. This system the Conqueror afterwards imposed upon England with a remarkable uniformity.

The knights in their turn held their lands from the barons by the same military tenure. The knight, if he held a 'knight's fee' of land, had to follow the banner of the baron from whom he held it, whenever the baron followed the Duke to the field or made war on his own account,—such at least was the custom in Normandy.

This military service was due nominally for forty days in the year, but it was possible sometimes to exact it for rather longer in order to finish the campaign. A few weeks would serve for the private wars of baron against baron, or for the Duke's campaigns in Brittany and Anjou. But for a prolonged adventure like the conquest of England a voluntary long-service agreement had to be improvised, distinct from the feudal obligation. The period of military service due was wholly inadequate for distant enterprises; that is one of the chief reasons why feudalism broke down as communications improved. Feudalism had been originally advised for the defence of a countryside against Danish and other raids, and for the purposes of private war: it was not suited to the growth of great states or for the

high mounds like those of the Norman barons. The English thegn's house was usually unfortified. Hence the English outcry against the high mounds crowned by timber forts which the Normans erected in great numbers immediately after their arrival in England. It was only gradually that stone replaced timber work in the Norman castle —except in a few special cases like the Conqueror's Tower of London, which was of masonry from the first.

conduct of prolonged and extensive military operations.

From the top to the bottom of society the feudal relation of lord to man in Normandy was fixed, territorial and heritable—passing from father to son. At the top was the Duke, under him the barons, under each of them the knights, and under all the peasants. The peasant was a serf bound to the soil and to his lord as owner of the soil. In Normandy neither peasant nor knight could transfer his vassalage at will to another lord, as many freeholders were still able to do in the less territorialized feudalism of Anglo-Danish England. Norman society was therefore less free than Scandinavian or even Anglo-Saxon, but it was more stable, and more efficiently organized for peace and war.

Although in Normandy the social and military system was more strictly feudal than in Saxon England, the political system was less feudal, for the Duke had begun to impose on his barons an authority which the Kings of strictly feudal countries could never hope to wield. The feudal King of France claimed a vague suzerainty over the Norman Duke, but enjoyed no power in his territories, nor in any other province of France except in the small royal domain round Paris. On the other hand the Norman Duke was much more than feudal lord in his own remarkable Duchy. The traits of real monarchy in the Norman State were neither Scandinavian nor French in their character. They were peculiarly Norman. The Conqueror and his sons carried these monarchical peculiarities of their Duchy to the island soil, where they re-enforced the English Kingship and developed it into that great mediæval monarchy which had no parallel in France, Germany or Spain.

In the first place there were no large baronies inside Norman territory, and no single baron was strong enough to defy the Duke with impunity. Government by great feudal Earldoms, which prevailed in the England of Edward the Confessor and in contemporary France, had no place in Normandy. The Norman Duke had real administrative officers of his own who exercised functions properly public, as distinct from the work of a bailiff of the ducal domains. These officers were called *vicomtes*; they col-

lected the Duke's revenues, commanded his troops, held
his courts and maintained his peace. The King of France
had no such officers. The subsequent identification of the
Norman *vicomte* with the old English sheriff greatly
strengthened the position of the latter, and made the sheriffdom the chief pillar of the mediæval English monarchy.
Norman finance was the best in Europe and the Duke was
proportionately powerful; he collected a revenue in hard
money, while his suzerain King of France lived as best he
could on rents paid in kind, moving round for his bed and
board from farm to farm upon his domain. In Normandy no
one besides the Duke dared to mint money. Private castles
could be erected only by his license, and were to be
handed over on demand. Private war, though not yet illegal, was limited by the Ducal power.

It will therefore be seen that when England was invaded
in 1066, she was being attacked not merely by a band of
cosmopolitan adventurers enlisted for the nonce under a
single war-chief—though that was one element in the affair;
England was also being attacked by the most highly organized continental state of the day, which possessed peculiar institutions capable of rapid development in the free
field of a vast and inchoate conquered territory. And even
more important to England than the institutions of the Norman State were the habits of mind and action which the
Norman Duke and his subjects brought over with them.
William, before ever he invaded England, had fought and
conquered his rebellious barons in Normandy. A bastard,
called to his doubtful inheritance as a boy of eight, he
had seen feudal anarchy at its worst, trampled it down
and taught men to obey.

Last but not least, the Church in Normandy was in
league with the Ducal power. The later Dukes, zealous
converts from Danish Woden to the French Christ, had
restored and re-endowed the Abbeys and Bishoprics overthrown by their heathen ancestors. In return they appointed all the Bishops and most of the Abbots. The leaders
of the Church were therefore servants of the Ducal policy.
Some of them, indeed, were merely fighting barons dressed

up as churchmen. The Conqueror's most powerful subject
was his brutal and turbulent brother Odo, whom he had
thrust into the Bishopric of Bayeux while still a boy. Odo
led his own hundred and twenty knights to war, and since
the Church objected to priests shedding blood with the
sword, swung his mace in the thick of the melee at Hastings.

Others of the Norman prelates were of a higher type.
Since the beginning of the Eleventh Century there had
been a strong movement of reform, and the Cluniac monastic revival had been favoured and guided by the rulers
of the Duchy. In a land remote from the Italian centres of
religion and learning, a land where barbarism might long
have reigned undisturbed under heathen or Christian
forms,[2] there had grown up monasteries like that of Bec
capable of attracting the greatest intellects of the day from
beyond the Alps. Lanfranc of Pavia and Anselm of Aosta
were successively Priors of Bec and Archbishops of Canterbury. No fact illustrates more clearly the cosmopolitan
character of learning and religion in the Middle Ages, in
striking contrast to the isolation in which most men had to
pass their lives, bound never to leave their native village,
either by their legal status as serfs or by want of means to
travel. The physical and social barriers that impeded the
communication of man with man were very great, but national barriers scarcely existed. Lanfranc and Anselm, from
far Italy, brought the knowledge of Roman and Canon Law,
and the latest theology and philosophy of the day, first to
Normandy and thence to England. And few complained of
them as 'foreigners.' Before the age of Universities, monasteries like Bec served as the chief centres of learning.
Meanwhile architecture was already laying its massive and
imperishable impress on the Norman landscape. Though
the great age of stone castles was delayed till the Twelfth
Century, the Norman Abbeys and Cathedrals that we know

[2] As late as 1001 a Burgundian monk declared that
scarcely a priest in Normandy could read. Haskins, *Normans in European History,* p.164.

were already beginning to rise when the Conqueror sailed for England.

Yet although the Normans were ahead of barbarous Europe in certain respects which proved of the first importance in the future development of England, they were not what we should recognize as a civilized people. In spite of a few learned priests, the upper class were ignorant of the rudiments of letters; there were no lawyers and practically no professional men except the clergy; the luxury, art, commerce and chivalry of the later Middle Ages had not yet come into existence, and nothing of that kind was to be found in the timber fortresses and occasional stone 'donjons' of this primitive baronage. The Normans were quite as inhumane as the Anglo-Saxons or Danes of contemporary England, and being more active and industrious they committed many more deeds of revolting cruelty. The lopping-off of hands and feet and the gouging out of eyes of prisoners and rebels, wholesale massacre of populations, and deliberate devastation of whole districts, were among the Norman methods of warfare, as England was soon to learn to her cost. The Norman, devoted servant of the Church as he had now become, had advanced little if at all beyond the heathen Viking in point of humane conduct. But in knowledge and organizing power he had advanced. The Church taught barbarians to organize society, and it was this better organization of society, even more than the precept and example of the Church herself, that eventually taught men to take the first halting steps in the direction of humanity and justice.

Although the Ducal power in Normandy, when transferred to England, would help to make the King's Peace supreme there, the Normandy of the Conqueror was an unquiet land, perpetually disturbed by private and public war, violence and outrage of all kinds, like the typical feudal province of the Middle Ages. It is an error to suppose that the mediæval world was safe and peaceful because its inhabitants were theoretically conscious of the unity of Christendom. It was indeed free from our modern dangers of race hatred and war organized on the national scale, for the low level of organization and transport prevented France and Germany from conceiving the idea of racial patriotism and making war on one another as nations; but they were both in a state of constant internal war between the petty feudal powers composing them, wars conducted with the utmost ferocity, although for purely personal motives. In the feudal world the hand of neighbour was perpetually raised against neighbour, and death, injustice and outrage were the daily lot. But in the Norman Dukes' conception of their office there was that which looked distantly towards better conditions of life; if this conception could be realized in the ring fence of an island State, it might lead in the course of a few generations to a better society than the chaos of the ordinary mediæval kingdom.

Meanwhile the inhabitants of England, left to themselves, were making little or no progress towards a more united island or a stronger monarchy. The failure of Canute's sons to perpetuate his Nordic Maritime Empire or to govern England as a Danelaw, had resulted in the restoration of the House of Alfred in the person of Edward, whom after ages called the Confessor. [1042–66.] He was the son of Ethelred the Redeless and of Emma, daughter of a former Duke of Normandy. [SEE p. 155, BELOW.]

The return of the English line to the throne, though it put an end to the Scandinavian supremacy, failed to set the Anglo-Saxon nation again on the path of progress. If an Alfred or even a Harold had inherited the unchallenged throne at a juncture so favourable, something at least might have been done to unite and reform England without Norman interference. But the Confessor was, at heart, not an English King but a French monk. He was entirely without political vision and almost without political ambition. What stirred his enthusiasm was the religious life as he had seen it lived among the new school of Norman clergy. He had spent among Norman monks his long years of exile, from boyhood to middle age, during the Danish rule in England. Norman by birth on his mother's side, he was at the moment of his restoration even less of an Englishman than Charles II when he landed at Dover. Edward spoke, and probably thought, in French. His rôle in English history was to prepare the way for the Norman Conquest, both by the little that he did and by the much that he left undone.

His only active policy was to introduce Normans into the high places of Church and State. He was prompted to show them favour not only by his personal tastes and friendships based on the experience of the best years of his life, but by the desire to find loyal and able adherents of his own to counterbalance the overpowering influence of Earl Godwin. Godwin had placed him on the throne, and like other kingmakers expected to act as Mayor of the Palace. Without his Normans, the King would have had neither the wit nor the strength of will to resist his too powerful subject.

Edward raised several Normans to be Bishops, and made one of them, Robert of Jumièges, Primate of England. A group of Sussex ports, the gateway of the continent, was placed in Norman hands. Herefordshire was entrusted to the Norman Earl Ralph; his wardship of the Welsh March, which this post implied, enabled him to introduce the Norman military system into that remote woodland shire, while some of his followers gave the inhabitants a foretaste of Norman violence and greed. Ralph and his knights built private castles, a novel portent on which the Saxon freemen looked askance, and he attempted in vain to teach the thegns to fight from the saddle in their contests with the Welsh tribesmen. The characteristic refusal of the English to learn the now indispensable art of cavalry fighting from Ralph or anyone else, sealed their doom in the Hastings campaign.

At court the Confessor's secretaries and chaplains were Normans. In the heart of London, the wine merchants of Rouen held a wharf of their own at the mouth of the Wall Brook. When therefore the Conqueror landed at Pevensey, he set foot on an island where for a quarter of a century there had been a Norman party in politics, and where Norman methods and customs were known, feared and admired.

But what Edward left undone was even more important than what he did, in preparing the way for the Norman Conquest. In the first place he deliberately left behind him a disputed succession by his personal adherence to the monkish ideal of chastity, in spite of the fact that he went through the idle ceremony of marriage with Earl Godwin's daughter. Secondly, he never tried to unite the island administratively or to improve its laws and institutions. It would have been a hard task, impossible perhaps for anyone but an armed conqueror to complete, but Edward never even attempted it.[3]

The most serious bar to all national progress was the government of England in half a dozen great Earldoms, each presided over by a feudal magnate, instead of in single shires, each ruled by a royal official. It is true that the evil was no new thing in Edward's day, that England had never really been united since the departure of the Romans, and that a similar system prevailed in yet worse forms in Germany and France. But since England under the Confessor enjoyed more than twenty years of external peace, unassailed by Normandy or Scandinavia, a strong King would have used a respite so unusual to try at least to promote greater national unity, before the inevitable next onset of the foreign foe. But Edward's policy, so far as he

[3] 'In after days,' writes Maitland, 'the holy but imbecile Edward won not only the halo of the saint, to which he may have been entitled, but the fame, to which he certainly was not entitled, of having been a great legislator. In the minster that he reared, king after king made oath to observe the laws of the Confessor. So far as we know, he never made a law. Had he made laws, had he even made good use of those that were already made, there might have been no Norman Conquest of England. But then had there been no Norman Conquest of England, Edward would never have gained his fictitious glories. As it was, men looked back to him as the last of the English Kings of the English,—for of Harold, who had become the perjured usurper, there could be no talk,—and galled by the yoke of their French masters, they sighed for Saint Edward's law, meaning thereby the law that had prevailed in a yet unvanquished England.' *Social England*, I., p. 169.

can be said to have had any consistent plan besides the
introduction of Normans, only served to encourage provincial feeling and to divide North from South. For he was
fain to play off the power and the jealousy of the Northern
Earls of Mercia and Northumbria against Wessex and the
other Earldoms of the South presided over by the House
of Godwin.

[1051.] By this means the Confessor on one occasion succeeded in having Godwin and his family driven from the
realm. But next year a counter-revolution took place. Godwin and his son Harold came back from their places of
exile in Flanders and Ireland. They sailed up and down the
Channel, landing at various points to ravage after the cruel
manner of warfare in those days; none the less South England rose to fight on their side. The seafaring population
swarmed out of the Channel ports to join their flotilla,
while forces from Sussex and Surrey marched on London,
all vowing to 'live or die' with Earl Godwin. When finally
he floated up the Thames, the men of London let his ships
pass unopposed under their bridge. [1052.] Then and there
he dictated terms to the King, for whom no one seemed
eager to fight. Godwin's chief Norman enemies fled the
land, and his House was restored to all its private estates
and public offices.

The underlying motives of the politics of this troubled
reign are obscure. The evidence we have is fragmentary,
and modern historians equally well informed of all that
there is to know have differed widely from one another in
their estimate of the character and policy of the chief
actors. It is probably safe to say that dislike of the Normans
was a strong motive in the popular reception of the ambitious Earl, a year after his outlawry had been so easily
decreed. But to speak of him and of his son Harold after
him as 'national heroes' may be misleading, because 'national' feeling as we know it had not come into existence.
The men of Wessex, of the Severn valley and of Danelaw
might each and all dislike the Normans, but they knew
not one another and had no common loyalty. The appeal
to unite in defence of England as a whole was never made

Map 8   England in Earldoms: Eve of the Norman Conquest

to them in the Eleventh Century, because it would not have been understood. If it had been understood, a few thousand armoured cavalry would not have been able to conquer and share up England after Hastings.

[1053.] Godwin died the year after his triumphant return, bequeathing to his ablest son Harold the chief direction of the King's government, the Earldom of Wessex, the affection of England south of Thames, and vast estates scattered over many shires. These last had been accumulated in a single generation by arts which would perhaps not bear too close an inquisition. For Godwin's fortunes were of his own making. A simple thegn of Sussex, he had not inherited but acquired the vast wealth and the power unparalleled in a subject, which he left to his son. He must have been a remarkable man, but we know too little about him to estimate his character and career.

For the dozen years after Godwin's death, the King was never able openly to defy Harold. It was a state of equilibrium which prevented any real steps towards national consolidation. Not all the Normans had disappeared, and, when Edward died, the two great Earldoms of Mercia and Northumbria belonged to Edwin and Morcar, representing interests alien if not openly hostile to Harold's power. The Earldom of East Anglia, indeed, had been consigned to his brother Gyrth. But the fact that two of his brothers, Sweyn and Tostig, were ne'er-do-wells who proved unfit for public trust had helped to prevent the closer union of the whole island under the ægis of the House of Godwin.

Such was the political situation when the mild King died in his new Palace at Westminster [JAN. 1066.], after a futile reign in which Saxon England had wasted its last opportunity of setting its own house in order. The continued decadence of Anglo-Saxon prose and poetry in this period had been all of a piece with the political failure. The Norman Conquest did not cause the decline of Anglo-Saxon literature, though it may have prevented its revival. The decline might with more plausibility be ascribed to the Danish conquest of half a century before.

Like the Third and Sixth Henries and other 'sore saints for the Crown,' the Confessor left behind something that pleads with posterity against his political failures. Though Westminster Abbey was destined to be rebuilt once more in a greater age of architecture, it was Edward's endowments and buildings that prepared for Westminster the high place that it holds in ecclesiastical history and its supreme place in the political development of England. He moved the King's dwelling from inside the walls of the City to a new Palace on the rural 'island of thorns' two miles up the river, in order to be near the great church that he was building there to St. Peter, an operation on which his whole heart was set. Mighty consequences flowed from the royal flitting to Westminster. As time went on, the centre of government was inevitably drawn more and more from the old Wessex capital at Winchester to the area of London. And if the strong Norman Kings, like their Saxon predecessors, had lived actually inside London walls whenever they were in the neighbourhood, the political independence of the City would have been nipped in the bud. Yet the political independence enjoyed by the Londoners was to be the bulwark of the liberties of England in times to come, from the days of King John to the Stuart era. It was well, therefore, for British freedom that the great Plantagenet bureaucracy which grew up round the King's Palace, struck root not in the City itself, but in Westminster; it was no far-seeing political philosophy that had fixed it there, but chance and Edward the Confessor's pious whim.

At the end of the Saxon period London was beginning again, for the first time since Roman days, to be a great centre of North European commerce. London was a whale among the fishes beside the other English boroughs. Within the circuit of its Roman walls, which five hundred years before had stood unrepaired and almost empty, the chief arteries of traffic and many of the narrow lanes were already laid out on the sites they occupy in 'the City' of to-day. The houses, indeed, were of wood, many of them mere market booths, and there was much open ground behind and around the buildings. But the busy, cosmopolitan character of the great port had already something about it prophetic of the future 'London.' Scandinavian, Fleming, German and Norman all had their share in the place, but the East Anglian type prevailed among the common people. Close outside the walls spread the ploughlands and pastures of Moorfields, Smithfield and other 'fields,' growing food for the citizens, and loud with the noise of water-mills turned by streams flowing to the Thames. On the northern horizon lay wooded hills, where the lords of the London sokes and the merchant warriors of the City hawked after herons and hunted the stag, the boar and the wild bull, in St. John's Wood, in Hampstead, in Enfield Chase, and in the Hertfordshire forests beyond.

The death of the immaculate Edward left the succession to the throne in a fine confusion. The nearest heir was Edgar the Atheling, but he was a boy. If, indeed, the English State had been more highly organized, and if Englishmen had been more conscious of their nationality, they would have proclaimed the boy King and rallied round him against all comers. But as the world went then, there was great fear of anarchy if a minor should ascend the throne, especially one who had no strong connections and no party of his own. It is small wonder that men turned rather to the tried ability and long established power of Harold. He was, indeed, more distant from the royal line, but the blood of Scandinavian Kings was in his veins through his mother's side; and with all his experience, and his wide family estates in Southern England, he bade fair to defend and rule the land in troubled times better than the Atheling.[4]

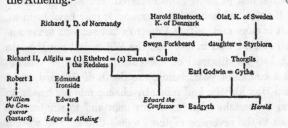

It may be that Harold would have done better if he had resisted the suggestions of vaulting ambition, and set himself as the guardian lion on the steps of the Atheling's throne. But his acceptance of the crown, even if ill-advised, cannot be stigmatized as a usurpation. England had never observed a strict law of hereditary succession; the passing over of minors was quite usual though not obligatory; the dying Confessor had named Harold his heir; and, above all, the Witan chose him King. But his weak title invited Scandinavia and Normandy to compete for the conquest of England—as probably they would have done even if the Atheling had been chosen in his stead, though scarcely if the Confessor had left a son. The autumn of 1066 saw England attacked by Harald Hardrada, King of Norway, and by William, Duke of Normandy, in two almost simultaneous invasions. It was the dramatic climax of the long competition between Scandinavia and Latin Europe for the prize of England. Harold might have repelled either enemy alone; he sank beneath the double attack, and the Norman, through luck and conduct, rose the only winner.

William's claims to the throne—if indeed we are willing to set aside the not altogether unimportant fact that he was a bastard—were genealogically better than Harold's, though worse than the Atheling's. But Harold had been chosen King by the Witan and William had not. William, however, won the sympathy of continental Christendom by certain arguments which appeal very little to modern minds, though they served conveniently to brand Harold for many centuries as a perjured usurper.

In the first place William declared that Edward had at one time named him as his successor. It may have been so, but it is more certain that Edward's last act was to recommend Harold, and in any case the Witan and not the late King had the disposal of the Crown. Secondly, William had, a couple of years before the death of Edward, compelled Harold, who had fallen by chance into his hands, to swear on certain relics to be his man and to support his claims to the reversion of the English throne. The solemn

oath and its flagrant breach weighed heavily in the minds
of contemporaries, in whose every-day lives and legal
proceedings oaths sanctioned by religion played a very
much larger part than in our own.[5] The less formal modern
mind is more impressed by the fundamental injustice of
William's proceedings; he took advantage of an accident
to compel his guest, as a condition of safe return home,
to swear away his own chances of succession and those of
Edgar Atheling, and his country's freedom to decide its
own destiny. It is one of the points on which mediæval
and modern ethics stand honestly at variance.

Last of all, William raised prejudice against Harold as
the patron of Stigand, whom the Godwin faction had irregularly thrust into the Primacy of England, but who was
regarded by the Papal party on the continent as little better
than a schismatic on account of his dealings with an anti-
Pope. The age of Hildebrand was approaching upon the
continent; that great man was not yet Pope, but he already
enjoyed considerable influence at Rome, and he used it
with effect on William's side at this crisis. The reforming
and Hildebrandine party in the Church, eager to press
clerical celibacy and high Papal claims upon the easy-going
English Christians, was in traditional alliance with the
Dukes of Normandy, and had long been at enmity with
the House of Godwin. The Papal banner and blessing were
a useful asset to William in an undertaking that otherwise
looked more like a robbery under arms than a crusade.

In that day of small feudal States, Normandy counted
as a great European power, and its ruler was a statesman
well versed in the intricacies of foreign politics. Like his
namesake six centuries later, William prepared the way
for his invasion of England by propaganda and diplomacy
ably conducted in many distant countries, and by skilful

[5] For instance, the oath of 'compurgators' swearing to a
man's innocence, or to his character, even if they did not
know the facts of the case at issue, held the place which the
examination of evidence holds to-day in criminal justice.
It was the oath more than the evidence that was valued.

settlements with his neighbours which rendered his homeland safe during his absence. Harold's case was unheard
abroad and went by default. The French-speaking feudal
world felt a glow of righteous enthusiasm for the bandits'
league into which it entered under the great chief.

The armament that landed at Pevensey was not a feudal
levy, though its members were strongly imbued with the
feudal spirit and were to be rewarded by strictly feudal
holdings in the conquered land. William had no power
under feudal law to call out his vassals to a campaign which
must last a great deal longer than forty days. But many of
the barons and knights, not only of Normandy, but of
Brittany and of Flanders which owed him no allegiance,
had voluntarily engaged themselves to serve under his
flag. It was a joint-stock enterprise for the sharing out of
the English lands. On much the same principle the conquest of Ireland in Cromwell's day—also regarded at the
time as a great religious work—was carried through by
military service to be paid in estates won from the conquered and by loans raised on the same speculative security. William and his confederates were at the expense of
building a fleet of transports during the spring and summer
of 1066, for it was essential to carry across not only the
armoured men but the trained war-horses which gave them
their chief hope of breaking the shield wall of Harold's
famous housecarls.[6]

It was a great armament, but its strength lay in its training and equipment rather than its size. In those days even
officials were unable to count large numbers accurately,
but modern historians reckon that at the highest figure
the expedition did not exceed 12,000 men, of whom probably less than half were cavalry. It is certain that when
England had been divided up among the conquerors,
many of whom came over after Hastings, the total number

[6] The invading Danes in Alfred's time could 'horse' themselves in England, because they wished to march as
mounted infantry, but not, like the Normans, to fight as
cavalry.

of knights enfeoffed did not exceed 5000.[7] That a country of a million and a half people should have been subdued, robbed and permanently held down by so small a band, gives the measure of the political and military backwardness of the English system as compared to the Norman.

There was also an element of luck, decisive of the narrow margin by which William conquered at Hastings. For six weeks contrary winds had held him weatherbound in port. During that interim Harald Hardrada, King of Norway, landed with another great host to conquer England, and defeated Earls Edwin and Morcar and their local levies two miles from York. The English Harold had perforce to break up the armed watch he was keeping on the southern coast against the expected Norman armada, and hurry off to save the North. His housecarls,[8] the finest mounted infantry in Europe, began their last admirable and tragic campaign by riding hot-spur to the gates of York, and fighting foot to foot against the great Viking host at Stamford Bridge until it was utterly destroyed. [SEPT. 28, 1066.] Three days later William landed at Pevensey.

Harold had removed from the Normans' path a most formidable opponent, and in doing so had reduced his own strength by many gallant warriors hewed down at Stamford Bridge. He and his housecarls rode back to London in four days, reaching it on October 6th. The battered forces of the North were following more slowly on foot; the fyrd of the South-West had not yet arrived. Rightly or wrongly Harold determined to give William battle at once in Sussex, with the thegns and fyrd of the South-Eastern counties alone, gathered round the strong nucleus of his remaining housecarls. Since infantry contending against cavalry must needs stand on the defensive, he defied William from a well-chosen position on an isolated spur of hill six miles north-west of Hastings; it stood on

[7] Round, *Feudal England*, pp. 265, 289–92. Haskins, *Norman Institutions*, p. 78. Oman, *England before the Conquest*, p. 641. Stenton's *William*, p. 196.

[8] For the Anglo-Danish institution of the housecarls see p. 139, above.

the southern edge of the great forest of Andredsweald from which the Saxon army had emerged. The hill, afterwards crowned by the village and Abbey of Battle, then bore no dwelling and no name, and was distinguished only by a forlorn feature on its skyline, 'the hoar apple tree.'[9]

[OCT. 14, 1066.] The storming of that hill proved a day's task almost beyond the power of the invaders, in spite of their great superiority in arms and tactics. The two hosts represented different developments of the old Nordic method of war, the outcome, respectively, of two different social and political systems. Norman knights and English housecarls wore indeed much the same defensive armour; the primitive shirt of ring-mail of their common ancestry had been lengthened into a garment of the same material ending in a divided skirt convenient for riders. Both sides wore the conical helmet and nose-piece then in fashion, and bore shields no longer round but in most cases of the new kite shape, long and tapering so as to protect the warrior's thigh when on horseback. Both armies contained also a number of unarmoured or half-armoured men with inferior weapons—the 'fyrd' of the neighbouring shires swelling the ranks of the Saxons in this particular. But here the similarity between the opponents ceased. The Anglo-Danes, leaving their horses in the rear, still fought on foot in the shield-ring, and still used the long Danish battle-axe, which Harold plied so manfully in his last fight. The Normans fought from the saddle, casting and thrusting with the spear[10] and striking down with the sword. But even the shock tactics of their splendid cavalry proved unable to destroy the shield wall on the top of the hill, without the

[9] In the Middle Ages the action was called either *Battle* or *bellum*, or the battle or *bellum* of Hastings. It was hardly ever called Senlac until the end of the Nineteenth Century by Freeman and his school. See Round, *Feudal England*, pp. 333–40. See the same authority on the course of the battle; he has shown that the English had no artificial defences to their position.

[10] The long heavy spear of the 'tourney' type was a later development in mediæval war.

aid of another arm. The Normans as warriors had not only learnt the new but remembered the old; they had learnt cavalry tactics from the French, but they had preserved the old Scandinavian practice of archery which the Anglo-Danes had neglected. Between the charges of horse Harold's infantry were exposed to the shafts of archers, inferior indeed to the future long-bowmen of Crecy, but superior to any who drew bow for England that day. Infantry with only striking weapons fight at desperate odds against cavalry supported by missiles. At Waterloo the English squares had missile weapons on their side against the French cuirassiers; it was otherwise at Hastings.

When night fell, Harold and all his housecarls around him were lying dead in their ranks on the hill-top, like the Scots round their King at Flodden; and the surviving warriors of the 'fyrd,' battle-scarred and sick at heart, were trailing to their distant homes in every direction along the darkening tracks of the Andredsweald.

CHAPTER EIGHT

The Norman Conquest Completed, and Norman Institutions Established. 1066–1135

KINGS: William I, 1066–87; William II, 1087–1100; Henry I, 1100–35

The shock of the battle of Hastings would have rallied the forces of a well-organized feudal kingdom, and stirred the patriotic resistance of a nation. It had no such effect in the Anglo-Danish realm. Earls, thegns, Bishops, sheriffs, boroughs thought only of making their private peace with the Conqueror. Even Stigand, the foremost man in Harold's party, and the special object of aversion to the Pope's Norman allies, vainly sought to retain the throne of Canterbury by an immediate submission, made while William was in the act of crossing the Thames at Wallingford. Edwin and Morcar had come south too slowly to help Harold at Hastings—whether from treachery, slackness or unavoidable

delay no one will ever know. They now slunk back to the
North, leaving Southern England to make the best of the
situation. Probably they reckoned that, whoever wore
the crown in Wessex and on the banks of Thames, they
themselves would continue to enjoy virtual independence
as Earls of Mercia and Northumbria. But it was not so that
William conceived of the Kingship he had won.

South England meanwhile offered little resistance. Winchester, the old Wessex capital, led the way in submission.
As to London, William had not force enough to be sure of
taking it by storm, and he desired to enter it in peaceful
guise as Edward's acknowledged heir. He began therefore
to make a wide circuit round the city to west and north,
destroying as he went the villages of Buckinghamshire and
Hertfordshire to hasten the surrender of the English. The
policy was successful. London, after a few weeks' hesita-
tion and a futile proclamation of Edgar Atheling as King,
sent to acknowledge William and invite him to his coronation at Westminster.

There, on Christmas Day, 1066, he was crowned as lawful heir of the Confessor, while his followers, on a false
alarm of treachery, were setting fire to the houses of the
English outside. The noise of strife and outrage interrupted
the service, and all save William and the officiating priests
rushed out of the Minster to take part. Here were grim
realities, in dramatic contrast to William's theory of a lawful and natural passage of the Crown. The claim to be heir
to the Confessor and guardian of his 'good laws' thinly
covered over the brute facts of conquest, and seemed of
little avail to protect the country against French robbery
and violence. Nevertheless, in the days of the Conqueror
and his sons after him, the occasional alliance of the Norman King with his Saxon subjects against rebellious members of the Franco-Norman baronage, and the revival and
strengthening of the fyrd and the shire-court, gave importance to the constitutional formula on which William had
based his claim to the throne of England.

In the first critical months after Hastings, when the English let slip the opportunity of united resistance, many of

them hoped by submission to suffer no more loss of lands and liberties than they had suffered under the foreign rule of Canute and his men from Denmark. They were soon undeceived. On the ground that everyone who had acknowledged the usurper Harold had forfeited all his possessions, the confiscation of Saxon estates for the benefit of the foreign conquerors began directly after the battle, and went on year after year as rebellions or other less good reasons gave excuse.

Nor was the yoke of Norman King or Norman baron like the easy yoke of Canute and his Earls. The new monarchy and the new feudalism were riveted on the land by the new military system. Everywhere huge circular mounds, like those still visible at Lewes and in a hundred other places throughout the land, were piled up by the forced labour of Saxon peasants, and crowned by royal or private fortresses first of timber and ultimately of stone.[1] In front of the mound there was an outer court, called a 'bailey,' protected by an earthwork enclosure. From these impregnable citadels the armoured horsemen issued forth to dominate the countryside, sometimes in the interest of order, sometimes on errands of plunder and misrule. The Londoners saw with alarm the royal masonry of the Tower donjon gradually overtopping the eastern walls of their city, and curbing though not destroying their cherished independence.

After a successful campaign in the South-West, where the power and estates of the House of Godwin had chiefly been concentrated, William by the end of 1068 was true lord of Southern England, and in the North was at least

---

[1] See note, p. 142, above. The mound was known as the 'motte' and the timber or stone tower on it as the 'turris,' 'donjon' or 'keep.' The Bayeux tapestry represents the throwing up of such a mound at Hastings to support a timber fortress. The character of the timber fortresses of the Normans is more exactly delineated in the siege of Dinant castle in the same tapestry. We see there the attackers applying fire to it; that danger no doubt hastened the 'stone age' of Norman castle building in the time of Stephen.

acknowledged as King. But only a portion of the landed estates of the country had as yet changed hands; in particular, Mercia and Northumbria were very much as they had been before Hastings. The *status quo* in the North would have lasted longer, had the two Earls, Edwin and Morcar, remained passively loyal. But they rebelled, were suppressed and pardoned, and then rebelled again. Their second rising was rendered formidable by the help it received from another Viking invasion, led by the sons of the King of Denmark. [1069.] In Mercia the wild Welsh poured across Offa's dyke to aid the war against Norman rule.

Such was the occasion of William's great campaign in the North and of his cruel vengeance. Between York and Durham he left no house standing and no human beings alive that his horsemen could search out. As Domesday testifies, many scores of villages were still without inhabitant seventeen years later. Most of the North Riding and much of the East Riding of Yorkshire were depopulated by massacre. In Durham County the houses and cattle were destroyed, but the inhabitants had warning and escaped across the Tyne. Many sold themselves as slaves, not a few in the Lothian district of Scotland which thus obtained a strong infusion of Scandinavian blood. Devastation and massacre were let loose in more spasmodic fashion in Cheshire and the midland shires. The wooden hovels of that day could be rebuilt from the neighbouring forests more easily than houses in civilized times, but the loss in men, cattle and farm utensils could be less easily repaired. The 'harrying of the North' was a vengeance Turkish in its atrocity, but fully in accord with the ideas and practice of the most zealously Christian warriors in mediæval Europe.

This foul deed served its purpose. There could be no more rebellions after such wholesale destruction. It decided the question whether William and a few thousand armoured knights could conquer all England and coerce her inhabitants into a new manner of life. It put an end to the age-old separatism of Northern England and of the Danelaw in opposition to the kingship seated in Wessex and London. And it broke the resistance of Scandinavian society to Norman feudalism. The Durham Castle and Cathedral that we know, rose as the symbol of a new Latin civilization, superimposed on these wild Nordic lands by a foreign soldiery and clergy: the splendid architecture that crowns the rock, much of it raised within one generation of the 'harrying of the North,' in a region that had been poor and barbarous to a degree even before that terrible catastrophe, bears witness to the energy of the French-speaking rulers, builders and churchmen, the handful of men whom William's Conquest sent to govern and transform those distant regions.

Not only the lands north of Humber, but Lincolnshire and East Anglia, the richest agricultural districts in England, received the new civilization, but at a heavy price in human freedom. The freemen of the Danelaw had hitherto kept at arm's length even the Anglo-Saxon forms of feudalism. Many of them could 'go with their land' to what lord they would, and some villages had no lord at all. The proportion of freemen was much greater in the Danish and Norse districts than elsewhere in England. But the Normans put an end to these old-fashioned liberties, and imposed the French system of strictly territorial feudalism on the Scandinavian North and East as well as on the Saxon South and West. The Danish freeman in most cases sank into the villein of the manor. Yet in prosperous Lincolnshire some of the villeins remained well-to-do and in certain legal aspects free men.

'The harrying of the North' diminished the number of Danes in England and especially in Yorkshire. But it appears that, as time went on, the Norsemen who had settled so thickly on the Western coast in Cumberland and Lancashire moved eastward into the depopulated regions, so that the actual acreage of Scandinavian occupation in England was perhaps not greatly reduced in the end.[2] But

[2] Lancashire as a county was only created after the Conquest: it is one of the newest of the Shires of England. The status of Rutland as a county is also post-conquest. For the movement of Norsemen from the West into the depopulated districts of Yorkshire, see W. G. Collingwood, *Scandinavian Britain*, pp. 176–81.

Scandinavian ideals and civilization gave way to Norman. The North England of the Middle Ages, with its great families of Umfraville and Percy, its great Yorkshire Abbeys and its Palatinate of Durham, was a land very completely feudalized and Normanized in its governing class.

The same influences, by peaceful penetration across the Border in the reign of King David of Scotland, laid the impress of Norman ruling families on Scottish society and religion. [1124–53.] The Bruces and Balliols, Melrose and Holyrood, were but a further extension of the Norman Conquest. South England, indeed, owing to more rapid economic progress, moved out of the feudal age in Tudor times more quickly than the northern part of the island. Yet the North, completely feudalized as it became and long remained in its social forms, retained the old Nordic temper of independent manhood all the while, underneath the feudal form of its society. The peasant of Scotland and North England, however much bound by law and attached by affection to his lord, seems to have suffered less degradation of spirit than the peasant of the Saxon South from the long centuries of feudal subjection.

The military drama of the conquest closed with the vast siege operations conducted by William against the Isle of Ely defended by Hereward. [1070–71.] Hereward was a man of the Fenland district, with a genius for amphibious guerilla warfare in that difficult country. But his resistance only began after the rest of England had been conquered, and the event was therefore never in doubt. It was but the last and noblest of a series of regional revolts undertaken too late. There had been no general movement of patriotism, no Wallace or Joan of Arc. England was still a geographical expression, an aggregation of races, regions and private jurisdictions. She still needed to be hammered into a nation, and she had now found masters who would do it.

The fact that England had been conquered piecemeal, as a result of a series of spasmodic local rebellions, gave William an excuse for depriving English landlords of their lands, and glutting his followers, lay and clerical, with feudal baronies, till every shire was divided up into knights' fees held by French-speaking knights from French-speaking Barons and Prelates, who in their turn held of the King.

The gradual character of the conquest and of the confiscation, which had moved step by step across England during a number of years, was one cause of a peculiarity in English feudalism: each individual Baron held lands in many parts of the country; his estates were not gathered in a single province as was frequently the case on the continent. Because the possessions of the typical Norman magnate in England were scattered far and wide, the royal power remained stronger than that of any single subject within the boundaries of the shire. It was therefore possible to govern it through the sheriff, a man usually of baronial rank, but removable by the King, and acting solely as his officer. The old English 'shire-reeve' was henceforth identified with the Norman *vicomte*, and the old English 'shire' was also known by the foreign title of 'County.' The sheriffdom reached its moment of greatest political power as the instrument of the Norman Kings, alike against Saxon and French-speaking malcontents.[3]

[SEE MAP 8.] To make way for direct royal government in each shire, William deliberately broke up the half-dozen great Earldoms into which later Saxon England had been divided for purposes of administration. First Wessex disappeared with the House of Godwin, and has never again been a unit except in Mr. Hardy's novels. Mercia and Northumbria vanished no less completely on the fall of Edwin and Morcar after their second rebellion. [1069.] East Anglia was preserved for a while under a Norman Earl, but was resolved back into its component shires after the Norman Earl had himself risen in revolt against the Crown. [1075.] When William Rufus died, there remained only three counties governed otherwise than by the King's officers,—the hereditary Earldoms Palatine of Chester and Shrewsbury, and the County Palatine of Durham, gov-

[3] For the early history of the 'shire-reeve' and *vicomte*, see pp. 128, note, and 144–45, above.

erned by its Prince Bishop, the secular and spiritual lord of the Border. Such as they were, these exceptions were tolerated by the Norman Kings only to keep the military guard strong against Welsh and Scots.

Outside the Counties Palatine, William the Conqueror governed England by a dual system: indirectly through the feudal contract with his vassals, and directly through sheriffs and through special commissioners like those who made the Domesday survey. Those perambulating inquisitors recalled the *missi* of Charlemagne's Empire, and foreshadowed the Justices in Eyre and the Justices of Assize. There had been nothing like them in Saxon England. He would have been a bold servant of the Saxon Crown who had set out to enquire through the sheriffs and the good men of the townships into the affairs of Godwin's Wessex or Edwin's Mercia.

The French-speaking Barons had hoped to obtain in England the privileges usually enjoyed by their caste upon the Continent. Some of these men turned with fury upon William when they realized the restrictions he was laying upon their power. In the last dozen years of his reign he was frequently called upon to suppress their turbulence, with the help not only of the loyal members of their order, but of the conquered English themselves. Racial feeling was in those days little developed, and the Saxons had been schooled to suffer the tyranny of the strong even under their native rulers. The wrongs done by the French conquest were therefore soon forgotten, enough at least to permit of the combination of the disinherited English with William himself. Yet the great King had done them wrongs such as Irishmen never forgave to England in later and more sophisticated times.

The Barons' rising of 1075 and its suppression by the King shows that the Norman Conquest proper was already complete. The robbers could afford to fall out over the spoil, and to make appeal to their victim. The subsequent rivalry in arms of William's sons for the succession, compelled Henry I to appeal to the favour of his subjects irrespective of race and rank. Charters of liberties, general and particular, were the price by which the Kingship was purchased; and the special importance of London, as a makeweight in the balance of these disputes for the succession, removed any inclination that the Norman Kings might otherwise have felt to tamper with the privileges of the City.

The Conqueror, while establishing a rigorously feudal system of land tenure, had successfully prevented England from falling into the anarchy of political feudalism prevalent on the continent. And he had cleared the ground for the gradual development of a great monarchical bureaucracy. But he did not enjoy unlimited despotic power, nor by right did anyone who ever succeeded him on the throne of England. William was doubly bound by law,—by the old Saxon laws which he had ostentatiously sworn to observe, and by the feudal customs of continental Europe to which his followers from oversea were one and all devoted. It was from the marriage of these two systems that in the course of long centuries the laws and liberties of modern England were evolved. The concentration of power in a single person 'carrying the laws in his own breast' was opposed to the mediæval spirit, at least in secular affairs. The omnicompetence of the modern State, the omnipotence of the monarch who says '*L'état c'est moi,*' would both have been alien to the mediæval mind, which conceived of public law as a mosaic of inalienable private and corporate rights. Between the King and the baronage stood the Church, who satisfied her interest and her moral sense alike by holding the balance between the two secular forces. Again and again, from the days of Lanfranc through Langton to Grossetête, we find the Church justly maintaining the balance of the constitution; lay tyranny and lay anarchy were alike unwelcome to her, and therein she was able to speak for the dumb multitudes of the common people, in matters where her own privileges were not too directly involved to bias her judgment.

In the mediæval State anarchy was a greater danger than despotism, though the opposite was the case in the mediæval Church. The mediæval State was a 'mixed polity' of King, Barons and Prelates. The relation between lord and man, which was the essence of feudal politics, was based on mutual obligation. A breach of contract on either side involved penalties, and as law was ill-defined and ill-administered, resort was continually had to war to decide points of feudal right. Non-resistance to the Lord's Anointed was opposed to the central current of thought and practice of the Middle Ages. In the mutual obligations of feudalism lay the historical reality of that 'original contract between King and people' long afterwards proclaimed by the Whig philosophers in reaction against the Renaissance despots.

It was at once the privilege and the duty of a feudal King to consult his tenants-in-chief,—that is the men who held land from him direct. It was at once the privilege and the duty of the tenant-in-chief to give advice to his lord the King. From this arose the royal *consilium* or *curia* common to all feudal states. Such was the 'Council' or 'Court' of William. The Witan, though not in the strict sense feudal, had been a somewhat similar body, but the strong and self-willed Norman monarchs were less governed by their vassals in Council than the Saxon Kings had been by the magnates of the Witan.

In Norman times the words *consilium* and *curia* were two words used indifferently for the general body of the advisers of the Crown, not yet divided up into administrative, judicial and legislative organs such as Privy Council, King's Bench and Parliament. Indeed no distinction was made in the minds of even the subtlest clerks between administrative, judicial and legislative acts. The King consulted whatever members of his 'Court' or 'Council' happened to be with him, on the question of the moment whatever its character. He appointed Committees and sent Commissioners down to the shires for this purpose or that, according to the apparent need of the hour, without being guided by rules. As yet there were no bodies, like the House of Lords or the Court of Common Pleas, consisting of definite persons, with a right and duty to meet periodically for special purposes with a fixed procedure. This very vagueness gave an able King immense power, but he needed it all to bring any semblance of order out of the chaos of the Anglo-Norman State.

The earliest step towards differentiation of function was taken in the reign of Henry I, when certain 'Barons of the Exchequer' evolved a procedure and an office of their own, inside the larger Court or Council, for the purpose of dealing with the most important of all the royal interests, the proper receipt of his multiform dues and money payments from his sheriffs, feudatories, chartered boroughs and domain lands.

All other procedure in what we should now call legislation, administration and justice was left undefined. The form to be adopted in any given case was decided by the will of the King, subject to very strict practical limitations in a land full of armed barons accustomed to maintain their rights by the sword. But the theoretical obligation under which the King lay to consult his tenants-in-chief, however little defined by law, and however irregularly observed in practice, was never denied, and it was the seed out of which the liberties of England grew in the constitutional struggles of the Plantagenet epoch.

The greatest of the inquests carried through by the power of the King was the Domesday Survey of 1086. Its text is the surest proof we have of the obedience to which that 'stark' man, the Conqueror, had reduced Norman, Saxon and Celt, from remote Cornish 'trevs' hidden away in woodland creeks of the sea, to the charred townships and wasted dales of Yorkshire. No such uniform set of answers to an unpopular inquest could have been wrung from any equally large district on the continent, nor again from England herself until the days of Henry II's bureaucracy. 'So narrowly did he cause the survey to be made,' moans the Saxon chronicler, 'that there was not one single hide nor rood of land, nor—it is shameful to tell but he thought it no shame to do—was there an ox, cow or swine that was not set down in the writ.'

Domesday is primarily a 'geld book,' that is a collection of facts made for a fiscal purpose, the proper collection of the Danegeld. But although all the questions asked and answered may have helped the collection of the geld, it is going too far to say that William the Conqueror could have had no further end in view. The final form in which Domesday Book itself was laboriously recast out of the original returns, points to other objects and ideas besides the Danegeld. The Book presents to the King,—as lord paramount of the feudal system, from whom henceforth every acre in the realm is held,—an exact account of the power and resources of his feudatories and of their vassals in every shire. The government was engaged in supplementing the Saxon scheme of local administration by a network of new feudal bodies for military, fiscal, judicial and police purposes. Therefore,—although the original evidence for Domesday was taken by the Commissioners from sworn juries consisting of the priest, the reeve and six villeins of each township,—the form in which the returns were rearranged grouped every township or section of a township in its new position as a manor in the feudal system.

Domesday Book takes full cognizance of one organ of Saxon life,—the Shire. Everything is grouped under the Shire or 'County,' for it is through the Shire organization that the King intends to act. But inside each Shire the unit under which all the information is rearranged is the feudal holding of the tenant-in-chief, however widely scattered his lands may be over all the Hundreds of the County. And the lesser unit in Domesday Book is not the village regarded as a township, but the village regarded as a manor belonging to a lord, be he tenant-in-chief or vassal. Thus the final form in which the Report was drawn up established the feudal maxim—*nulle terre sans seigneur,*—'no land without its lord,'—with a uniformity unknown before.

In the collection of the Danegeld, the Norman King and Council laid on each Shire a round sum, which was reallotted locally among the Hundreds. But the officers of the Shire or Hundred made their demands not from the men of each township, still less from each peasant, but from the lord of each manor, who 'answers for the manor' in the matter of taxation and must wring the geld from his tenantry as best he may. With that the Shire officers have nothing to do. In the eyes of the law the man who 'answers for the manor' becomes more and more the owner of the manor, and the old village organization slips ever more into the background. It was a process begun long before in Saxon times, but it now reached its theoretic perfection and was made uniform for the whole country, including the sullen Danelaw.[4]

The lowest unit of the new England was the lord's manor, into which the township had been transformed. Every manor had its manor court.[5] Nor was that the only or the most important of the courts of private jurisdiction in Norman England. Other higher courts sprang up, as necessary adjuncts of complete feudal tenure: a tenant-in-chief could hold a court to decide questions of feudal law among his vassals. Last, but not least, many valuable franchises, surviving from Saxon days, gave to Lords and Prelates criminal jurisdiction equivalent to that of the Hundred Court. It was only very gradually, in the course of the three centuries following the Conquest, that the King's courts took the place of nearly all these private jurisdictions, because the King's justice was found to be a better and cheaper article than any which private courts could supply: but that was far in the future. In Norman times the public courts were those of the Hundred and the Shire, and after the conquest the Hundred Court rapidly declined. In the Shire Court the King's Sheriff presided, but the judges were the principal freemen of the County, administering the traditional law of the district, and such bits of law common to the whole realm as might be known and approved in that Shire. But English Common Law and the

[4] See pp. 133–34, above. For a typical Domesday extract see note at end of chapter, pp. 180–81, below.

[5] See pp. 199–205, below, where the agricultural methods and social structure of the manor are described.

great legal profession capable of administering it in the King's courts, were still in the womb of time.

One class of royal court was indeed brought into existence by the Conqueror,—the Forest Court—more odious to Norman and Saxon alike than any private jurisdiction. For it represented the King only in his personal and selfish capacity. The forest law and the forest courts of Normandy were transplanted to England, with lamentable results in human suffering and servitude. In the following century as many as sixty-nine forests belonged to the Crown, computed at almost a third of the whole acreage of the Kingdom. Inside that vast but thinly inhabited area the King's peace indeed reigned, but in a form hateful to God and man. The special courts of the forest deprived all who dwelt within their jurisdiction of many of the ordinary rights of the subject. Poaching deer was punished under the Conqueror by mutilation, under his successors by death.

The alienation of so huge an acreage of land from national uses and national liberties remained for hundreds of years a source of constant bickering between the King and his subjects. The gradual deforestation of district after district marked the economic and moral progress of the country. When in Stuart times the King's power passed to the squirearchy, the modern 'game laws' grew up, like 'a bastard slip,' as old Blackstone called them, of the dying forest laws of the King, less ferocious indeed but equally opposed to the freer spirit of the English law of the day.

It was William the Conqueror who brought this plague into our island:

He made large forests for deer (wrote the Anglo-Saxon Chronicler), and enacted laws therewith, so that whoever killed a hart or a hind should be blinded. As he forbade killing the deer, so also the boars. And he loved the tall stags as if he were their father. He also appointed concerning the hares that they should go free. The rich complained and the poor murmured, but he was so sturdy that he recked nought of them.

In the Church the Conqueror effected a revolution hardly

less important than in the State. Just as the French Barons
and knights ousted the Saxon Earls and thegns, so foreign
clergy replaced native Englishmen in Bishoprics and Ab-
bacies and in the Chapters of Cathedrals. Obedience was
enforced to the doctrines and standards of the reforming
party on the continent in the age of Hildebrand. Some of
these changes, particularly the change in the persons of
the hierarchy, meant greater efficiency and a higher standard of learning and zeal. There followed four centuries of
splendid ecclesiastical architecture, starting with the Norman builders, who hastened to replace the largest Saxon
churches with structures yet more magnificent. But the
changes effected by the foreign churchmen meant also the
further Latinization of religion in ways not permanently
endurable to the Nordic temper and genius.

'On the day King Edward was alive and dead' a large
proportion of the English parish clergy were living with
their lawful wives. The compulsory celibacy of all priests
was introduced at the bidding of the Pope, not without a
prolonged struggle in the reigns of the Conqueror and his
sons. It meant that not only the parish priests, but almost
all professional or educated men could have no legitimate
children. The monastic ideal of chastity, however suited to
the more zealous churchmen of that age, was at total variance with the outlook on life of many types of useful citizens and public servants who were then as a matter of
course numbered among the clergy. To prevent almost all
educated men from having wives and lawful children
scarcely tended to improve the breed of the race, and had
lamentable results upon its moral standard.

The Conqueror's great ecclesiastical reform was his division of the spiritual from the secular courts. Hitherto
Bishop and Sheriff had presided together over the Shire
Court, where both spiritual and secular causes came up
for decision. By William's order the Bishop now retired to
hold a court of his own, concerned only with spiritual
affairs. The separate jurisdiction of the Church covered
great tracts of human life which in modern times have
been made over to the King's courts and the law of the

land,—such as felonies committed by persons in holy orders, and the great fields of marriage, testament, and
eventually of slander. It included also many matters which
are not now dealt with by any court at all, such as penance
for sins and jurisdiction over heresy.

The differentiation of the functions of lay and spiritual
courts was a long step towards a higher legal civilization.
Without it neither Church nor State could have freely developed the law and logic of their position. The English
Common Law could never have grown to its full native
vigour, if its nursery had been a court shared by ecclesiastical lawyers and judges trying to measure English law
by Roman rules. And the separate existence of her own
courts rendered it easy for the Church to adopt the Canon
Law, as fast as it was formulated on the continent in the
great legal age now coming on. The Papal Canon Law was
enforced in the Church Courts of England throughout the
later Middle Ages. The Church as a spiritual body was
subject to the Pope, but the King, representing the secular arm, dealt with the Papacy as with an honoured but a
rival power. The limits to Papal power were therefore set,
not by churchmen as such, but by the King acting in defence of his own authority, often with the goodwill of many
English priests.

It was essential to William's conception of Kingship that
he should be able in practice to control the nomination of
Bishops and Abbots. Without that privilege he might have
reigned but could scarcely have ruled in England. He used
this great power for the benefit of the reforming party in
the Church, but he also used it in the secular interests of
the Crown. His secretaries, his judges and most of his civil
servants were churchmen, for there were no learned laymen. Men who were learned, took orders as a matter of
course. The King and his successors, right down to the
Reformation, used a large part of the wealth and patronage
of the Church to pay for services rendered to the State.
Judges and civil servants were rewarded with benefices
and even with bishoprics. Viewed ecclesiastically by mod-

ern standards, this was an abuse. But the system served
the country well and rendered the enormous wealth of the
mediæval Church useful and tolerable to a society that
might otherwise have revolted against it before the age
of the Tudors. The mediæval Church served not only the
purposes of piety and religion strictly defined, but all the
purposes of learning and knowledge. Only when learning
and knowledge spread into the lay world, a new system
had to be adopted involving a limitation of the sphere of
the clergy and a consequent reduction of the wealth of the
Church.

William the Conqueror, a generous patron of the
Church, yet a strong protector of the rights of the Crown,
had ruled the country with Lanfranc as his right-hand
man, in spite of occasional quarrels. But William Rufus
[1087–1100.], though not without kingly qualities, was a
ruffian only pious when on his sick bed. In pursuit of revenue
he abused the position he had inherited from his father
in relation to the Church, just as he strained his feudal
rights over his lay vassals. After Lanfranc's death he refused to appoint a new Primate, and enjoyed for five years
together the revenues of the See of Canterbury. [1089–
93.] At length he was taken ill, thought he was dying, and
appointed the most unwilling Anselm. Then, to the surprise and grief of his subjects, he recovered, and for years
led the saintly Archbishop such a life as fully explains the
comic and almost cowardly reluctance that Anselm had
shown to accept the post, to which the voice of the whole
country had called him. The events of the reign show how
the secular power, in the hands of a passionate and un-
scrupulous prince, could hamper the religious life of the
country. Such facts must be borne in mind in judging of
the undoubtedly extravagant claims put forward to secure
the 'liberties' of the Church, the championship of which
Hildebrand, the great Pope Gregory VII, had bequeathed
to his successors.

In the reign of Henry I [1100–35.] the inevitable clash
came. Henry 'the clerk' was a very different person from

his barbarian brother Rufus.[6] But though he did not abuse
he steadily maintained the rights of the Crown, while
Anselm stood for the new claims of the Church. The question was that of 'investitures,' then convulsing all Europe:—
should prelates be appointed by the Crown or by the Pope?
After a fierce struggle a compromise was arranged. [1106.]
The King of England ceded to the Pope the right of in-
vesting the new Bishops with the spiritual staff and ring.
But he retained the right of claiming their feudal homage
as Barons. And the choice of the man who was to be
Bishop tacitly remained with the King. The King's power
of naming the Bishops whom the Cathedral Chapters were
to elect, though not absolute and often subject to the ap-
proval or interference of the Pope, was the basis of the
friendly relations of Church and State. During the centuries when laymen were ignorant and the States of Europe were small and weak, the mediæval Church was so
truly 'universal,' so powerful in opinion, knowledge and
wealth, so strongly organized under the Pope and dominant over so many sides of life that have since been left to
the State or to the individual, that if she had then enjoyed
all the 'liberty' of a voluntary religious denomination of
modern times it would have meant the complete enslave-
ment of society to the priesthood. That at least the mediæval Kings were able to prevent.

We have unfortunately no picture of the parish clergy,
as they were in the days of the Normans, like the charming
portrait of the village priest drawn three hundred years
later by Chaucer. The poor parson was a Saxon and one of
the conquered. The riches of the Church, distributed
among the conquering race, concerned him not. His status

[6] In the Middle Ages, almost every King of England who
was a political failure left us something particularly good
in stone. Rufus left us Westminster Hall, destined to be the
spacious nursery of the English Common Law. Richard II
gave it its present character by removing the pillars that
once supported the roof. Henry III rebuilt the Confessor's
Abbey. Henry VI began King's College Chapel.

in the manor was parallel to that of the villein.[7] The social class from which the parish priests in England were chosen, rose steadily from the Conquest until the Nineteenth Century. In the later Middle Ages, when the number of freemen was again on the increase, the Church attempted to lay down the rule that no villein was to be a priest, though with only partial success. In Tudor and Stuart times the parish priest was usually drawn from yeoman stock or from one of the numerous middle classes of that day, though not infrequently from the gentry. In the age of Jane Austen the wheel has come full circle, and the parson appears normally as one of the upper class, very often the son or the friend of the squire.

One outcome of the Norman Conquest was the making of the English language. As a result of Hastings, the Anglo-Saxon tongue, the speech of Alfred and Bede, was exiled from hall and bower, from court and cloister, and was despised as a peasants' jargon, the talk of ignorant serfs. It ceased almost, though not quite, to be a written language. The learned and the pedantic lost all interest in its forms, for the clergy talked Latin and the gentry talked French. Now when a language is seldom written and is not an object of interest to scholars, it quickly adapts itself in the mouths of plain people to the needs and uses of life. This may be either good or evil, according to circumstances. If the grammar is clumsy and ungraceful, it can be altered much more easily when there are no grammarians to protest. And so it fell out in England. During the three centuries when our native language was a peasants' dialect, it lost its clumsy inflections and elaborate genders, and acquired the grace, suppleness and adaptability which are among its chief merits. At the same time it was enriched by many French words and ideas. The English vocabulary is

[7] 'The parish priest with his virgate, half-hide or hide, appears as one of the villein shareholders of the township, though his tenement is held free of the common service on account of his special obligations.' Vinogradoff, *Eleventh Century*, p. 455.

mainly French in words relating to war, politics, justice, religion, hunting, cooking and art. Thus improved, our native tongue re-entered polite and learned society as the English of Chaucer's Tales and Wycliffe's Bible, to be still further enriched into the English of Shakespeare and of Milton. There is no more romantic episode in the history of man than this underground growth and unconscious self-preparation of the despised island *patois,* destined ere long to 'burst forth into sudden blaze,' to be spoken in every quarter of the globe, and to produce a literature with which only that of ancient Hellas is comparable. It is symbolic of the fate of the English race itself after Hastings, fallen to rise nobler, trodden under foot only to be trodden into shape.

BOOKS FOR FURTHER READING (FOR THE LAST TWO CHAPTERS): C. H. Haskins, *The Normans in European History* (Houghton Mifflin, 1915); F. M. Stenton, *William the Conqueror* (Heroes of the Nations Series); Oman, *England before the Conquest,* and *The Art of War*; H. W. C. Davis, *England under the Normans*; J. H. Round, *Feudal England*; Dean Church, *Anselm*; J. F. Baldwin, *The King's Council,* Chap. I.; Maitland, *Domesday Book and Beyond*; Vinogradoff, *The Manor,* Book III., especially pp. 291–306 on Domesday, and his Chap. XVIII. of *Cam. Med. Hist.,* III., on Feudalism; Pearsall Smith, *The English Language* (in the Home University Library); F. M. Stenton, *Anglo-Saxon England,* 1943, Chaps. XVI.–XVIII.

NOTE ON DOMESDAY: Here is a typical Domesday extract, translated from the Latin; it differs from the more usual purely agricultural Manor in that it also records the existence of a small market town of 52 burgesses.

'Count of Mortain's land. In Tring hundred. Count of Mortain holds Berkhamsted. It is rated for 13 hides. The arable is 26 *carucates*. In the lord's domain 6 hides, and there are 3 teams of oxen for ploughing: there is land for 3 more. Here is a priest with 14 villeins and 15 bordars, having 12 teams of oxen for ploughing and there is land for 8 more. There are 6 slaves. A certain ditcher has half a hide, and Ralph, a servant of the earl, one virgate.

'In the borough of this vill are 52 burgesses who pay 4 pounds a year for toll and they have half a hide, and 2 mills of 20 shillings rent by the year. And there are 2 arpends of vineyard, meadow 8 *carucates*, common of pas-

ture for cattle of the vill, wood to feed 1000 hogs, and 5
shillings rent by year.

'In the whole value it is worth 16 pounds. When he
received it 20 pounds. In the time of King Edward 24
pounds. Edmar, a thane of Earl Harold, [=King Harold,]
formerly held this manor' [before it was confiscated for
Count of Mortain's benefit].

The 'certain ditcher' mentioned is probably the local
Vauban, who kept the earth-works of Berkhamsted Castle
and its fine new Norman mound in a state of military
preparedness.

BOOK TWO

The Making of the Nation. From the Conquest to the Reformation

INTRODUCTION

The mediæval period, as distinct from the Dark Ages, may be said to begin about the time of the First Crusade, that startling outward thrust of the new Europe reorganized by the feudal system. [1095–99.] Feudalism is the characteristic institution of the Middle Ages; it implies a fixed and legal subordination of certain classes of society to certain others, to obtain civilized order at the expense of barbaric anarchy. Feudal society divided up the surplus product of the labour of the rural serf among Barons and knights, Bishops and Abbots. By stereotyping and regularizing the inequality of incomes derived from the land, it enabled wealth to accumulate in the hands of Lords and Prelates, and so stimulated the rich man's demand for luxuries, whence grew the trade and the higher arts and crafts of the merchant cities. In this way the Dark Ages progressed into the Middle Ages, and barbarism grew into civilization, —but decidedly not along the path of liberty and equality.

Another aspect of feudalism was that it organized military, political and judicial power on a local basis. Not the Empire as in Roman times, or the nation as in modern times, but the barony, or the manor was the unit of power. Feudalism was a confession of the disintegration of the Empire and the extreme weakness of the State. Over against this disintegrated secular society of feudal Barons and knights, each with an outlook limited to his province or his manor, stood the pan-European Church organized from

Rome, as centralized as secular society was decentralized, and, therefore, if for no other reason, its master. Furthermore, since the clergy enjoyed an almost complete monopoly of learning and clerkship, the control of Church over State in the early Middle Ages was very great.

Mediæval society began as a rude arrangement, between knight, churchman and peasant serf, for the protection of a poverty-stricken rustic village against marauders and devils, in return for its due exploitation for the benefit of knight and churchman. It was an arrangement in the making of which there were elements of force and fraud, as also of religious idealism and soldierly heroism in defence of the community. But gradually, out of these primitive arrangements of feudalism, the Middle Ages built up the Europe of Dante and Chaucer; of the Cathedrals and Universities; of the English monarchy and Parliament; of the Canon, Civil and English Law; of the merchant communities in Italy and Flanders, and of London 'the flower of cities all.' Which of these two pictures is the true Middle Ages? The feudal village, with its ragged, frightened, superstitious, half-starved serf, leaving his chimneyless cabin to drive afield his meagre team of oxen, and fleeing to the woods at the approach of armed horsemen—or the Florence of Dante, the Flanders of Van Artevelde, the Oxford of Grossetête and of Wycliffe? Which is the true Middle Ages, the barbarism or the civilization? We may answer—'both.' The one was developed out of the other and the two continued side by side. The Dark Ages were in four hundred eventful years transformed into the full splendour of the Renaissance, although the darkness of poverty and ignorance still lay thick in many districts of the new Europe.

The aim of the greatest minds of the Middle Ages was to provide man upon earth with a permanent resting place in unchangeable institutions and unchallengeable beliefs; but their real achievement was very different; the true merit of mediæval Christendom was that as compared to Islam and Brahminism it was progressive, and that society moved constantly forward from 1100 to 1500 towards new

things,—out of uniformity into variety; out of feudal cos-
mopolitanism into national monarchy; out of a hegemony of
the priesthood into lay emancipation; out of the rule of the
knight into the world of the craftsman, the capitalist and
the yeoman. The spirit of mediæval Europe was not static
but dynamic. The best and the worst of the Middle Ages
was that they were full of wolfish life and energy. Their
sins were the vices not of decrepitude but of violent and
wanton youth. It is useless to seek in the Middle Ages for
a golden age of piety, peace and brotherly love. It is an
equal mistake to fall back into the error of the Eighteenth
Century, of despising the great epoch that led man back
out of barbarism into the renewed light of civilization. We
should think of the mediæval era not as a fixed state but
as a living process; we should not conceive it as a motion-
less picture in a Morris tapestry, but as a series of shifting
scenes, some brilliant, some terrible, all full of life and pas-
sion.

Throughout the mediæval period the British islands were
still in the extreme North-West angle of all things. No one
dreamt there were lands yet to be discovered beyond the
Atlantic rollers,—unless indeed, in remote fiords of Iceland
and Norway, tales about 'Vineland' lingered among the descendants of those bold Viking crews who, a thousand years
after Christ, had beached their long-ships on some point
of the North American shore.

But although, when William landed at Pevensey, Britain
still seemed to be poised on the world's edge no less than
when Cæsar first beheld the cliffs of Dover, the world itself had shifted its centre northward and drawn nearer to
the British angle. [SEE MAPS 2 and 3.] Western civilization
was no longer, as in Græco-Roman times, Mediterranean,
but properly European. North Africa, the Levant and part
of Spain had been lost; they had become portions of Asia
and of Islam. Germany had been gained instead, and was
thenceforth the trunk of the body politic of Europe, with
Britain and Scandinavia its northern limbs. The cultural
leadership was divided between Italy and France, but

political and military power lay decisively to the north of the Alps, among the feudal knighthood of the French and German states. Flanders, Normandy and Paris, closely connected with South England in commerce, politics and literature, did as much for the development of mediæval civilization as Italy herself. Because the centre had been shifted northwards from the Mediterranean, the Norman Conquest left more permanent traces than the Roman had done upon the life of our island.

Until the middle of the Eleventh Century, both Scandinavia and Britain had been somewhat loosely attached to the civilization of Europe. They had their own Nordic traditions and literature, perhaps the noblest product of the Dark Ages,—the spirit of the Eddas and Sagas. But the Norman Conquest severed Britain from Scandinavia of the Vikings and connected her with France of the feudal knights.

The mediæval Europe to which England was closely attached for four hundred years after Hastings found its unity only in its social, religious and cultural insitutions. Unlike the ancient Roman world, it was not held together as a single State. Its political structure was the legalized and regulated anarchy of the feudal system. The only name by which Europe knew itself was Christendom, and its only capital was Papal Rome. There was no political capital; the so-called 'Empire' existed in theory, but lacked administrative force. Real unity was given by the customs of feudalism, chivalry and Roman Christianity, which were then common to all lands from the Forth to the Tagus, from the Carpathians to the Bay of Biscay. The agrarian feudal economy with its lords and villeins, the orders of clergy with their judicial powers and social privileges, feudal custom and the Canon Law, were universally accepted, as no equally important institutions could be accepted after the rise of the middle classes and of nationality had given greater variety to European life. The English knight, speaking French, and the English churchman, speaking Latin, could travel through Europe from castle to castle and from abbey to abbey, and find less that was strange to them than Englishmen touring in the same parts in Stuart or Hanoverian times.[1]

Britain, reorganized after the Norman Conquest, became strong enough to defend herself behind the narrow seas; henceforth they served 'as a moat defensive to a house,' and no longer as an open pathway to her enemies. As she gathered strength, she became the hammer instead of the anvil, the invader of France instead of the invaded. And as the French influences of the Norman Conquest became absorbed in the island atmosphere, the Norman overlords became identified with the life of their English neighbours, particularly after the loss of Normandy in the reign of John. Britain began, before any other European State, to develop a nationhood based on peculiar characteristics, laws and institutions. Because she was an island, her life drew apart once more. Already in the reign of Henry III, the Barons of the land, the descendants, or at least the successors, of those victors of Hastings fight who had scorned everything English, had learnt to say 'Nolumus leges Angliae mutari' ('We don't want the customs of old England changed').

Foreign chivalry and foreign clericalism had been the two chief methods of progress for Englishmen under the Norman and early Plantagenet Kings. High above the wooden huts and thatched roofs of the Saxon villeins towered the great stone castle and the great stone cathedral: mighty works they were, and strong the arms and subtle the minds of the men who reared them and dwelt in them. Nevertheless it was the despised English people and not their alien tutors who would prevail in the end, emerging once more, strengthened, instructed, elevated, prepared for tasks that would have astonished William and Lanfranc.

The leaders in this great work of evolution were the

[1] These remarks are of course quite untrue of that semi-detached portion of Christendom, the Byzantine or Eastern Roman Empire seated at Constantinople that ultimately fell before the advance of Islam. Its form of government was a bureaucratic, erastian despotism, inspired by Orthodox religion, Hellenistic culture, and Roman political tradition.

Anglo-French Kings. The Norman Conquest and the Angevin succession gave us, by one of those chances that guide history, a long line of Kings more vigorous than any in Europe. They used the new feudalism to enforce national unity, though elsewhere feudalism meant disruption; they built up a strong but supple administration, centralized, yet in touch with the life of the localities; their courts evolved a single system of native law for the whole realm; they stretched out their royal hands to the subjugated English, protected them against feudal oppressors, helped them to find new organs of self-expression in cities, law courts and Parliament, and even in foreign wars won by the long-bow of the English yeoman.

Under such kingly leadership England acquired, during these centuries of foreign rule and influence, great institutions undreamt of before in the life of man; representative assemblies, Universities, juries and much else on which our modern civilization still rests. In the Middle Ages institutional and corporate life flourished and grew, while the individual was held of little account. Some of these institutions, like the Universities, the legal profession, the city guilds and companies, and Parliament itself, had their origin or analogy elsewhere; they were characteristic products of mediæval Christendom as a whole. But our Common Law was a development peculiar to England; and Parliament, in alliance with the Common Law, gave us in the end a political life of our own in strong contrast to the later developments of Latin civilization.

Yet even as late as the Fourteenth and Fifteenth Centuries, England was not yet fully conscious of her life apart, nor of the full value of her island position. Under the later Plantagenets, she abandoned her task of completing the British Empire by the assimilation of Ireland and Scotland, and tried instead to revive the Norman and Angevin Empire on the continent. The preoccupation of England with the Hundred Years' War secured Scottish freedom; left half-conquered Ireland to permanent anarchy; hastened the ruin of mediæval society in France and England, and stimulated the national self-consciousness of both—leaving to the victors of Agincourt memories on which two hundred years later Shakespeare could still look back with pride as the central patriotic tradition of his native land, only in part replaced by the Armada story.

At the same time in Chaucer and Wycliffe we see a new English culture struggling to be born, not the old Saxondom of *Beowulf,* Bede and Alfred, but something far richer and stronger,—thanks to the French and Italian schoolmasters, soon to be peremptorily dismissed by full-grown Tudor England. In the Fifteenth Century we see all the conditions of mediæval society silently dissolving, sure prelude to the coming revolution. The villein is achieving his emancipation under a new economic order. New middle classes in town and country are thrusting themselves in between lord and serf, the two isolated pillars of the old feudal structure. Commerce and manufacture are growing with the cloth trade, and are bursting the boundaries of mediæval borough and guild. Laymen are becoming learned and are thinking for themselves. Caxton's press is replacing the monastic scribe. The long-bow of the English yeoman can stop the charge of the feudal knight, and the King's cannon can breach his donjon wall. As climax to all these profound changes, slowly at work through many passing generations, the mist is suddenly rolled back one day off the Atlantic waves, revealing new worlds beyond the ocean. England, it seems, is no longer at the extreme verge of all things, but is their maritime heart and centre. She has long been half European; she shall now become oceanic—and American as well, and yet remain English all the while.

CHAPTER ONE

The Anarchy and the Restoration of Royal Power.
Henry II. Knights and Villeins at the Manor.
The Village Economy

KINGS: Stephen, 1135–54; Henry II, 1154–89

The Norman Kings had kept their Barons in order, revived
the shire organization as the instrument of royal government, and established in the Exchequer an effective system
of collecting the multifarious revenues of the Crown. But
the peace of the land still depended on the personal activities of the King. As yet there was no automatic machinery of State that would continue to function even when
the crown had been set upon a foolish head. Between the
First and Second Henries, between the Norman and
Angevin Kings, intervened the anarchy known as the reign
of Stephen. It was, in fact, not a reign but a war of succession [1135–54.], waged by Stephen of Blois against Matilda,
widow of the Emperor and wife of the great Plantagenet
Count, Geoffrey of Anjou.[1]

The miseries of this period prepared all men to accept
the bureaucratic and judicial reforms by which Henry II

It is remarkable that the citizens of London, in support of
Stephen, asserted with some success their right to choose
who should fill the throne. This shows how little the crown
was then held to devolve by divine right of hereditary
succession. It shows also how the country as yet lacked
an institution like Parliament to settle such disputes.

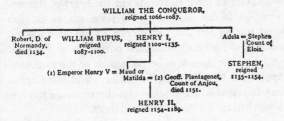

WILLIAM THE CONQUEROR,
reigned 1066–1087.

Robert, D. of Normandy, died 1134.

WILLIAM RUFUS, reigned 1087–1100.

HENRY I, reigned 1100–1135.

Adela = Stephen, Count of Elois.

STEPHEN, reigned 1135–1154.

(1) Emperor Henry V = Maud or Matilda = (2) Geoff. Plantagenet, Count of Anjou, died 1151.

HENRY II, reigned 1154–1189.

afterwards extended the authority of the King's courts, and laid the basis of the Common Law, in a spirit alien to true feudalism. Of true feudalism England had enough under Stephen.

The feudal anarchy rose out of a disputed succession between a man and a woman equally unfit to fill the throne. Stephen and Matilda raised rival armies by giving a free hand to their baronial supporters, and by granting away to private persons those rights of the Crown which the Norman Kings had laboriously acquired. For two generations past, the sheriff had been a real King's officer, removable at will and subject to the inquisition of the central *Curia*. But the typical figure of the new age was Geoffrey de Mandeville, whom Matilda and Stephen in turn made hereditary sheriff and justiciary of Essex, granting to him and his heirs for ever the right of holding all the King's judicial and administrative power in the county. He was perpetually changing sides and perpetually raising the price of his allegiance. Finally he secured from Stephen these royal rights not only in Essex but in Hertfordshire, Middlesex and London, the very heart of the Kingdom. He was a ruffian of the worst order, and the most powerful man in the East of England, not excepting the King. But, in spite of the royal charters, 'his heirs for ever' were not destined to rule those regions.

By men such as these, in local possession of sovereign power, whole districts were depopulated. The Thames valley, the South-West and part of the Midlands suffered severely, but the worst scenes of all were enacted in the fenland, where Geoffrey de Mandeville kept an army afoot on the plunder of the countryside. In the heart of this unhappy region, in the cloisters of Peterborough, an English monk sat tracing the last sad entries of the Anglo-Saxon Chronicle, first compiled under the patronage of the great King Alfred, now shrunk to be the annals of the neglected and oppressed. In it we hear the bitter cry of the English common folk against the foreign chivalry to whom the foreign Kings had for a while abandoned them.

They greatly oppressed the wretched people by making them work at these castles, and when the castles were finished they filled them with devils and evil men. They then took those whom they suspected to have any goods, by night and by day, seizing both men and women, and they put them in prison for their gold and silver, and tortured them with pains unspeakable, for never were any martyrs tormented as these were.

Then follows the passage so often quoted in our history books, the inventory of the tortures used, of which the mildest were starvation and imprisonment in oubliettes filled with adders, snakes and toads. If we remember that two generations later King John starved to death a high-born lady and her son, we may well believe the worst of these tales of horror wrought under the anarchy upon the friendless and the poor.

While such atrocities were things of every day in the stone castles that now covered the land, the feudal nobility who had reared them were also engaged with a peculiar zeal in founding and endowing monasteries. In Stephen's reign a hundred new foundations were made. Those who caused and exploited the anarchy were foremost in making liberal grants to the Cistercian monks, who first came over from France at this period. We need not suppose that religious motives of a very high order were always at work, any more than that they were always absent. A Baron, whose imagination was perturbed by some rude fresco in the church of a long-clawed devil flying off with an armoured knight, would reflect that a grant to a monastery was an excellent way of forestalling any such unpleasant consequences that might follow from his own habits of torturing peasants and depopulating villages.

[1153.] At length, by the help of Archbishop Theobald, an accommodation was brought about between the claimants. Stephen was to wear the crown till his death, but Matilda's son should succeed as Henry II. Meanwhile unlicensed castles, reckoned at over a thousand, were to be destroyed. It was a coalition deliberately made by both parties against the too apparent evils of unchecked feudalism. But Stephen was not the man to cure the ills of the

State, and it was one of England's great good fortunes that he died next year. He was a gallant warrior, a knight-errant of the new chivalric ideal, capable of giving the Lady Matilda a pass through his lines to his own great disadvantage, but careless of the public welfare and wholly unfit to be King.

Of all the monarchs who have worn the island crown, few have done such great and lasting work as Henry Plantagenet, Count of Anjou. [1154–89.] He found England exhausted by nearly twenty years of anarchy, with every cog in the Norman machine of State either broken or rusty with disuse, the people sick indeed of feudal misrule, but liable at any moment to slip back into it for want of means to preserve order. He left England with a judicial and administrative system and a habit of obedience to government which prevented the recurrence of anarchy, in spite of the long absences of King Richard and the malignant follies of King John. After the death of the First Henry, the outcome of bad government was anarchy; after the death of the Second Henry, the outcome of bad government was constitutional reform. And the difference is a measure of the work of the great Angevin.

Henry II was as little of an Englishman as the Norman or the Dutch William. There are advantages as well as disadvantages in having a King who is a foreigner: he may see the wood more clearly for not having been born among the trees. The Angevin brought to bear on English problems not only his fierce and tireless energy and imperious will, but a clerkly mind trained in the best European learning of his day, particularly in the lore of the legal renaissance then spreading northward from the Italian Universities; he was able therefore to be the pioneer of the new jurisprudence in a land that only since his day has been famous for its native law. He was wise too in all the administrative arts of the various provinces of the empire that he ruled. For he was not merely Duke of Normandy but ruler of all western France. By marriage, diplomacy and war, the House of Anjou had accumulated such vast possessions that the Monarchy at Paris and the Holy Roman Empire itself were for awhile of less account in Europe.

Since Henry reigned from the Cheviots to the Pyrenees, he was the better able to control the English baronage, who dared not defy the lord of so many lands. The last baronial revolt of the old feudal type was in 1173, and Henry crushed it. In this way the continental power of the early English Kings was indirectly of service to the internal development of England, when the chief thing needed was a strong monarchy.

Henry's ever-moving court[2] was filled with men of business, pleasure and scholarship from every land in Western Europe. To the great King, who was to leave so deep an impress on English institutions, England was merely the largest of his provinces. The dominions which he administered were not divided by conscious national cleavage, but were all part of the same cultural civilization. In England the upper class still talked French, and continued to talk it till well on in the reign of Edward III. In the English village the distance between the lord and his villeins was accentuated, no longer indeed by racial feeling and the memory of Hastings, but by the ever-present barrier of a different language. The deep social gulf, characteristic of feudalism, was not in the Twelfth Century filled up by a

[2] It was no sinecure to be a courtier of Henry II. Here is an account of the life by Peter of Blois, who shared it: 'If the King has decided to spend the day anywhere, especially if his royal will to do so has been publicly proclaimed by herald, you may be certain that he will get off early in the morning, and this sudden change will throw everyone's plans into confusion. . . . You may see men running about as though they were mad, urging on the pack-horses, driving chariots one into another, and everything in a state of confusion. . . . His pleasure, if I may dare to say so, is increased by the straits to which his courtiers are put. After wandering about three or four miles in an unknown forest, frequently in the dark, we would consider our prayers answered if we found by chance some mean filthy hut. Often were there fierce quarrels over these hovels, and courtiers fought with drawn swords for a lodging that it would have disgraced pigs to fight for.'

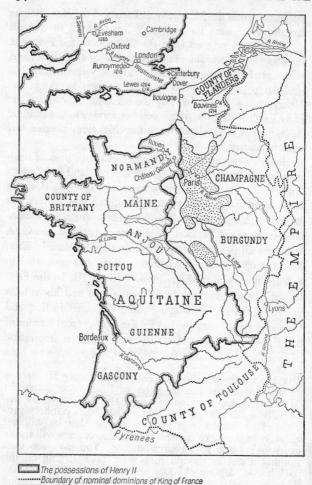

Map 9   The Angevin Empire

numerous middle class of yeomen or traders. Such as they
were, the bailiff, men-at-arms, and other go-betweens who
linked the lord to the peasant serf, must have spoken both

French and English. The priest dealt in yet a third tongue—Latin, which was therefore the language of official documents. Mediæval England was a polyglot community—even without taking account of the numerous provincial variations of 'old' and 'middle' English, or of the Celtic tongues spoken in Wales and Cornwall.

English snobbery was already at its beneficent task, unending down the ages, of spreading the culture of the upper class outwards and downwards among the people. As late as the reign of Edward III, a chronicler tells us that 'uplandish men will liken themselves to gentlemen and strive with great business for to speak French, for to be i-told of,' and we may be sure it was so even more in the time of the Angevin Kings. It is then no wonder that the great wave of French poetry and French narrative that was sweeping over Europe in the Twelfth Century, invaded and conquered England. The alliterative poetry of the school of *Beowulf* must have lingered on obscurely, since there was a modest revival of it two centuries later in the time of Langland's *Piers Plowman*. But the England of Henry II and his sons, inhabited by a good-humoured folk devoted, as foreigners remarked, to outdoor sports and games and jokes, was carried away by the lilt and swing of French songs for music and the dance, by the *verve* of French epics and tales, and by English songs made in imitation. Here we must seek the origin of the forms taken by the great English poetry of later times.

In remote Iceland a literature not inferior to the French romances and carols was flourishing and decaying, neglected by the world. If the prose Sagas had been known and appreciated in England, they might have changed much in the history of letters. But they were left to a little clan, hemmed in by the stormy seas, while England and Germany were conquered by the literature of Italy and France, which made all Europe one in culture no less than in religion. The Nordic humour and poetry, when it reawakened in Chaucer and Shakespeare, poured its impetuous forces into Latin forms, transmuting them into something rich and strange.

The progress of mediæval England in the arts and

crafts, in wealth, civilization and good humour, was due to the relative peace that she enjoyed as compared to the rest of mediæval Europe. Her French-speaking Kings not only prevented the constant invasions which had characterized the Anglo-Saxon period, but after the reign of Stephen stopped the private wars which continued to be a feature of continental feudalism. In England, a Baron did not enjoy the right to wage war on another Baron; and the knights whom he had enfeoffed to render the services he owed to the Crown, were not permitted to fight in his private quarrels, least of all against the King.

The knights, in fact, were ceasing to be called out on any feudal service at all, even in the King's wars. A great foreign ruler like Henry II wanted troops whom he could take to Aquitaine or beyond, and keep on foot for more than the feudal forty days. He therefore extended a system begun by Henry I, by which payments called 'scutage' or 'shield-money' were, if the King wished it, received by the Exchequer from Prelates and Barons, in lieu of the military service of their knights enfeoffed upon their lands. The cash could be used by the King to hire mercenaries either foreign or English.

And so in the reigns of Henry II and his sons, an English knight, though trained to joust and fight from the saddle, might never have seen a siege or a stricken field. His interests were growing every day more peaceful and more agricultural. He was always plotting to improve the yield of his domain lands, watching the villeins at work upon them, and going the rounds with his friend and servant the bailiff, whom he could instruct to 'sow the headland with red wheat.' He was in process of becoming that pre-eminently English figure—the country gentleman.

For these reasons the stone castle typical of Stephen's reign was gradually replaced by the stone manor-house, typical of the Plantagenet epoch. The movement was hastened by Henry II's demolition of unlicensed castles and his unwillingness to grant new licences. The stark donjon-keep was replaced by a high-roofed stone hall of the type of a college dining-hall at Oxford or Cambridge, the lineal descendant of the high timber hall of the Anglo-Danish thegn. In front of it was a walled courtyard partly surrounded by buildings. The manor-house was only to be entered through the gateway of the courtyard, and was often protected by a moat. It was built to be defensible against a mob or a troop of horse, but could not, like the castle, stand a regular siege. The men who built the Plantagenet manor-houses lived among armed neighbours easily moved to violence, but they were not preoccupied with the thought of serious war, their chief desire being to enjoy in safety the fruits of the soil and to cultivate the arts and crafts of peace.

There were indeed infinite varieties and grades of manor-house and hall, and I have here described only those of the better-to-do gentry. But some must have been very humble abodes in the Middle Ages, for even in Tudor times there were some 'halls' of the gentry that are now only used as barns, and very many that are now farmhouses.

English knights, down to the age of Chaucer and beyond, often hired themselves out to their own or other Kings to fight in Scotland, in France, or even as far afield as 'Alisandre when it was wonne.' But they were soldiers only when on campaign, and could return to their peaceful country homes. Others never left the manor except to ride to the Shire Court on county business. The more fashionable and adventurous were devoted to the sport of the tournament and to the trappings and romance of the new school of chivalry coming over from France, rather than to actual war.

Such at least was the state of the southern and midland counties, but the social landscape grew more grim as one approached the Welsh or Scottish borders. There dwelt the Marcher Lords in their high stone castles, soldiers ever on watch for the beacon fire and the raid of the racial enemy. It was these warrior nobles of the Welsh and Scottish Marches who supplied the chief fighting element in the constitutional troubles of Plantagenet times and in the pseudo-feudalism of the Wars of the Roses.

There followed, indeed, one remarkable consequence of the feudal and warlike origin of the English country gentleman. After the Norman Conquest the rule of primogeniture had gradually been adopted for land, to secure that a feoff should not be broken up among the sons of a vassal and so become unable to supply the military service due to the lord. In Saxon times an estate had normally been divided among the sons. In Plantagenet times it normally went to the eldest son alone. And therefore the younger sons, after being brought up as children of the manor-house, were sent out into the world to seek their fortunes. This had the effect of increasing the adventurous and roving spirit of the new English nation, and of mingling classes as they were not mingled in Germany or France. The English upper class never became a closed caste, like the continental nobles who married only inside their own order, and despised merchants and commerce. If English history followed a very different course, it was partly because the custom of primogeniture, though originated to meet a feudal requirement, had become part of the land-law of an England that was rapidly escaping from feudalism.

We are watching an important step towards the higher stages of civilization—the growth of a leisured class. At a time when the island held about as many people as New Zealand to-day, and when these few inhabitants were still so poor that we should not have expected any of them to be people of leisure, the feudal system had established a class of warriors living at the expense of the cultivators of the soil. And now that the Monarchy had caused war to cease in the island, this warrior class found its occupation gone. The time and endowments which it was to have spent on war and the preparation for war had become an endowment of leisure. In the Plantagenet manor-houses, time lay heavy on the peace-bound knights, and to kill time they took to a number of different devices, each according to his tastes,—to drink, sport, tournament, agricultural improvement, local administration and politics, music, letters and art. In the primæval Saxon forest, hunting had been the duty of the thegn; it was now the pass-time of the disoccupied knight. As game and wasteland became more scarce, he struggled with the King above and with the peasantry below to preserve enough for his own diversion. Increasing wealth was supplied him by the manorial system of agriculture, by the rising population, by the increasing acreage under plough, and by the disinheritance of his younger brothers under the law of primogeniture; he spent the surplus on comforts and amenities for his manor-house, on art and minstrelsy in the hall, in a thousand ways discovering for the behoof of a barbarous age what a spacious and beautiful thing man can make of life. The rich Abbot and Bishop did the like. The accumulated wealth of the feudal classes and their call for new luxuries caused the rise of the English towns, and the new middle classes engaged in manufacture, trade and overseas commerce. The arts of civilized life were forced into being in mediæval England by the unequal distribution of wealth under the feudal and manorial system, by the stability of these harsh social arrangements, and by the good peace which the King imposed on all.[3]

It remains for us to examine the feudal system of the manor from the point of view of the peasant; to him it was a less unmixed benefit than to the privileged classes, lay and clerical, whom it was specially designed to support.

In the Twelfth Century the proportion of freeholders in an English manor was very small. The day of the yeoman freeholder only came with the breakdown of the old manorial system and the feudal economy proper, which were still in full vigour under the Angevin Kings. The slave, who had composed nine per cent. of the population recorded in Domesday, had risen into the villein class, but the free man was not markedly on the increase. The lord and his villeins shared the manor and its produce between them.

The serf or villein was by birth and inheritance bound to

[3] Mediæval commerce chiefly supplied luxuries for the rich. The food, furniture and clothing of the poor were produced and manufactured locally in the villages. It was the Industrial Revolution of modern times that devised methods of mass-production and distribution of common articles for the common man.

the soil; he and his family were sold with an estate when it changed hands. He could not marry his daughter save with the lord's consent and the payment of a heavy fine; when he died, his best beast, sometimes his only cow, was seized as 'heriot' by the lord of the manor. He could not migrate or withdraw his services at will. He could not strike. He must work on his lord's domain so many days in the year without pay, bringing his own team or half-team of oxen for the plough. It was by these services of the villein, and not by hired labour, that the lord's home farm was worked. The bailiff had to keep his eye on the unwilling workmen lest they should sit down for half-an-hour at a time at the end of every furrow.

But the villein, half slave as he was in these respects, held lands of his own which he tilled on those days of the year when his lord had no claim upon him or his oxen. And he had his share in the use and profit of the village meadow, the village pasture and the village woodland and waste, where the swine and geese were turned loose.

How was his position secured? There was for him no 'equality before the law.' As late as John's reign the safeguards given by Magna Carta to the 'free man' touched him not at all. He could not sue his lord in the King's courts. But he had a double protection against ill-usage. First, the lord and bailiff found it to their interest to receive from him willing rather than unwilling work and to give him no motive to run away. For he could not be easily replaced, like an overworked slave in old Rome, or in the West Indies before Wilberforce; nor might he be driven to work with the whip. And secondly, he had the security of village tradition, legally expressed in 'the custom of the manor,' and enforced in the Manor Court, which was held sometimes in the lord's hall, sometimes under the time-honoured oak tree in the middle of the village.

How much protection was the Manor Court to the villein? It was indeed his lord's court, not the King's. But at least it was an open court, in which there is reason to think that the villeins shared with the freemen the duty of acting as judges or assessors. It was at least better than

the mere arbitrary word of the lord or his bailiff. Against
a rapacious and wicked lord the protection seems but
slender, and doubtless there was often terrible oppression,
especially in Stephen's reign. But in Plantagenet times the
English peasant never fell to the level of the French peasant of the *Jacquerie*.

No ancient system must be judged in the abstract, or by
purely modern standards. The great merit of the manorial
system in its day was this, that among men of primitive
passions and violent habits it promoted stability, certainty
and law. A court that focussed public opinion and tradition,
and that actually kept written records from the Thirteenth
Century onwards, was established as part of the normal
life of the English village. When the system worked properly, a peasant knew what services he owed his lord, and
he knew that the bailiff would exact those and no more. It
is true that the peasant could not strike and could not legally emigrate without his lord's consent; but neither
could his lord evict—in fact, whatever may have been the
case in theory. Nor could the lord raise the rent or services
due, once they were fairly established by custom of the
Manor Court.

During the centuries when this system flourished in England, wealth slowly accumulated; more land came under
plough; flocks and herds multiplied in spite of frequent
murrain; and in spite of no less frequent famine and pesti-
lence the population went up from perhaps one-and-a-
quarter or one-and-a-half million when Domesday was
compiled in 1086, to perhaps three-and-a-half or four millions when the Black Death of 1349 temporarily checked
the increase.

But at the best of times life on the manor was hard, and
the villeins were very slow in rising above the level of
Anglo-Saxon rural barbarism towards the type of jolly English yeoman of later days. The serf was what poverty and
submission made him,—shifty, fearful, ignorant, full of superstitions Christian and pagan, trusting to charms and
strange traditions of a folk-lore of immemorial antiquity;
cheating and sometimes murdering the lord or his officers;

incompetent and fatalistic in presence of scarcity and plague in the village and murrain among the ill-kept beasts. The soil was undrained and sodden to a degree we can now hardly conceive. The jungle kept rushing in, weeds overspreading the ploughland, as bailiffs complained. Under the open-field system with its unscientific farming, the soil after centuries of use became less fertile, and the yield per acre was reduced.

The English weather was at least as bad as it is in our day, and when the crop failed, as it often did after a wet summer, there was nothing to avert famine in the village. Animal food was less available than in Saxon times, for the vast forests of the Norman Kings and the private warrens of their vassals were guarded by cruel laws. The wild birds, the preserved pigeons and rabbits, and the other animals with which the island swarmed, often came marauding into the peasants' crops with the direst effects, and were taken and cooked on the sly in spite of laws and penalties. Cattle and sheep were not for the peasant to eat, though 'beef' and 'mutton' figured in the bill of fare of the French-speaking lords at the manor-house. Pig's flesh was commoner in the cottage. In fen regions fishers and fowlers supplied eels and water-fowl good and cheap.

The mediæval English village, at the end of its muddy riding tracks, with its villeins bound for life not to stray from the precincts of the manor, was subject to physical and intellectual isolation that governed its life in every respect. One result of isolation was that the village had to manufacture for itself. Among the villeins were craftsmen, who might or might not be husbandmen as well. The 'wright' or carpenter could knock together the cottages, their furniture and the wooden part of the farm machinery; the thatcher and the blacksmith could finish his work. The women and children were all 'spinsters,' and village weaving of the coarser kind of cloth preceded fine weaving in England by many centuries—and indeed stretches back to prehistoric times. Much of the peasant's clothing was of hides roughly tanned. The neighbouring market town, itself an agricultural village, supplied what else had occasionally to be bought. Only the inhabitants of the manor-house were likely to go further afield in their purchases and to patronize the commerce of the towns and the traders oversea.

In Henry II's reign, the lord's dwelling, whether Abbey, castle or manor-house, was often built of stone. But the villeins' cottages were still hovels, without chimneys or glass, and sometimes without any aperture but the door. They were built either of split logs, erected side by side in the old Saxon fashion, or, where timber became scarce, of 'half-timber' walls, with mud filling in the oaken frame-work. The art of baking bricks had died with the Romans and had not yet been revived. The roof was of turf or thatch. A small orchard, garden or yard surrounded the villein's cottage, even when it faced the village street.

In the West and North and in districts still chiefly wood-land, the cottages often stood in small hamlets of one, two, three, or half a dozen farms, and each little farm often had its own consolidated lands, sometimes surrounded by per-manent enclosures.[4] But in the best agricultural districts in East and Middle England, the prevailing system was the large village of two to five hundred souls, grouped round the parish church and manor-house, in the middle of the open field. This 'open' or 'common field,' was not cut up by hedges into the chess-board appearance presented by rural England to-day. It was divided into hundreds of little strips each of an acre or half an acre, divided by 'balks' of grass or footpath. It must have looked somewhat like a group of allotments of our time, but on a gigantic scale, and all under corn.

Each of these strips was a separate holding, a unit of pro-prietorship as well as of agriculture. Each peasant had his property scattered about in the field in a number of sepa-rate strips, and a single freeman or villein might hold any number from one upwards; thirty formed a usual holding. The lord's domain, though part of it might be in a con-tinuous tract separate from the village field, was in part scattered about among the peasant holdings.

4 See above, p. 27, and note, p. 29.

Lord, freeman and villein were perforce subject to the general village policy as to the cultivation of the 'common field,' of which the private strips were the component parts. There were in fact three separate fields, in each of which every man had his share, small or great. Each year one of these three huge fields lay fallow with the cattle grazing over it; one was planted with wheat or rye, and the third with oats or barley. While under cultivation, the area was generally enclosed by hurdles. Agricultural improvements and private enterprise were severely handicapped by such a system, yet it lasted in some of the best agricultural districts of England from times long before the Conquest to the great age of agricultural change in the Eighteenth Century. The chief improvements took place in that part of the lord's domain which formed a self-contained whole, and could be enclosed, or let as a separate block to leasehold farmers.

Apart from the 'fields' lay the meadow, if possible down beside the brook. The meadow was common hayfield and common pasture, subject to elaborate rules and 'stints' discussed and enforced in the Manor Court. Astride of the brook or mill-stream stood the water-mill, usually belonging to the lord, who could make the villeins bring their own corn to be ground there at his price, which was sometimes so exorbitant that the right to use hand mills at home was striven for as a rare privilege. Windmills were uncommon in mediæval England: the first of them are said to have come from the East after Richard I's crusade.

It will be seen that this was not a communist society, or a 'village community' in the strict sense. But individualism was shackled. The manor consisted of a number of private holders, including the lord, very unequal in wealth and in their relations to one another, but with closely inter-related rights, and all dependent on one another for co-operation on a traditional system. Cash nexus, freedom of contract, fluidity of labour were the exception and not the rule.

Beyond the 'fields' lay the 'waste'—the marshes, heaths and forests that had once clothed the whole acreage of the

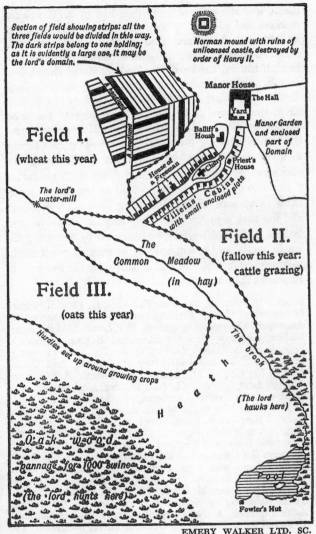

Section of field showing strips: all the three fields would be divided in this way. The dark strips belong to one holding; as it is evidently a large one, it may be the lord's domain.

Norman mound with ruins of unlicensed castle, destroyed by order of Henry II.

Manor House

The Hall

Yard

Manor Garden and enclosed part of Domain

Field I.

(wheat this year)

Bailiff's House

House of a Freeman

Church

Priest's House

The lord's water-mill

Villeins' Cabins with small enclosed plots

The Common Meadow (in hay)

Field II.

(fallow this year: cattle grazing)

Field III.

(oats this year)

Hurdles set up around growing crops

The brook

H e a t h

(The lord hawks here)

O a k   W o o d

pannage for 1000 swine

(the lord hunts here)

Pool

Fowler's Hut

EMERY WALKER LTD. SC.

Map 10 Cowstead: an Imaginary English Village under the Manorial System

island, and still covered more than half of it. The Saxon pioneers had pierced its heart of darkness and broken it up with their 'hams' and 'dens' planted everywhere in its midst. Generation after generation, down the length of English history, the heath, fen and woodland shrank and shrank, as new hamlets and farms sprang up, as village 'fields' were enlarged and multiplied, and as the hunter-Kings were forced to disgorge to their subjects one forest jurisdiction after another. At length, in Hanoverian times, the 'waste' dividing township from township had shrunk to a couple of village commons. Last of all, during the enclosures of the Eighteenth and Nineteenth Centuries, the remaining commons disappeared so fast that in many cases every acre of the land lying between one village and the next is to-day divided up into the chess-board of hedged fields. The townships have ended by devouring the whole 'waste' and forest, unlikely as such an event might have seemed to a bird in mid-air surveying the tree-tops of England a thousand years ago.

BOOKS FOR FURTHER READING: *For Book II. (Middle Ages) in general*: Davis, *England under the Normans and Angevins*; Vickers, *England in the Later Middle Ages*; Stubbs, *Lectures*, and *Constitutional History* (3 vols.); Pollock and Maitland, *History of English Law* (2 vols.); Maitland, *Constitutional History of England*, and *Canon Law in the Church of England*; Holdsworth, *A History of English Law*, Vols. I., II. (the less technical parts are of great value to historical students, whether lawyers or not); Oman, *Art of War in the Middle Ages*; W. C. Bolland, *The General Eyre* (Cam. Press, 1922); A. L. Smith, *Church and State in the Middle Ages*; H. O. Meredith, *Outlines of the Economic History of England*; Coulton, *Social Life in Britain from the Conquest to the Reformation*, and *The Mediæval Village*, and *Five Centuries of Religion*; Various writers, *Social England* (ed. Traill), Vols. I.–II.; W. P. Ker, *English Literature, Mediaeval* (Home University Library); Tout, *Relations of France and England in the Middle Ages*; Quennell, *A History of Everyday Things in England*; J. F. Baldwin, *The King's Council*; C. H. McIlwain, *The High Court of Parliament* (Yale Univ. Press); Stawell and Marvin, *The Making of the Western Mind*; A. F. Pollard, *Evolution of Parliament*; Barnard's *Mediaeval England* (ed. 1924. H. W. C. Davis); M. Deanesly, *A History of the Mediaeval Church* (1926).

For Chapter One only: Relative parts of general works above, especially Davis; J. H. Round, *Geoffrey de Mandeville, a Study of the Anarchy*; Hubert Hall, *Court Life under the Plantagenets* (reign of Henry the Second).

CHAPTER TWO

> Henry II continued. The Cistercians in the North. Becket. The King's Courts. The Common Law and the Jury

KING: Henry II, 1154–89

Some features in the manorial system described in the last chapter were only developed after the period of Henry of Anjou. It was in the reign of his grandson, Henry III, that the keeping of written records by the Manor Court became usual. And in the same reign scientific treatises on agriculture and estate management began to be circulated. The home-staying feudal knights began to imitate on their own estates the methods of account-keeping and record with which the King's Justices, Sheriffs and Barons of the Exchequer had made them unpleasantly familiar. They also took lessons from the managers of Church estates, particularly those of the Cistercian monasteries.

In spite of the enthusiasm with which abbeys were being founded and endowed in the reigns of Stephen and Henry II, and the puritan severity of the original English Cistercians, the monks of that order were not for long a great moral and intellectual force among the people of the land, such as the friars became in the following century. But they led the way in estate management, and especially in growing fine wool for the Flemish looms. If, as has been said in relation to the export of raw wool, Plantagenet England was the 'mediæval Australia,' the monks were among the first great 'squatters.' The famous monasteries under the steep, wooded banks of Yorkshire dales began the movement that in the course of four or five hundred years converted most of North England and Scotland from unused wilderness into sheep-run. By a process too slow to be observed or recorded, the nibbling flocks destroyed the dwarf oak-rods, birch and scrub which had cumbered the water-logged wastes of the North since time immemorial, leaving us instead the prairies of white grass and heather under the drying western wind.

The Cistercians in England perhaps did as much good by their methods of estate management as in any other way. Good and evil are hard to disentangle, for the order was most heartily abused by contemporaries for its proverbial greed, which led the monks into chicane, forgery and oppression, but led them also to keep estate accounts and to develop sheep farming sooner than most landlords. If it is once admitted that monks who have renounced the world and its vanities have nevertheless as good a right to acquire riches as people with fewer pretensions to virtue, then the same measure of mingled praise and blame must be allotted to the early Cistercians as to the improving lay landlords of Tudor times and of the Eighteenth Century.

Many of the new foundations were not subject to the control of the English Bishops, but only of their own Abbots and of the Pope—a liberty, of doubtful benefit to the Church at any time, that ultimately hastened the destruction of the monasteries in England. But some abbeys were within the jurisdiction of the Bishops, and the reports of the episcopal visitations supply the best evidence we have from which to form a judgment on the vexed problems of English monasticism.

In this connection, there is a story told by Giraldus Cambrensis in his malicious *Speculum Ecclesiæ*. One day when Henry II was riding back from the chase, the prior and monks of St. Swithin at Winchester fell on their knees before him and besought him with tears to save them from the Bishop, who proposed to cut down three out of their thirteen dishes at dinner. 'By God's eyes!' said the King. 'Look at these monks! I thought from their howling, their abbey had been burned down. And this is all the story.

May the Bishop perish if he does not cut down their dishes to three, with which I am content at my royal table.' Whether this tale be true or not, many similar stories, jests and sayings show that the popular reputation of the monastic body for sanctity was not very much higher in the reigns of Henry II and his sons than in the time of Chaucer. But in the early days some monasteries were of great service as centres of scholarship before the rise of the English Universities, and as the homes for chroniclers and copyists before the rise of lay historians, scriveners and printers. Carlyle's hero, the noble Abbot Samson of St. Edmondsbury, kept his monks on stricter fare than their contemporaries at St. Swithin's. But the scandals of the Evesham case in the reigns of Richard and John show how easy it was for the heads of monastic houses to abuse their autocratic powers, and how utterly unfitted some of them were for such trust. There was as much variety between one abbey and another as between one manor and the next. Idealization and sweeping censure are equally dangerous with regard to any period—whether Past or Present.

In deciding about the dishes proper to a refectory table, and in more weighty matters of the law, Henry II would have worked well enough with his Bishops, whom he had himself appointed, if he had not made the memorable mistake of naming his Chancellor and friend, Thomas Becket, to be Archbishop of Canterbury. The new Primate, freed from the King's service, held himself to be representative only of the Church and of the Pope. [1162.] It rejoiced his combative nature and litigious intellect to stand up almost single-handed against a combination of King and Barons and a varying proportion of the Bishops themselves.

The sympathies of the English Church and nation were divided, but on the whole they inclined to the King—for Becket was both violent and inconsistent in his conduct of the case. Unfortunately Henry's ungovernable temper broke out in a cry of rage that inspired four of his knights to steal away from his court and murder his enemy in Canterbury Cathedral. [1170.] The wave of reaction caused by this appalling deed deprived the State of many important rights only recovered at the Reformation. The cult of St. Thomas the Martyr remained for three centuries the most popular in England. So many myriads besides Chaucer rode to Canterbury 'the holy blissful martyr for to seek,' that the word *canter* passed into the language for the pace at which pilgrims bound thither should ride—presumably between one tale and the next. It was left for another masterful King Henry, in an age when much had changed, to grind the shrine to powder as being not only the chief centre of a relic worship which the pupil of the Renaissance reformers wished to destroy, but as the monument of the famous triumph of clerical privilege over the King and the King's law. [1538.]

The matter of the criminous clerks on which Henry II was worsted by the dead man was this. In the Constitutions of Clarendon, [1164.] when a grand council of Barons and Prelates had defined the boundaries of Church and State, the King had successfully claimed that clerks who committed felony should be accused first in the lay court, then handed over to the Church court for trial, and, if condemned and degraded from holy orders by their spiritual superiors, should finally be brought back by the King's officers to the lay court for sentence and punishment. This, he argued, was agreeable to ancient usage and not inconsistent with the Canon Law. He did not claim that lay courts could try persons in holy orders.

To many even of the clergy this had seemed a reasonable compromise. But Becket, after a temporary acquiescence, threw it over. His intransigence was approved by his martyrdom, and the result of his posthumous victory was that not only monks and parish priests, but professional men, and an enormous crowd of menials and minor officers of clerical establishments, and in later times anyone who could make some show of being able to read, were safe from the dread of any serious penalty for such crimes as burglary, rape and homicide, at any rate for the first offence. It was only too easy to obtain minor orders, and the attraction to baser spirits of such privileges and protection was great. 'One of the worst evils of the later Middle Ages,' wrote Maitland, 'was the benefit of clergy.'

Although Henry's rash outcry and the knights' wicked deed saved the skins of felonious clerks for more than ten generations to come, in many matters Henry successfully set up the barrier of the lay courts against the encroachments of the clerical power. During the atrophy of the State under Stephen, the Church had naturally and deservedly improved her position and prestige. Supported by the high Papal claims from oversea, the Church courts now threatened to invade many provinces not their own. Henry stayed this tide. The 'benefit of clergy,' that he was forced to concede, only affected cases of felony. For minor offences and in civil actions arising from contract and delict, clerks must appear as defendants in the lay courts of England, to the scandal of high churchmen.

Above all, advowsons were declared lay property and cases about Church benefices were to be tried in the lay courts. This victory of the Common over the Canon Law set some limit to the power of the Pope over the English Church. Cases decided in the spiritual courts could be carried by appeal to Rome, and the Pope was in the habit of stopping cases while they were still pending and calling them up to Rome or before tribunals appointed by himself in England. The Church was in no position to resist this procedure, for she admitted its legality. In matters spiritual she was subject to the Pope, and therefore the only way to protect her against him was to restrict the frontiers of the spiritual field, and compel her to take refuge behind the lay power in the King's courts.

Henry II's firm stand in the matter of advowsons, which he insisted were temporal property, prevented appointments to benefices in England from passing wholesale, by the route of the Church courts, into the hands of the Roman Court.

Even as it was, the Pope soon learnt how to make appointments by 'provisors,' largely for the benefit of Italian priests. The struggle between the Pope and the patrons of English livings, whom the King sometimes championed and sometimes betrayed, went on for centuries, and led to the Statutes of Præmunire and other anti-Papal enactments of Parliament under the later Plantagenets, all tending towards the far-off event of the full Tudor solution.[1]

The greatest of many benefits that Henry II conferred upon England was legal reform. The new judicial procedure that he introduced was destined to shape the future of English society and politics, and to give distinctive habits of thought to all the English-speaking nations 'in states unborn and accents yet unknown.' For the increase of power and jurisdiction that he gave to the King's central courts and to their offshoots travelling in the shires, rendered possible the rapid growth of English 'Common Law,' that is to say a native system 'common' to the whole land, in place of the various provincial customs still administered in the Shire and Hundred Courts and in the countless private jurisdictions.

The organs of old Anglo-Danish life, the communal courts of Shire and Hundred, could never have become instruments for creating the supremacy of the Common Law. They were the courts of the middling class of gentry, and could not have been clothed with enough power and prestige to wrest jurisdiction from the feudal and ecclesiastical courts held by the great nobles and prelates. Moreover, the knights and freeholders who were judges in the Shire Court were themselves too much wedded to various local customs, and their intelligence was too untrained and too provincial to evolve by the light of their own wisdom a new jurisprudence for all England. Even the sheriffs who presided there were not lawyers bred in one great central school like the King's Justices. If a common law was to be created for the nation it must emanate from a single source. That source was the royal *curia*, the King's Court.[2]

Henry II, with his foreign legal learning and his gift for choosing men, made a famous bench of royal judges. Some

[1] Maitland, *Canon Law in the Church of England*, especially pp. 84–107.

[2] See pp. 170–71, above.

were in holy orders, but others, like Glanvil himself, were of the feudal warrior class. These men and their intellectual progeny in succeeding reigns evolved the Common Law from the procedure of the King's central courts. And the same men went forth to every corner of the land as Justices of Eyre or of Assize, carrying with them the Common Law as fast as it was made, teaching its new doctrines and enforcing its new procedure among 'uplandish men' in every shire.

The Common Law, the great inheritance of the English-speaking nations, has in modern times sharply divided them in their habits of thought from the world of Latin and Roman tradition. Nevertheless it was an outcome of the Norman Conquest. The men who made it between the reigns of Henry II and Edward III were lawyers who thought and pleaded in French, while making their official records in Latin. 'How shall one write a single sentence about law,' said Maitland, 'without using some such word as *debt, contract, heir, trespass, pay, money, court, judge, jury*? But all these words have come to us from the French. In all the world-wide lands where English law prevails, homage is done daily to William of Normandy and Henry of Anjou.'

The Common Law owes only a little to the Anglo-Danish codes and customs with their barbarous procedure, their compurgation and their weregild, representing a by-gone stage of society. It owes something to the feudal custom of all Europe, particularly as regards land tenure. But the favourite subject of study in the Twelfth Century was the 'Civil Law' of the old Roman Emperors, and the Canon Law of the Church, then in process of elaborate definition. These two Roman 'laws' served as the exemplar in legal method and science for the men who were making the very different Common Law of England. From about 1150 to 1250 the Universities of Bologna and Paris, where the 'two laws' could best be studied, drew across the sea and the Alps young English clerks, lawyers and archdeacons by the hundred, who returned, as their countrymen complained, Italianate Englishmen full of foreign vices, but full also of strange legal learning. Oxford, almost as soon as she became a University, had flourishing schools of Civil and of Canon Law.

The question then arises—why did the law of England grow upon lines so native and so free in spite of the intellectual attraction exercised during the most critical century of its growth by these potent alien forces? No doubt the Barons of the land, already an English and a conservative body, eyed the Civil Law askance as something foreign and as favouring autocratic kingship, and they had shown in the Becket controversy that they had no love for the Church courts. These feelings on the part of the grandees of the land had to be respected by the King's lawyers, who, moreover, shared them at least in part. And so, while they used the Civil and Canon Law as lesson books in method and spirit, they rejected their positive contents, all except a few great maxims. The English 'Common Law' was not a code imitated from the Code of Justinian but was a labyrinth of precedents, cases and decisions of the various royal courts, a labyrinth to be unravelled by the help of clues held by the legal profession.

Throughout early Plantagenet times the King's *curia* or Court began to specialize its work among various subordinate committees, each gradually acquiring a special function and a procedure of its own, as the financial Exchequer had begun to do as early as the reign of Henry I. A bench of judges, known in after times as the Court of Common Pleas, was by John's reign fixed for the convenience of the subject at Westminster, where the Exchequer also sat, thereby 'giving England a capital.' Otherwise, parties to a suit in the *curia regis* had to chase the King about on his bewildering journeys. The King's courts were as yet judicial committees of the *curia*, rather than law courts in the modern sense. But they, and the itinerant justices in the shires, had enough regularity of procedure to manufacture 'case law,' the precedents which composed the Common Law of England.

By the procedure laid down in his writs, Henry II enabled the subject to bring many kinds of action in the

King's courts rather than in the local and private tribunals. The Crown at this period had plenary power to issue what writs it would, and they form a great original source of English law. Only in the more constitutional times of Henry III and de Montfort, when the King's power was being limited, were the permissible forms of writ defined, and the power of issuing novel writs circumscribed. But by that time the King's courts were well on the road to becoming the ordinary courts of the land.

Partly by writs, partly by 'Assizes,' which were royal decrees issued in an 'assize' or session of notables, the Kings from Henry II to Henry III enjoyed the power of creating new legal remedies, new modes of litigation, new forms of action, to the detriment of the feudal and ecclesiastical courts. Other 'legislation' in our sense of the word there was none. But Henry II, by offering the subject alternative and preferable methods of procedure in the royal courts by his 'Assizes,' in effect stole from the feudal courts most of their jurisdiction as to the title and possession of land. He thereby threw the shield of the royal justice over small landowners whose estates were coveted by some great feudal neighbour.[3]

By this Assize legislation Henry II at the same time introduced the new procedure of trial by jury.

The barbarous Anglo-Saxon method of trial by 'compurgation,' when a man proved his case by bringing his friends and relations in a sufficient number to swear that they believed his oath; the superstitious 'ordeal' by hot iron, originally heathen, but latterly Christian; the Norman warriors' favourite 'trial by battle,' always unpopular with the English, when the parties knocked each other about with archaic weapons of wood and horn, till one of the two was fain to cry the fatal word 'craven'—all these were

[3] The Assize of Novel Disseisin (1166) and of Mort D'Ancestor protected the possessor and his heir against unwarranted eviction. The Grand Assize (1179) regulated proprietary actions, and the Assize of Darrein Presentment disputes as to advowsons. All these added greatly to the jurisdiction of the King's courts.

methods which resulted perhaps as often as not in a wrong verdict, frequently in an unjust sentence of mutilation or death. In looking back over the martyrdom of man, we are appalled by the thought that any rational search after the truth in courts of law is a luxury of modern civilization. It was scarcely attempted by primitive peoples. In mediæval England the first step in that direction was taken by Henry II, when he laid the foundation of the jury system in place of these antiquated procedures.

The jury which he established was not the jury we know to-day—persons empanelled to hear the evidence of others and decided on the facts laid before them. Henry's jurymen were themselves witnesses to the fact. Yet even this was a great advance, because hitherto courts had too seldom asked for witnesses to fact at all. Henry's Grand Assize enabled a man whose right to property in land was challenged, instead of defending himself through trial by battle, to claim trial by jury. [CIRCA 1179.] If such were his choice, twelve neighbours who knew the facts were to testify before the King's Justices as to which party had the better right to the land.

Another kind of jury, the jury of presentment or accusation, was instituted by the Assizes of Clarendon [1166.] and Northampton. [1176.] Twelve sworn men representing each 'Hundred' were to 'present' to the court those of their neighbours who had committed crimes. Like the jurors of the Grand Assize, these jurors of presentment were not judges of fact but witnesses to fact—at least to the facts of the local reputation of the accused. Their 'presentment' sent the culprit to the ordeal, but even if the so-called judgment of God was given for him, though he escaped the gallows, he was to abjure the realm! When in 1215 the Lateran Council abolished the long-discredited ordeal, by forbidding priests any longer to conduct the mummery of the hot iron, the way was opened in England for further developments of the jury system. In the course of the later Middle Ages the jury were gradually transformed from givers of sworn evidence to judges of the evidence of others. In the Fifteenth Century the jury system, more or less as we now have it, was already the boast of Englishmen, proudly contrasted by Chief Justice Fortescue with French procedure where torture was freely used.[4]

Henry's new justice was popular and was eagerly sought. Cruelty, violence and oppression were things of every day in a society slowly emerging from barbarism, and the royal writ at least afforded to the defenceless occasional help and remedy. Yet there was a less attractive side to the justice of the King. His courts were a means of extortion, to fill his ever-gaping Exchequer. It was not only the disinterested desire to give his people true justice that caused Henry II to extend the profitable domain of the royal courts. Richard, John, and Henry III cared even less than he about abstract justice, and even more about money, and they all continued to foster the royal jurisdiction. The Justices were quite as busy collecting the King's revenues as enforcing the King's peace. They were two aspects of the same operation.

Specially extortionate, unpopular and monstrous, from the time of Henry III onwards, were the proceedings of the 'General Eyre,' when a King's Commissioner was sent down to some unhappy shire to overhaul every judicial and financial action of the sheriff and freemen since the last Eyre perhaps seven or more years before, and extort heavy fines for every trifling oversight. In 1323 the men of Cornwall fled with their families to the moors and woods to escape the dreaded visitation. In Edward III's reign, partly on account of their unpopularity, the General Eyres came to an end—the itinerant Justices thenceforth holding smaller commissions. Although royal justice was the chief method of progress under the early Plantagenets, it no more deserves unqualified praise than other human institutions.

[4] The jury system as created by the Plantagenet Kings and judges was suggested by the methods used by Norman Kings to take the evidence of townships on the Domesday and other inquests. But Anglo-Danish customs had already in Ethelred's time a system curiously like Henry II's jury of presentment. See p. 116, above.

Henry II was an autocrat, but like his Tudor namesakes he lived in times when people wished for strong government more than anything else. And like them he was an autocrat who ruled by law, who trusted his people, and who had no standing army, but encouraged his subjects to be armed, as unpopular tyrants dare not do. The Assize of Arms of 1181 decreed in detail what weapons and armour the men of every rank to the lowest freeholders and artisans must keep ready for the King's service in time of need. It was a measure anti-feudal in tendency, looking back to the Saxon fyrd, and forward to the new England in the making.

It was owing to Henry of Anjou that anarchy was quelled in the early morning of our history, instead of the late noon, as happened in the feudal lands of the continent. And it was due to him that the King's Peace was maintained through a native Common Law, which, unlike the systems more directly drawn from the civil law of the Roman Emperors, made law itself the criterion, and not the will of the Prince.

CHAPTER THREE

Richard I and the Crusades. Hubert Walter and the Middle Classes. Constitutionalism Grows Out of Feudalism. John and Magna Carta. Henry III and Simon de Montfort.

KINGS: Richard I, 1189–99; John, 1199–1216; Henry III, 1216–72

Christendom in the Ninth and Tenth Centuries had been ringed round by foes encroaching upon her from east, from south and from north. Europe had been, not the attacker, but the attacked; not the explorer, but the explored. If her enemies no longer, after the days of Charlemagne, threatened her very life, they bade fair to deny her the use of the sea, the possession of her own coasts, and therewith the prospect of the commerce and the world expansion which we associate with the destiny of the European peoples. In the North, the heathen Vikings held both sea and shore. Most of Spain and Sicily were under Saracen rule. The Mediterranean was swept by Moslem and Viking craft. From the lower Danube the heathen Magyars pushed into the heart of Germany and across the Lombard plain. Both by sea and by land Western Europe was being cut off from everything outside herself, even from Constantinople, the hearth of Eastern Christianity and learning.

[SEE MAP 3.] In the course of the Eleventh and Twelfth Centuries the situation was reversed. The slow conquest of Spain from north to south began. Norman instead of Saracen reigned in Sicily. The Vikings were repelled or converted, and their splendid energies, renewed in Norman warriors and statesmen, became the spearhead of Christian chivalry. The Magyers too were baptized, and their kingdom of Hungary gave the crusading armies free access by land to the Balkan territories, the Byzantine Empire, and thence into Asia Minor and on to the Holy Land. Sea power passed into the hands of the Italian maritime Republics of Genoa and Venice, who were therefore able to convoy the soldiers of the Cross to the Levant.

This brilliant change in the prospects of Europe had been achieved in the main by feudalism. Feudal Christianity, for all its faults, had imposed its ideals on Viking and Magyar as something superior to their own social order. And it had turned back the Moslem advance. When the feudal knight charged, as he had now learnt to do, with heavy lance in rest, no one could resist his onset. Infantry were no longer of great account till the rise of the English bowmen. And during the Twelfth and Thirteenth Centuries the military power of feudalism was crowned by improvements in the science of castle building. Richard I's famed Château Gaillard in Normandy and the fortresses of the Crusaders in the East were vastly superior to the mound-and-stockade castles with which the Normans of the Conquest had held down England. They were superior even to the square donjon-keeps whence

the anarchy of Stephen's reign had emanated, for the
scheme of the new military architecture was a long curtain wall, defended by towers placed at intervals along
its circuit, and enclosing a single great courtyard. The
type is to be seen in Conway, Carnarvon and Harlech,
with which Plantagenet England held down the Welsh,
and in Bodiam Castle in Sussex.

In these altered circumstances and with these improved
methods of warfare, the recovered self-confidence of feudal Christendom was bound to seek outward expansion.
The Crusades satisfied at once the dictates of piety and the
craving for battle, exploration and plunder. They were
the policy not of the national statesman but of the knight
errant, a characteristic figure in real life during the Twelfth
and Thirteenth Centuries. The Crusades were the first
phase in that outward thrust of the restless and energetic
races of the new Europe which was never to cease till it
had overrun the globe. It was the same spirit which had
inspired the Vikings, but it was directed no longer inwards
against the vitals of Europe, but outwards against her
Asiatic neighbours.

As yet these adventurous energies, which were one day
to cross the Atlantic and Pacific Oceans, were turned to
the South-East, by the reopened routes of Danube and
Mediterranean. England, in the North-West corner of the
world, was left in a backwater. Individual English knights
long continued to go on crusade, but the movement never
became a national undertaking and tradition, as it did in
France. The reason is obvious. France had a Mediterranean seaboard and England had not.

[1095–99.] England, then, had practically no share in
the First and most successful of the Crusades, when
Godfrey of Bouillon liberated Jerusalem and set up the
Frankish states of Syria. In the Third Crusade [1190–93.],
for the recovery of these territories most of which had
been lost to Saladin, King Richard Cœur de Lion won
personal glory as the greatest of knight errants. He took
with him other Englishmen of an adventurous disposition,
but not the solid part of the baronage, who stayed at

home to govern the island in his absence. As for the English common folk, the emotions of the Third Crusade touched them just enough to produce some shocking pogroms of Jews.

But indirectly the effects of the Crusades upon England were very great, because they enriched and enlarged the mentality of mediæval Christendom, of which England formed part. They brought many of the ablest men of the half-developed society of the West into fruitful contact with the trade, arts, science and knowledge of the East. Both Saracen enemy and Byzantine ally were the heirs of civilizations older and better equipped than that of contemporary Europe. Even the art of fortification was largely imitated from the castles the Crusaders found in Asia. The settlements and ports founded by the Franks in Syria gave a great impetus to commerce between the two continents. The Crusades raised Venice, as the principal carrier of that commerce, to the pinnacle of her wealth and glory, enabled her citizen Marco Polo and many Italian traders and missionaries to traverse the heart of Asia sometimes as far as the Chinese littoral, and flooded Europe and England with luxuries and crafts imported or imitated from the East; while the nascent intellectual curiosity of the West, taking shape in Universities and in heresies, was deeply affected by Eastern philosophy and science. The rich, many-coloured fabric of later mediæval life, the world of Dante and of Chaucer, would never have come into existence if barbarous Europe had remained as much shut in upon herself as she had been before the Crusades.

Such were the prizes that Europe carried back from the East. Her ardour was not rewarded by the permanent liberation of the Holy Sepulchre; nor by the fraternal unity of Christendom, of which the tale of the Crusades is one long negation; nor did she permanently strengthen the Byzantine Empire, the true bulwark of our civilization against Islam, which the Crusaders of 1203 basely betrayed for their own ends. What the blood and the zeal of the Crusaders really purchased for their descendants was the increase of commerce, craftsmanship and luxury, the lust of the eye and of the ear, the pride of intellect, the origin of science, everything that was most despised by Peter the Hermit and the zealots who first preached the movement in the simpleness of their hearts.

[1189–99.] Richard as King of England was a negligent, popular absentee, as befitted the character of knight errant. He left the island on his long Crusade, after making provisions for the government that ensured its disturbance by his brother John. In the hands of that man, already a proved traitor and ne'er-do-well, he placed half a dozen counties, which were to pay nothing into the Exchequer, and which no royal justices were to visit. It was a dangerous blow at the system of direct royal government built up by Henry II, but that system had taken such firm root that even a rebellion plotted by John against his absent brother failed to shake the State. Richard had just appointed Hubert Walter to be Archbishop of Canterbury and Justiciar or Chief Officer of the Crown. [1193–94.] Hubert, backed by the official baronage and by the Mayor and Citizens of London, suppressed the treason of John, and purchased Richard's deliverance from the Austrian prison into which his fellow crusaders had thrown him on his way home. He rewarded England's loyalty by draining her of money once more, and going off again at once to defend his Angevin inheritance. He never returned to England. Five years later he received his death wound in some obscure dispute with a vassal, beneath the walls of a petty fortress. [1199.]

Hubert Walter, indeed, governed England better than Richard would have done in person. He not only enforced the King's Peace, but began a new policy of trusting the middle classes of town and country, an important preparation for the great constitutional changes of the next two reigns.

With the doubtful exception of London and one or two more, the English towns were not, even those few of them that stood on Roman sites, survivals of Roman *municipia*, as were the French and Italian cities. They were for the most part villages or forts that had grown into market-towns in Saxon times.[1] In the Twelfth Century, therefore, the towns still lay under seignorial, prelatic or royal government, according to the owners of the land on which they were built. The era of their emancipation now began, but most quickly on royal land.

It had not, indeed, been any part of Henry II's policy to favour municipal any more than feudal autonomy. Both had been equally suspect to him as encroachments on the direct authority of the Crown. But, if we may guess at Hubert Walter's mind by his actions, that wise prelate and statesman perceived that, while the power of the State would be weakened by feudal privilege, it would be increased by municipal growth.

He granted charters to various towns, conveying the privilege of self-government through elected officials. The old English word 'Alderman' and the word 'Mayor,' imported from France, reflect the dual origin of the liberties of the mediæval English towns. Hubert, indeed, like Henry II before him, seems to have feared the peculiar power which the citizens of London derived from their wealth, numbers and geographic position. Nevertheless, during the period of disturbance caused by John's intrigues, the Londoners had secured once for all the right of electing their own Mayor—the first officer so called in England. When John came to the throne he continued and expanded the policy of selling municipal independence to the towns.

But Hubert Walter's policy of trusting and using the middle class as instruments of government was no less observable in the affairs of the shire. The class of rural gentry, the knights who were settling down on their manors to agricultural and peaceful pursuits, were increasingly employed for county business by the wise Justiciar. It is here that we see the first sure signs of that peculiarly English system of government whereby the Crown depends largely on the amateur services of the local gentry for the enforcement of the King's Peace, instead of depending

[1] See p. 119, above.

wholly on the sheriff and Judges, or on a centralized bureaucracy of the later continental type. The new policy reached its full development in the Justices of the Peace of later times. In Richard I's reign the gentry were not yet performing their tasks under that name, but already, if not earlier, they were being compelled by the government to act as Coroners to 'keep the pleas of the Crown,' that is to defend the King's judicial and financial rights in the shire. Their services were not always voluntary; it was indeed a function of the mediæval Kingship to force the English to acquire the habits of self-government. The Crown found in the knights of the shire a useful check upon the sheriff, who was suspected by both King and people of frequently abusing his great powers.

[1194–98.] Nor did Hubert Walter keep the appointment of Coroners in his own or in the sheriff's hands. He ordained that the suitors of the Shire Court, in other words the local gentry, should choose four of their own number to serve as Coroners. On the same principle, he ordered that the juries, instead of being chosen as heretofore by the sheriff, should be chosen by a committee of four knights who also were to be chosen in the Shire Court.

Here we have the self-government of the shire not through its great Barons but through its gentry, and here also we have the principle of representation. Thus by the end of the Twelfth Century, two hundred years before the Franklin of Chaucer's *Prologue*, a rural middle class was arising in England, accustomed to the transaction of public business and to the idea of electing representatives. When these local activities of the smaller gentry and the idea of representation were carried up to the larger sphere of a national Parliament, mighty consequences followed to England and to the world.

In the reign of John [1199–1216.] the feudal resistance of the Barons to the exorbitant demands of the Crown began gradually to turn into constitutional resistance, embracing all other classes of freemen. The King by his plenary power had familiarized the country with the idea of a Common

Law of the land. In the reigns of John and Henry III after him, men began to formulate more precisely the conception of law as something with a life of its own, distinct from the regal power—something above the King, by which he must rule.

What we should now call 'constitutional ideas' were growing, slowly but steadily, all through the Thirteenth Century. Our constitution was the child of Feudalism married to the Common Law. For feudalism is the opposite of despotism. It may often be tyranny and it may sometimes be anarchy, but it is never despotism; for it is an elaborate balance of defined rights and duties as shared by the King and the various holders of land. The Barons and knights were protected from the King by feudal law and custom. When he claimed service, aids or reliefs on a scale larger than the custom allowed, they resisted him on point of feudal law. That was the beginning of the Constitutional and Parliamentary movement. The King, instead of arguing each disputed case with each separate lord, found it quicker to come to an agreement with them collectively in Council or in Parliament.

Moreover there is another sense in which English constitutionalism was feudal in origin. The resistance to royal despotism in the Thirteenth Century was successful because the feudal class, unlike the squires of later times, was still to some extent a warrior class. Although, as we have seen, many of them were unused to war, they all had chain-armour and war-horses, some had gone on the Crusades, and many lived in a state of chronic skirmishing with their Welsh and Scottish neighbours. That is why the Barons of Magna Carta and the followers of Simon de Montfort were able to put up a fight against the King. That is why Barons Bohun and Bigod so confidently replied to the threats of Edward I 'By God, Sir King, we will neither go nor hang.' Sir John Eliot would never have dared to answer Charles I in such terms; Pym and Cromwell had to tread the paths of revolution in order to procure the armed force which the Parliamentarians of the Middle Ages normally and legally possessed.

John was the very man to arouse a movement of constitutional resistance. A false, selfish and cruel nature, made to be hated, he showed pertinacity and tactical ingenuity in pursuit of his designs, but he had no broad political strategy or foresight. He strained the feudal law and misused the splendid machinery of State, to extort money from all classes of his subjects, lay and clerical, rich and poor, burgher and Baron—and then spent it in clumsy and unsuccessful attempts to defend his Angevin inheritance against the rising power of the Capet Kings of France. The loss of Normandy to Philip Augustus took place in 1204, and ten years later John's scheme to recover it through a grand European coalition against France was shipwrecked by the defeat of his German allies at Bouvines. [1214.] These events, together with the long-drawn-out quarrel of John with the Pope involving the interdict on England, were the prelude to Magna Carta. John's prestige was shattered, and the strength which previous Kings of England had drawn from their foreign possessions was turned into weakness.

Bouvines, besides helping England to become a constitutional country, ensured the reunion of France under the monarchy of Philip Augustus. The poetry-loving French Court, and the University and architectural schools of Paris, were the cultural centre of chivalric and crusading Europe. It was but natural that the Court should also become, after Bouvines, the political centre of the French feudal provinces. But it failed to develop administrative institutions like those with which the Plantagenets strengthened the English throne, and the French monarchy was therefore destined, in the days of Crecy and Agincourt, to go down once more before renewed English attack from without and feudal treason from within.

[SEE MAP 9.] But meanwhile, between the reigns of John and Edward III, the possessions of the English Kings abroad were reduced to reasonable dimensions. Their Angevin Empire was no more; but they still retained Gascony and the port of Bordeaux, a stimulus to overseas trade, supplying cheap and excellent wine to replace mead and ale on the tables of the English middle class, and so putting an end to the pathetic efforts of our ancestors to grow grapes under our sunless sky. But the connection with Gascony had not the intimate character of the old connection with Normandy, when so many Barons had lands or relations on both sides of the Channel. During the century and a quarter that intervened between the loss of Normandy and the beginning of the Hundred Years' War, the English Kings, nobles and knights, though still talking a caricature of the French tongue, interested themselves in questions proper to England—her relations with Wales and Scotland, and the development of her law and of her Parliament. This return to a more insular outlook saved us from too close an identification with France. If the England of the Thirteenth Century had been occupied in defending the Angevin Empire against the French Kings, the energies and thoughts of our leaders would have been drawn away from national interests and internal problems. When at length, in 1337, Edward III resumed the conquest of France, the English law had already acquired, and Parliament was fast acquiring, well-defined native forms, and the English people had become conscious of its own identity.

[1215.] The first great step on the constitutional road was Magna Carta. The Barons in arms who extorted it from King John at Runnymede were none of them, so far as we know, remarkable men, but their ally, the Archbishop Stephen Langton, had both moral and intellectual greatness. He was all the greater man because his support of the constitutional cause was contrary to the wishes of the great Pope Innocent III, who, in return for John's politic submission in 1213, backed him at every turn in his quarrel with his subjects and declared Magna Carta null and void. Considering that Stephen Langton owed his election to Canterbury to the Pope's support, his stoutness on political questions in England was doubly remarkable.

The Barons were acting selfishly and class-consciously to just the same degree—no more and no less—as other

English classes and parties who in successive centuries have taken part in developing 'our happy constitution' by self-assertion ending in a practical compromise. Doubtless they would have sworn mouth-filling oaths if they could ever have been made to comprehend the idealised misinterpretations of the Charter which held the field in Stuart and Hanoverian times—such for instance as the belief that Clause 39 demanded trial by jury for the meanest villein, and that Clauses 12 and 14 required all taxes to be voted by a national Parliament. Their demands were more limited and more practical, and for that reason they successfully initiated a movement that led in the end to these yet undreamt-of liberties for all.

The Barons had come together to prevent the King from abusing feudal incidents and from raising aids and reliefs on their lands beyond what feudal custom allowed. It has been called a 'tenant-right' movement on the part of an oppressed upper class against their landlord the King, though it must be remembered that what the King unjustly extorted from the Barons had most of it to be extracted by them from the classes below. The Barons also wished to put some limit to the King's plenary power of withdrawing case after case from their courts to his own, through the procedure of writs. We may sympathize less with the latter object than with the former. But, taking the situation as a whole, it was time that the King's plenary powers were curbed or nationalized, and no one but the Barons could have made such a movement effectual.

Stephen Langton was an enlightened guide to his baronial allies, but even without him the circumstances of the age in England were forcing them into the path of true progress. For the strength of the Plantagenet State machinery precluded a return to pure feudalism, nor had the Barons any such thought in their hearts. They had no desire to destroy the work of Henry II which had become a part of their own and of the nation's life. Knowing it to be indestructible, they desired to subject it to some form of common control, to prevent it from being any longer the instrument of one man's will.

In England a hundred years before, and still in Scotland and on the continent, the policy of the Barons was each to maintain his individual independence and private 'liberties' upon his own estates to the exclusion of the King's officers. But in England after Henry II, that was no longer to be dreamt of. The new English baronial policy, enshrined in Magna Carta, is designed to obtain public 'liberties' and to control the King through the Common Law, baronial assemblies, and alliance with other classes. When the Barons extracted the famous concession that no extraordinary 'scutage or aid shall be imposed on our kingdom, unless by common council of our kingdom,' 'and in like manner it shall be done concerning aids from the City of London,'—although they proceeded to define the 'common council' as a strictly feudal assembly of tenants-in-chief—they were none the less taking a step towards the principle of Parliaments and of 'no taxation without representation.' It was a very short step, but it was the first, and it is the first step that counts.

Moreover the Barons of Runnymede were not strong enough to rebel against the son of Henry II without the aid of the other classes whom John had oppressed and alienated. The Londoners opened their gates to the baronial army and took the field in warlike array. The clergy gave their moral and political support. The *liberi homines* or freemen—roughly including all classes above the unregarded villeins—aided with their passive sympathy; it was useless for John to call out the fyrd of all freemen under the Assize of Arms, as Henry II would have done against baronial rebellion. The English people for the first time sided with the Barons against the Crown, because they could do so without fear of reviving feudal anarchy.

Each of the classes that aided or abetted the movement had its share of benefits in the clauses of the Great Charter. In that sense we may call it a national document, though no claim was made on behalf of 'the people' or 'the nation' as a whole, since those abstractions had not yet begun to affect the minds of men. Protection against the King's officers and the right to a fair and legal trial were assigned to all 'freemen.' The term was of limited scope in 1215, but owing to the economic and legal evolution of the next three hundred years it came to embrace the descendant of every villein in the land, when all Englishmen became in the eye of the law 'freemen.'

Several clauses in Magna Carta give expression to the spirit of individual liberty, as it has ever since been understood in England. And the constant repetition of these brave words in centuries to come, by persons who were ignorant of the technical meaning they bore to the men who first wrote them down, helped powerfully to form the national character:—

No freeman shall be taken or imprisoned or disseised or exiled or in any way destroyed, nor will we go upon him nor will we send upon him except by the lawful judgment of his peers or (and) the law of the land.

Numerous other clauses apply sharp checks to various lawless and tyrannical habits of the King's officers, both in his forests and elsewhere, which, if patiently suffered, would have created a tradition of the worst type of continental *droit administratif*.

The Charter was regarded as important because it assigned definite and practical remedies to temporary evils. There was very little that was abstract in its terms, less even than later generations supposed. Yet it was the abstract and general character of the event at Runnymede that made it a great influence in history. A King had been brought to order, not by a posse of reactionary feudalists, but by the community of the land under baronial leadership; a tyrant had been subjected to the laws which hitherto it had been his private privilege to administer and to modify at will. A process had begun which was to end in putting the power of the Crown into the hands of the community at large.

It is for this reason that a document so technical as the Charter, so deficient in the generalizations with which the Declaration of Independence abounds, so totally ignorant of the 'rights of man,' has had so profound and lasting an influence on the imagination—in every sense of the word—

of succeeding ages. Throughout the Thirteenth Century the 'struggle for the Charter,' with its constant reissues, revisions, infringements and reassertions, was the battleground of parties—although both sides were drifting away from the feudal 'consilia' of Clauses 12 and 14, towards the larger ideal of a national Parliament. But until the Edwardian Parliaments were fully established, the Charter remained in the foreground of men's thoughts.

In the Fourteenth and Fifteenth Centuries it fell into the background, its task apparently accomplished. Parliament held the place in men's minds which the Charter had once occupied. The later copyists and the early printers were never called upon to issue popular English versions of the great document. In Tudor times the Charter was even more utterly out of fashion, because it emphasized the distinction between the interests of Prince and people, which throughout the Sixteenth Century Prince and people were equally anxious to deny. Shakespeare's *King John* shows that the author knew little and cared less about the Charter; though he treated fully and freely the human tragedy of Richard II's deposition and death.

But when, under James I, Prince and people again began to take up opposing ground, Magna Carta came quickly back into more than its old splendour. The antiquarians and lawyers who asserted our Parliamentary liberties in the age of Coke and Selden, saw looming through the mists of time the gigantic figure of Magna Carta as the goddess of English freedom. Their misinterpretations of the clauses were as useful to liberty then as they are amazing to mediævalists now. Under the banner of Runnymede the battle of Parliament and the Common Law was fought and won against the Stuarts.

In the Eighteenth Century, the era of unchallengeable chartered liberty and vested interest, the greatest charter of all was worshipped by Blackstone, Burke, and all England. It had become the symbol for the spirit of our whole constitution. When, therefore, with the dawn of a more strenuous era, the democracy took the field against the established order, each side put the Great Charter in the ark which it carried into battle. Pittites boasted of the free and glorious constitution which had issued from the tents on Runnymede, now attacked by base Jacobins and levellers; Radicals appealed to the letter and the spirit of 'Magna Charta' against gagging acts, packed juries and restrictions of the franchise. America revolted in its name and seeks spiritual fellowship with us in its memory. It has been left to our own disillusioned age to study it as an historical document, always remembering that its historical importance lay not only in what the men of 1215 intended by its clauses, but in the effect which it has had on the imagination of their descendants.

The Barons, having no idea of Parliamentary institutions, could only devise the most clumsy means to enforce the treaty they had wrung from the momentary need of their shifty and able adversary. By one of the final clauses of the Charter, John was forced to concede to a revolutionary committee of twenty-five Barons the right, if he broke any of the terms, 'to distrain and distress us in all possible ways, namely by seizing our castles, lands and possessions and in any other way they can.' The situation immediately after Runnymede was as black as it could well be: John was incited by the Pope and his legate to repudiate the Charter, while the Barons called in the armed intervention of the French Prince. We were saved from having to choose between a cruel despotism and a foreign dynasty, by that fortunate surfeit of 'peaches and new cider.' John's death [1216.] afforded a last chance to reunite the nation on the principles of Magna Carta.

In the hands of patriotic statesmen like William Marshall and Hubert de Burgh, with Langton as mediator between parties, the cause of the infant King Henry III made successful appeal to the nation. In a few years the land was pacified. The Charter was reissued with modifications; the Frenchmen were expelled on the one hand, and on the other the growing Papal influence on our politics was kept in check. Castles which the feudal classes had built for themselves or seized from the Crown during the civil war, were pulled down or resumed into royal hands, in many cases after serious siege operations. The minority of Henry III [1216-27.], which began in the midst of war and bade fair to see a revival of anarchy, was turned to good account, thanks to the honesty and ability of the statesmen exercising power in the name of a King who never afterwards used it well for himself. This period saw an increase in the authority of the King's Council, through whom Marshall and de Burgh had to act during their regencies. Yet even so the Council was still a wholly indefinite body of men.

Henry III had so great a veneration for the memory of Edward the Confessor, whom he resembled in more ways than one, that he pulled down the church which it had been the chief life's work of the Confessor to erect, and built in his honour and round his high raised shrine, the Westminster Abbey that we know.

Henry's personal piety controlled his political action. It made him the instrument of the Pope's ambitions in England and in Europe. Since the clergy had no means of protection against the Pope except only the royal power,[2] the King's defection exposed them to the full blast of Roman covetousness. Italians and other foreigners, often of bad character, generally absentees, and nearly always unfitted for the cure of souls in England, were foisted into innumerable benefices by Papal 'provisions.' On one occasion the Pope rewarded the loyalty of the Romans with the promise of the next 300 benefices that should fall vacant in our country. Meanwhile the English clergy were pitilessly taxed to support the political schemes of the Papacy against the Emperor Frederic II and others. These experiences set going an anti-Papal current in English popular feeling, that went on increasing in force until it had accomplished the Reformation. In earlier times the English people, at least since the Norman Conquest, had been regarded as peculiarly loyal subjects of the Pope. Their new-born hostility to the Roman Curia, though shared by many of the clergy, had no logical basis in ecclesiastical theory until

[2] See p. 211, above.

the time of Wycliffe, but could find occasional expression through the acts of the State.

In further pursuance of the Pope's ambitions in Europe and Italy, Henry III allowed his second son Edmund of Lancaster to assume the disputed Crown of Sicily [1255.], and his brother Richard of Cornwall to be a candidate for the Imperial throne [1257.], England being expected to pay for the war of succession of the one and the election bribery of the other. These demands, unconnected with any conceivable English interest, roused the baronage and the nation to fury.

[1258–65.] Thus, for a whole generation after the King had come of age, misgovernment continued, keeping up discontent, till it burst out in another period of civil war and constitution-making. It was still 'the struggle for the Charter,' a continuance of the issues raised in John's reign, but with a significant difference. In the reign of John it had been a duel between the King on one side and the baronage supported by the people on the other. Under Henry III it was a triangular conflict. The 'bachelors,' that is the rising class of knights and gentry, accustomed to local work as Coroners and jurymen, now took a line of their own in national politics. Discontented with the self-ishness of the Barons as displayed in the Provisions of Oxford [1258.], they demanded and in the end obtained, that the baronage should concede to them as vassals and tenants the privileges that it extorted on its own behalf from the supreme landlord the King. And in the matter of royal against seignorial justice, the 'bachelors' favoured the King's courts.

The real strength of Henry's party lay in this division of its adversaries, which his able son Edward was eager to exploit. In opposition to the more popular movement, many of the Barons eventually went over to the King's side, while the constitutional or reforming party, that continued to follow the flag of Simon de Montfort, was almost as much democratic as baronial. The contest became, like the Civil War of Stuart times, less a class war than a war of ideas.

[1264, 1265.] In the final crisis, centring round de Montfort's victory at Lewes, and his overthrow in the following year at Evesham, his party consisted of the reforming section of the Barons; the more politically minded of the knights and gentry; the best of the clergy in revolt against the unnatural combination of Pope and King; the students of Oxford University; and the other popular elements to whom the preaching friars made appeal in the heyday of their democratic zeal for work among the poor. Though the Pope excommunicated him, Simon had the more potent religious forces upon his side. And among his partisans must be numbered the citizens of London, whose flying ranks Prince Edward at Lewes pursued in the fashion of Rupert, while Simon like Oliver was destroying the main of the King's army.

The political rhymes and treatises of the hour show that this reforming party of Simon's last years clearly conceived law as a thing above the King.[3] And many of them were filled, like their leader, with a religious spirit which they devoted to the cause of reform as being the will of God.

Simon de Montfort, Earl of Leicester, was of French extraction and education, but in an age when the English upper class talked French in its familiar intercourse, that did not prevent him from becoming an Englishman at heart. He was one of those commanding natures, like Cromwell or Chatham, who cannot play the second part, whom to accuse of ambition seems almost irrelevant. Like many such men he was not overscrupulous. But he too learnt to identify his cause with his country's, and the country felt it and knew it. He derived his broader conception of patriotism not a little from his long friendship with Grossetête, Bishop of Lincoln, [DIED 1253.] one of the noblest, wisest and most learned men of that remarkable century, who for many years stood out as the critic of royal and papal misrule in England. Simon was Grossetête's friend and successor, as Cromwell was Hampden's, and who shall say

[3] *E.g.*, from a political song of the time of Lewes:—'Nam Rex omnis regitur legibus quas legit. / Rex Saül repellitur, quia leges fregit.'

whether the forerunner would have approved all had he lived?

The party that Simon led in his last two years was indeed remarkably like the Cromwellian both in its strength and its weakness. Democrats before an age of democracy, they were in an impossible position, and could not themselves have effected any settlement. But their action dictated the future, at least negatively. Lewes, won like Naseby with prayer, psalm-singing and cold steel, was, like Naseby, a fact that could never be obliterated. The restoration of Henry III was no more a return to the old despotism than was the restoration of Charles II. In each case restoration was adopted as the only possible way to obtain government by consent.

But there were also differences. More of what Cromwell valued perished with him than in the case of de Montfort. It is no paradox to say that this was partly because Oliver had greater success than Simon as a ruler of the land. The Cromwellian rule was protracted by force for a dozen years, so that in the end the popular reaction against everything associated with it was much stronger. Simon's rule lasted hardly more than a year, and in fact he was never able to impose order on the North and West. And so it was Simon, dying for freedom on the field of Evesham, who became the beloved martyr in popular imagination—a part which Cromwell made over to Charles I.

There was a further reason why Simon's work profited by his death; he had made an intellectual conquest of his greatest enemy, the victor of Evesham. Henry III's son and heir Edward 'was one of those people whom revolutions teach.' He had learnt that the King must reign under and through the law, and that the Crown opposed to the nation was less strong than the Crown in Parliament.

What then was Parliament? The name 'Parliamentum'—'talking shop' as Carlyle translated it, 'parley' or 'discussion' as it might more fairly be rendered—was first applied in Henry III's reign to the purely feudal assemblies of tenants-in-chief sitting with the other members of the King's Curia.

The name 'Parliament' as yet carried no idea of election or representation, nor did it necessarily imply a legislative or tax-voting assembly. It was simply the King's Curia or Council, that elusive Proteus, in the largest and most majestic of its forms, when Barons and King's servants met together to 'talk,' to debate high politics foreign and domestic, to discuss petitions, grievances, ways and means, and new forms of writ, and to conduct State Trials. It was not more legislative than administrative, not more financial than judicial. Having 'talked,' it acted, for it was an epitome of all the powers in the State. But the method of selecting its members had not yet been defined.

In the course of Henry III's reign it became an occasional but not an invariable practice to summon to this great assembly two or more knights elected in each Shire Court to represent the county. This was not to create a new assembly, or to 'originate Parliament'; it was merely to call up some new people to the plenary session of the old *curia regis*. Neither was it a party move either of the King or of his opponents; both sides felt that it was best to know what the 'bachelors' were thinking. It was a natural evolution, so natural as scarcely to attract notice. For two generations past, knights elected in the Shire Court had transacted local business with the King's judges and officers.[4] It seemed but a small step to summon them collectively to meet the King among his judges and officers at some central point. Moreover representatives from individual shires and boroughs had long been in the habit of attending the King's Curia to transact the business of their community. To us, with our knowledge of all that was to come, the step of summoning them collectively and officially may seem immense. But in the mediæval world the representation of communities was a normal way of getting business done, and its application to the central assembly of the realm was too natural to cause remark. When the wind sows the acorn the forester takes little heed.

Then and for long afterwards the summons to Parlia-

[4] See p. 223, above.

ment was often regarded as a burden, grudgingly borne for
the public good, much as the companion duty of serving on
a jury is still regarded to-day. Communities, particularly
boroughs, often neglected to send their representatives;
and even the elected knights of the shire sometimes ab-
sconded to avoid service. Doubtless it was galling, when
you looked round the Shire Court to congratulate the new
member ironically on his expensive and dangerous honour,
to find that he had slipped quietly on his horse and ridden
for sanctuary, leaving the court to choose you in his stead!
'The elective franchise' was not yet a privilege or a 'right
of man.' In Edward III's reign, the borough of distant Tor-
rington in Devon obtained by petition the 'franchise' of not
being required to send members to Parliament; for the
payment of members' expenses then fell on the communities
that sent them up.

Nevertheless the presence of the knights of the shire
strengthened the authority and aided the counsels of the
Parliament of magnates. The Government found it convenient and advantageous to enforce the presence of the
'communities' or 'commons' of the realm through their representatives. And so in the year of revolution after Lewes,
Simon de Montfort summoned not only the knights of the
shire, but for the first time two representatives from each
of the chartered boroughs. [1265.] He probably knew that
the burghers would be of his faction, and he was the first
of our rulers to perceive that the general position of a
party government could be strengthened by calling representatives of all the communities together and talking to
them. It was a form of 'propaganda,' over and above any
financial or judicial use that was made of the Assembly.
We learn from the writs that the burghers were summoned,
but we do not know how many came, or what, if anything,
they did. That particular Parliament was a revolutionary
assembly to which only those Barons were summoned who
were of Simon's party, but it set a precedent for the summoning of burghers which was imitated in the more regular
Parliaments of Edward the First.

The English Parliament had no one man for its maker,

neither Simon nor even Edward. No man made it, for it
grew. It was the natural outcome, through long centuries,
of the common sense and the good nature of the English
people, who have usually preferred committees to dicta-
tors, elections to street fighting, and 'talking-shops' to revolutionary tribunals.

BOOKS FOR FURTHER READING: Kate Norgate, *John Lack-
land*; F. M. Powicke, *The Loss of Normandy*; McKechnie,
Magna Carta; Lives of *Simon de Montfort* by Creighton,
Charles Bémont and G. W. Prothero. Also see p. 206,
above.

CHAPTER FOUR

The Corporate Sense of the Middle Ages. The Universities. The Friars. The Jews. The Common Law
and Lawyers. Parliament under the Edwards. The
House of Commons. The Justices of the Peace

KINGS: Edward I, 1272–1307; Edward II, 1307–27

In the Middle Ages men thought and acted corporately.
The status of every man was fixed by his place in some
community—manor, borough, guild, learned University or
convent. The villein and the monk scarcely existed in the
eye of the law except through the lord of the manor and
the Abbot of the monastery. As a human being, or as an
English subject, no man had 'rights' either to employment
or to the vote, or indeed to anything very much beyond a
little Christian charity. The unit of mediæval society was
neither the nation nor the individual but something between the two,—the corporation.

By thus strictly formulating on the group principle the
relation of every man to his fellows, civilization emerged
out of the Dark Ages into the mediæval twilight. Only in
the later age of the Renaissance and Reformation, after
the emancipation of the villeins had shattered the economic system on which the feudal world rested, was it
possible to take another step forward towards personal free-

dom. Then indeed many of the mediæval corporations went down before the omnipotent State on the one hand and the self-assertive individual on the other. The monasteries and orders of friars disappeared from England, and the town corporations and guilds saw their more important functions divided between the individual and the State. But some mediæval institutions survived unimpaired. The secular clergy, the lawyers and the Universities adapted themselves to the service of the new nation, and the 'House of Commons,' where the 'commons' or 'communities' of the Realm were represented, became the chief organ of the national life.[1] Such has been the priceless legacy to England of the mediæval genius for corporate action.

In this chapter we are concerned with the rise of four great institutions, of which three have survived and one perished in England—the Universities, the orders of friars, the lawyers incorporated in the Inns of Court, and Parliament, more especially the House of Commons. The monastic and the feudal systems had arisen in the struggle against barbarism during the Dark Ages; but these newer institutions were the ripe fruit of mediæval society at its culminating point.

Universities, like Parliaments, were an invention of the Middle Ages, unknown to the wisdom of the ancients. Socrates gave no diplomas or degrees, and would have subjected any disciple who demanded one to a disconcerting catechism on the nature of true knowledge. Philosophy and science rose in the Hellenic world to a point far above any regained in the Middle Ages. But ancient learning and wisdom were never organized in Universities. Partly for this reason they decayed, and fell before the attack of the regimented Christian priesthood.

After that, during the long centuries when the Church

[1] Originally the House of 'Commons' represented, not as to-day statistical aggregations of individual voters, but certain definite communities—the City of London, the Shire of York—somewhat as the United States Senate represents the separate States.

supposed that all necessary knowledge was a simple matter, and the world agreed with her, no need was felt for any organization of learning outside the occasional efforts of monastic cloisters and Cathedral chapters. But the Twelfth Century saw a Renaissance of learning and thought, partly owing to the contacts set up by the Crusades, partly to the automatic increase of mental activity in a richer and safer Europe. The study of Civil and Canon Law, of classical Latin, of philosophy based on Aristotle, of mathematics and medicine based on Arabic numerals and treatises, seemed to require a new corporate life of their own.

The zeal for learning, like the contemporary zeal for the Crusades, was compounded of many diverse elements— pure fire of the spirit, professional ambition, greed for benefices, curiosity high and low, love of adventure and of travel. Like the Crusades, the impulse was international, leading men to desert their own country and wander over Alps and seas. Out of this intellectual ferment over the face of Europe, the Universities suddenly arose, first in Italy, then in almost all the lands of Christendom. Such was the genius of the Middle Ages for giving corporate life to an idea. Even when each land had set up its own Universities, the more famous centres of learning still had 'nations' of foreign students in their midst, for, so long as all educated persons talked and wrote in Latin, learning remained cosmopolitan in spirit.

The mediæval as distinct from the modern University was 'built of men' alone, not of stone and mortar, of colleges, laboratories and libraries, of endowments from capitalists and grants from the State. Nor was it burdened with over-much examining or too many regulations. It would have been the freest of all human societies had it not been for the control of the Church over heresy, which drove the keenest speculative abilities into narrow and arbitrary channels.

Just because the original Universities were not dependent on endowments or buildings, they were able to propagate their species all over Europe in the Twelfth and Thirteenth Centuries with amazing rapidity, without wait-

ing for the patronage of wealth. Thus it was that, owing
to trouble between Henry II and the King of France, the
English students at the University of Paris lightly migrated
to their native island and founded a University at Oxford.
It was a convenient spot, easy of access to all Southern
and Western England, with houses where the scholars
could lodge half a dozen in a room; taverns where they
could sit drinking, arguing, singing and quarrelling;
churches which could be borrowed for University functions; rooms where the Masters could lecture, each with
some precious volume open before him, while the students
on the floor took notes and applauded or hissed him like
a rowdy audience at the theatre.

[1209.] So too, it was probably an enforced migration
from Oxford, the result of town and gown feuds of the
murderous kind then usual, that gave birth to the rival
University. Cambridge was a meeting-place of waterways
and Roman roads convenient for the North and East of
England. Both Oxford and Cambridge were each just over
fifty miles from London, which had no University of its
own until the Nineteenth Century. Wales went to Oxford,
and Scotland to Paris and Padua, until at the beginning
of the Fifteenth Century the Scots set up a University of
their own at St. Andrews.

The early Universities were neither assisted nor cor-
rupted by great endowments, nor by the presence, as in
later times, of 'the noblest youth of the land.' Mediæval
Oxford and Cambridge belonged to the poor, in the sense
that the upper classes made relatively little use of them.
The knights and Barons thought themselves above University education. But the villeins, bound to the soil of
the manor, were below it. The actual students were for
the most part the cleverest sons of yeomen, retainers, and
citizens. When, abandoning their fathers' farms and crafts,
they took minor orders as the first step in the pursuit of
knowledge, they became indeed 'poor clerks' and 'poor
scholars,' the chartered beggars of learning.

For such men the University was the way to professional
honour. It was almost the only path to high promotion in

the Church for those who were not of noble family. And all who aspired to rise by their wits to be civil servants, secretaries of great men, physicians, architects or ecclesiastical lawyers, must needs take holy orders and pass through the University. The first profession to be laicized was the Common Law bar and bench, in the course of the Thirteenth Century. Yet even they were largely recruited from men who had once been at Oxford and Cambridge, in such minor orders as gave no indelible character of 'clergy.'

When, therefore, we imagine what the first English undergraduates were like, we must think of them as nearly all 'clerks' of a sort, protected by the shadow of Becket from the King's courts and hangman, but by no means of a type in which we should recognize the characteristics of a modern 'clergyman.' Any time before the Fifteenth Century, the typical student was a poor, clever lad of lower middle-class origin, coming up to Oxford or Cambridge at fourteen and staying probably till he was twenty-one or more, subjected all the while to slight discipline either of school or 'college' character. His morals have been depicted by the author of the *Miller's Tale* and the *Reeve's Tale* and by many others of less note, though Chaucer has also given us a nobler type in the Scholar of the *Prologue*. The songs of the student, Latin rhymes common to all the Universities of Europe and known as 'goliardic' verses, boast his resolution to 'die in a tavern,' and meanwhile to enjoy all the sweets of a vagabond life, now on the road, now in the city. They have small savour of any religion save that of Bacchus, Venus, and the heathen hierarchy as pictured by Ovid. Yet many of the students were pious, and all were devoted, at least in theory, to learning.

The atmosphere was that of the *Quartier Latin* rather than that of the later Oxford and Cambridge of the collegiate life, half aristocratic and half respectable. The mediæval student was neither. When Simon de Montfort raised his banner, the Oxford undergraduates flocked off in ragged regiments to fight for the cause of freedom, in the same mood as the undisciplined students of France, Italy and Germany fought on the barricades of 1848. In Simon's day it was still possible for youth to be the sectary at once of learning, licence, liberty and religion, and to feel no contradiction.

A sound and generous instinct has led people in modern times to compare themselves unfavourably with the 'poor clerks' of mediæval Universities who faced the direst poverty in pursuit of knowledge. But there was another side to the picture. Boys of fourteen sent, with little or no money and no advice or protection, to fend for themselves in a scene of riot, of debauchery, and frequently of murder, among practised extortioners who lived by cheating the 'silly scholars,' might often get as much harm as good from academic life.

When, therefore, the first Colleges were started, towards the end of the Thirteenth Century,[2] originally to provide food and maintenance for scholars to be placed 'on the foundation' of the College, it was soon perceived that the protection and control of the boys were hardly less valuable than the financial assistance afforded them. Careful English parents became more and more anxious to put their sons into one or other of these arks of safety; an increasing number of undergraduates who were not scholars 'on the foundation' sought and obtained a place in the envied life of the Colleges. The number, wealth and importance of these institutions increased generation after generation to meet a natural demand, characteristic of the English craving for the comfort and security of a settled 'home.' From the Fifteenth Century onwards an additional motive in the endowment of Colleges was to preserve the youth from the influences of Lollardry, Popery, Puritanism, Arminianism and similar evils of each passing age. Where

[2] Balliol, Oxford, 1261–66, and Merton, Oxford, 1263. Peterhouse, Cambridge, 1284. The numbers of mediæval Oxford students were probably always below 3000, and at Cambridge they were still smaller. There has often been gross exaggeration of this as of other mediæval figures.

a fold and shepherds were provided, the wolf could less easily prowl.

It is a mistake to suppose that Colleges were always peculiar to Oxford and Cambridge. Italian Universities had many Colleges or endowed residences for students, which have since disappeared with a very few exceptions. At Paris University upwards of fifty Colleges were founded between 1180 and 1500. But they never attained to the size, wealth and importance eventually reached by the corresponding institutions in England. They withered away and failed to preserve their property, and what was left of them finally disappeared in the French Revolution. The English Colleges grew in wealth and numbers until in Stuart times they had devoured their mother the University.

The chief study of mediæval Universities was a peculiar school of logic, much needed to reconcile Aristotle with the unchallengeable doctrines of the Church, a feat which St. Thomas Aquinas accomplished to the general satisfaction. A promising revival during the Twelfth Century of classical Latin on its literary side, took feeble root in the new Universities and withered away. The time for the poets, orators and historians of Greece and Rome was not yet. True vision of the ancient world, especially that of Hellas, only came with the second Renaissance in the Fifteenth Century. When it came, it gave the spiritual death-blow to the whole mediæval system, for men saw, or thought they saw, far back in time, something more wise, more noble and more free than the world of their own experience. The early doctors and students had no such disturbing vision.

Physical science did not get far in theological swaddling-clothes; the genius of friar Roger Bacon of Oxford shone like a star in the night, but with only scientific weapons he was, as Newton would have been in the Thirteenth Century, a powerless and unpopular victim of the prejudices of his age. Wycliffe, being a master of scholastic reasoning, was far more formidable a century later in his influence upon the minds of men.

The great work of mediæval logic and scholasticism was to train and subtilize the crude intellect of Europe. The intellectual progress of the Middle Ages is to be measured not by results in original thought, which was under an interdict, or at least in strict confinement, but by the skill with which men learned to handle their philosophic material. Though much of the subject-matter of their disputes seems to us as vain and nugatory as the much-debated problem 'how many angels can stand on the point of a needle,' the debt we owe to these ancient choppers of logic is none the less great for being strictly inestimable.[3]

Another great social change in Thirteenth Century England, besides the growth of the Universities, was the coming of the friars. We cannot indeed say of England, as was said with more plausibility of the continent, that the orders of St. Dominic and St. Francis saved the tottering Church. In the England of Henry III the Church as an institution was safe enough. There was much ignorance, neglect and practical heathenism, but there was no heresy and little anti-clerical feeling. There was nothing comparable to the Albigensian, Waldensian and other continental movements which were persecuted with ruthless and wholesale cruelty by the Inquisition, largely under the inspiration of the friars of St. Dominic. The Dominicans flourished in England, but as yet there were no heretics for the 'hounds of God' to hunt. It was the gentle Francis-

[3] Mr. Pearsall Smith, in his excellent work on the *English Language*, p. 187, says: 'If we were to study the history of almost any of the great terms of ancient or mediæval philosophy, . . . we should be able to observe the effect of the drifting down, into the popular consciousness, of the definitions of high and abstract thought. We should find that many of our commonest notions and most obvious distinctions were by no means as simple and self-evident as we think them now, but were the result of severe intellectual struggles carried on through hundreds of years; and that some of the words we put to the most trivial uses are tools fashioned long ago by old philosophers, theologians and lawyers, and sharpened on the whetstone of each other's brains.'

cans and their Umbrian evangel that most completely and rapidly won the hearts of the English after their landing in 1224.

Nor can the friars be said to have saved the Papal power in England. It is indeed remarkable that the anti-Papal feeling first grew strong over here in those very years of Henry III's reign when the friars were obtaining their greatest hold over the people. The two movements were not antagonistic. Grossetête took a leading part in both, and the commission which the friars held from the Pope did not prevent them from giving reign to their democratic sympathies and joining with the party of Simon de Montfort, which though religious and orthodox was openly at feud with the Roman court.

But if in England the friars cannot be said to have saved either the Papacy or the Church, they gave to religion a new spirit and new methods. The earliest Franciscans, themselves converts from the class of gentry, made a great religious revival among the poor, comparable in more ways than one to the Puritan, Wesleyan and Salvation Army movements. In the spirit of their founder, they sought out the poorest, the most neglected, the diseased, especially in the slums of the larger towns, insufficiently provided for by the parish system.

The secret of the friars' propaganda was preaching, in words which the common people could feel and understand. Parish priests were then seldom competent to preach, while the higher clergy had their heads full of matters of Church and State, and the monks abode in their convents or rode about on mundane business and pleasure. Before the coming of the friars, religion relied too exclusively on the sacraments she dispensed, nor were they always at hand for those who needed them. The friars not only made the sacraments more available, but erected preaching and religious instruction into a popular system. It was the destined method of the Lollards and Protestants in later times. By enhancing the importance of the pulpit the friars prepared the way for those who were to replace and destroy them, for they brought religion to the common people, endeavouring to make it intelligible to their minds and influential over their lives.

The monastic movement from the Fourth to the Twelfth Century had been the desperate resource of pious men in ages of decadence or of barbarism, to save their own souls and to make a garden of God in the midst of the world's wilderness. The garden had often served as a useful model for the cultivation of the wilderness, but the wall between the two had always been maintained. But now the friars, in a somewhat more hopeful and better ordered world than that which had generated many successive orders of monks, regarded the world itself as God's garden. They went down into the market-place and the slum to wrestle for the souls of men and women. The monk remained, theoretically at least, shut up in his cloister; when he wandered abroad, as he frequently did, he was more often than not breaking rules to escape the monotony of a life to which he had no real vocation. But it was the duty of the friar to walk from town to town, nursing the sick, preaching, and hearing confessions. The monk was supported by the income of broad acres and sheep-runs; but the friar was to live on the alms he received from door to door.

In theory, indeed, the friar might hold no property. But, contrary to the original intentions of St. Francis, his disciples acquired not only priories but libraries and great churches of their own. As their popularity increased, the ideals of their founder were forgotten or explained away with mediæval subtlety, until those who still stood by his tenets of evangelical poverty were persecuted inside his own order. Learning, which he had deprecated as a snare to the purity of the evangelical mission, was taken up with splendid results by the Grey Friars of Oxford University, under the patronage and guidance of Bishop Grossetête. His friend Adam de Marsh and Roger Bacon himself were among the earlier Oxford Franciscans; and in a later generation came Duns Scotus and William of Ockham. Philosophy, physical science and medicine owed much to the English followers of St. Francis.

As with all such movements, the true apostolic spirit gradually sank into its embers, while the institution survived. In the Fourteenth Century the English friars, Franciscan and Dominican, were two powerful corporations with a host of enemies. The secular clergy in whose parishes the friars poached, carrying off their flocks and their fees under their very faces, hated the friars scarcely less bitterly than did the Wycliffite reformers, who saw in Franciscan and Dominican their chief popular rivals; men of the world like Chaucer laughed at the hypocritical devices of 'brothers' who made gain out of popular superstition while pretending to observe rules of evangelical poverty; and the pious and orthodox Gower could write of the friars: 'Incest, flattery and hypocrisy and pandering to vices, these are the qualities have raised their minsters, their steeples and their cloisters.'

But even at the end of the Fourteenth Century the friars still had a strong popular following; to die in a friar's dress was still held by many to be a passport to heaven. During the Fifteenth Century, though they saw their Lollard enemies crushed, their own influence was declining. When the storm of the Reformation broke they were almost without friends. The secular clergy had always regarded them as interlopers and rivals. And when Henry VIII set out to destroy the Papal power, the disbandment of the friars was an essential part of the policy, for they were the Pope's special protégés and servants.

The coming of the friars was the last great wave of the flood of foreign influence that had been washing over England ever since the Norman Conquest. After that the waters recede, leaving a rich sediment, while the wind shifts and blows from inland woods. In the Edwardian and later Plantagenet period, England, instead of perpetually receiving, gives out of her own plenty. She becomes profuse in the creation of native forms. Her own law and Parliament develop under the First Edward, her own language and literature arise under the Third; and with Chaucer comes also Wycliffe and the beginning of the

distinctive English contribution to religion. Meanwhile the
English yeomen conquer France with the island weapon;
and the archer enshrines himself in the general imagination of a woodland people of sporting instincts, fun and
good-nature, as that exclusively English figure of the jolly
outlaw and radical—Robin Hood.[4]

All this was accompanied and aided by the growth of
English liberty in the emancipation of the villeins, and the
increase of English wealth in the substitution of the manufactured cloth trade for the export of raw wool. At the
same time, English finance and money-lending passed into
English hands in the course of the Fourteenth and Fifteenth Centuries; the way for that development was prepared by Edward I's expulsion of the Jews.

The Jews, like so many other foreigners, had come into
England in the wake of the Conqueror. Saxon England had
been so primitive as to require few money-lenders. But
the Norman and Angevin kings, like other continental
princes, employed the Jews to supply them with ready
cash in anticipation of revenue. The Jews throve on money-
lending for interest, a practice forbidden by the Church,
which Christian traders, having no gold to lend, were fain
to abandon with a curse to the infidels who had it. The
Jews were the King's sponges. They sucked up his subjects'

---

[4] Robin Hood, originally a woodland elf of infinite antiquity, was a 'good yeoman' in his greatest days towards the
close of the Middle Ages. He only became vulgarized as a
disguised Earl of Huntingdon late in the Sixteenth Century. His story, as it is known to us to-day, dates from
late Plantagenet to early Tudor times. The King with whom
the early ballads connected him was not Richard I, but
an Edward, probably the First. Robin's feats with the long-
bow (see p. 280, below) and his animosity against
rich Churchmen bespeak a period subsequent to the Thirteenth Century, and his 'friar' Tuck has had time to ac-
climatize himself to the island atmosphere. Maid Marian,
who seems to have had an earlier existence on her own
account, did not join Robin's troupe before 1500; yet the
fully developed idea of her is as distinctively English as
any part of the legend. Perhaps she owes most to Peacock
in the Nineteenth Century!

money by putting their own out on usury, and were protected from the rage of their debtors solely by the strong arm of the King, who in his turn drew what he wanted from their ever-accumulating wealth. They stood to the King as the villein to his lord; all they had was, theoretically, his. His 'exchequer of the Jews' aided them to collect their debts. They were utterly at his mercy, for he was their only friend in a hostile land. Their unpopularity was twofold, for were they not the arch-creditors when no one else had money to lend on usury, and the arch-infidels when everyone else, of course, believed?

Their operations in England, besides their dealings with the King, consisted very largely in lending money to the baronage and the warrior class. They supplied the sinews of war and government, but not yet of commerce and industry, for the day of commercial capitalism was still in the future.

Some of the English Jews became very rich, like Aaron of Lincoln in the reign of Henry II, who had the honour of a special department of the Exchequer, 'Scaccarium Aaronis,' to wind up his affairs. In the towns of wealthy East Anglia, the stone houses of the Jews, not easily broken open, stood as rivals to the stone castle and the stone church among the mud and timber hovels of the poorer Christians. But whenever the King drew in his protecting arm, horrible pogroms put an end at once to the Jews and their tell-tale parchments.

[1290.] In Edward I's reign this unhappy system came to its cruel end. Edward, perhaps, was only acting up to the best lights of his time, in driving the Jews out of the island. The expulsion was praised as an act of self-sacrifice on his part, and was of course intensely popular. It was a feasible policy because the time had come when it was just possible for a King and his nobles to get money elsewhere, from 'usurious' Christians. At first the money-lending business in England passed largely into the hands of the Flemings and Italians, like the great Florentine firms of Bardi and Peruzzi, from whom Edward III borrowed. Then English capitalists gradually became more impor-

tant. Merchants like William de la Pole of Hull, the first
commercial founder of an English noble family, and Richard Whittington, Mayor of London and hero of the cat-
myth, became money-lenders to the King and baronage,
financing the Hundred Years' War and the Wars of the
Roses. Edward IV lived on intimate terms with the great
London citizens, not only because he liked their wives but
because he borrowed their money. When, therefore, under the Tudors the age of commercial capitalism slowly
dawned, high finance was in native hands.

When the Jews returned to England in the Stuart and
Hanoverian era, they found the English in control of their
own money-market and of the other intellectual professions. And by that time the new Bible-reading culture of
the English had diminished the religious hatred against the
Chosen People. For these reasons the relation of the Jews
to the English was renewed under happier auspices than
even now prevail in lands where the natives have not had
the wit or the opportunity to contract the habit of managing
their own affairs.

Edward I [1272–1307.] has been called 'the English Justinian,' in reference to the Emperor [527–65.] who carried
through the codification of old Roman law on the eve of
its decline. It has indeed been said that to compare
the English law of Edward's time with the Roman law of
Justinian is to compare childhood to second childhood. But
Edward at least resembled his prototype in being a royal
definer of things legal. He did not, it is true, perpetrate
anything so definite as a code, which is unsuited alike to
the childhood of a nation and to the plastic genius of English law. But he gave closer definition to our land law, our
public law and our Parliament. Under him the institutions
of the mediæval State, hitherto fluid, began to take form.
Henceforth the distinction between Parliament and Council is, for practical purposes, clear.

The first eighteen years of Edward I saw the beginning
of our Statute Law. Surrounded by great lawyers, native
and foreign, the legal-minded King, in the prime of his

magnificent manhood, passed Statute after Statute through his Parliaments, with a legislative vigour comparable, according to Maitland, only to that of the Whigs in the first few years after the Reform Bill.

These Statutes are a new phenomenon, for they alter the very substance of the law. Hitherto there has always been 'law,' Anglo-Danish in origin, traditional, customary, unwritten, much of it local, most of it obsolete; and there has been feudal law, also customary; more recently there has been 'case law,' made by pronouncements of famous royal judges, and commented on in professional treatises like those of Glanvill and Bracton; there have been public treaties, like the Constitutions of Clarendon and Magna Carta, purporting only to restate and re-enforce the law, though perhaps in fact enlarging it; there have been royal Assizes or ordinances altering legal procedure, substituting for instance trial by jury for trial by battle. But now under Edward I we get for the first time 'laws' undoubtedly competent to alter 'law' itself—with the exception of an undefined residuum of 'fundamental law,' for neither King nor Parliament are as yet 'omnicompetent.' [5]

In these first Statutes of the Realm, especially *De Donis Conditionalibus* and *Quia Emptores*, feudal law was restated with alterations, in such fashion as to become the starting point of our modern land law. Indeed the two great Statutes of Edward I remained so long the basis of our law of real property that a knowledge of them has remained necessary for English lawyers up till our own day.

[5] 'The vigorous legislation' of Edward I 'has an important consequence in checking the growth of unenacted law.' Maitland, *Const. Hist.*, p. 21. While there was still no Statute Law the law courts had been more free to mould the law than they ever were again; *e.g.*, from the Eleventh to the Thirteenth Century it had lain with the King and his Judges to decide whether murderers and felons should be blinded or otherwise mutilated, or hanged. William I had decided for mutilation, the Judges of the Thirteenth Century for death. But in later times the list of capital offences is settled by Parliamentary Statute, in obedience to which the Judge must put on the black cap.

De Donis [1275.] originated the practice of entailing estates, which for so many centuries wrought widespread
mischief in rural England. *Quia Emptores* was passed by
Edward I and his tenants-in-chief to preserve to themselves the full value of their feudal dues by preventing
subinfeudation. But in fact this only hastened the decay of
feudalism. For when the tenants-in-chief wished to dispose
of land, they had in future to make the purchaser become
a tenant-in-chief like themselves. This caused a great multiplication of persons holding land direct from the King,
and a consequent levelling of classes and a further disintegration of the feudal spirit.[6] Before long a man was
more proud of being summoned to Parliament than of being one of the innumerable tenants-in-chief. And the King
had more prestige as head of the executive and as the
holder of Parliament than as the supposed universal landlord. From a feudal society we were becoming a Parliamentary nation.

Edward defined the land law, and the process of defining
the law courts was always going forward, not least in his
reign. In the course of the Thirteenth and Fourteenth Centuries, the Exchequer, Common Pleas, and King's Bench,
one after the other, became distinct courts, each with its
own records, procedure, permanent officers and judges.
The rise of the Court of Chancery was later and more peculiar.[7]

From the time of Edward I onwards the courts of Common Law, as distinguished from the Court of Chancery and
the Church courts, were manned by persons not in holy
orders. The Pope had for some time past taken objection
to the service and teaching of the secular law by the priest-

---

[6] *Quia Emptores* allowed land to be freely sold, but the
purchaser must hold it as the vassal of the King or of the
lord from whom the vendor held it, and not as the vassal
of the vendor himself. Scottish law continued to permit
subinfeudation—one reason why Scotland remained more
feudal than England.

[7] See note, pp. 266–67, at end of this chapter.

hood. The King's judges were ceasing as a rule to be ecclesiastics like Bracton, or warrior-statesmen like Glanvill. The normal movement of legal promotion in England was no longer from outside, but from bar to bench, whereas in many countries of Europe to this day judge and pleader belong to two distinct and mutually exclusive professions. In the professional atmosphere of the King's courts in Westminster Hall, where English law was perpetually on the anvil red-hot, the corporate sense of the Middle Ages was forming pleaders and judges into a single self-conscious society. Jealous of outsiders, rivals to the ecclesiastical lawyers, 'learned brothers' to one another, makers and guardians of a great intellectual and moral tradition, acquiring too all the faults and all the unpopularity of a powerful and highly organized profession, they were not a close 'noblesse of the robe,' but offered to any Englishman of brains and industry a ladder to wealth and greatness as attractive as the Church herself.

The common lawyers were, as a class, the first learned laymen, and as such were of great importance to the growth of the nation. Their place in English history is only a little lower than that of the Parliament men. Without the lawyers neither the Reformation nor the victory of Parliament over the Stuarts would ever have been accomplished. Yet their tradition and their society are a highly characteristic product of the Middle Ages, closely comparable to the Universities.

And as the English Universities developed Colleges, so the English lawyers built their Inns of Court. During the reigns of the first three Edwards they grouped their halls, libraries and dwelling places in and around the deserted groves of the Templars. Their place of public performance lay two miles further westward, in the shadow of the royal residence, where they were royally accommodated in Westminster Hall, the magnificent excrescence which William Rufus had added to the Confessor's Palace, as it were in rivalry to the Abbey. But the lawyers slept, dined and studied in their own Inns of Court, half-way between the commercial capital at London and the political capital at

Westminster, a geographic position that helped the English lawyer to discover his true political function as mediator between Crown and people.[8]

In the reign of Edward I the famous Year Books begin. They were unofficial verbatim reports of legal proceedings, taken down in court in the French tongue, which was then spoken by the upper classes and therefore by the lawyers in their pleadings. There was no such full reporting in any other country or in any other sphere of English life, political or ecclesiastical, for centuries to come. All that is of professional and much that is of purely human interest is recorded word for word as it was uttered, 'the shifting argument, the retort, the quip, the expletive.' These reports, carried on for generation after generation, stood in the place of the Code of Justinian or the Decretals as the authority and inspiration of the great students who, in apostolic succession through the ages, built up English law.

Proud of his courts of law, and jealous of any baronial franchises more extensive than the usual manor court, Edward I instituted a formal enquiry, known as the *Quo Warranto* inquest [1278–79], into the origin of the higher private jurisdictions, demanding to see a charter where in many cases there was only the prescriptive right of immemorial custom. The attempt was premature, seeking to achieve by a bold stroke of political authority what could more safely be left to the invisible action of time. The story goes, with somewhat doubtful authenticity, that in answer to the questions of the Justices, the Earl Warenne drew his old, rusty sword and told them that he held his land and franchises by that charter. King Edward did not press the issue, for he had seen enough of Barons' wars in his youth. But the *Quo Warranto* inquest at least put a stop to recent or future encroachments on the sphere of the King's tribunals, and the preference felt by suitors for royal justice gradually brought private courts to an end. When, during the Wars of the Roses [1455–85.], anarchy

[8] In the latter part of Queen Victoria's reign the Law Courts themselves were moved from Westminster to the neighbourhood of the Inns of Court at Temple Bar.

raised its head for the last time, the great lords no longer claimed extensive jurisdictions of their own, but were content to employ their retainers to overawe judge and jury in the King's courts.

England's characteristic institution, Parliament, was not devised on the sudden to perpetuate a revolution in which one power rose and another fell. It grew up gradually as a convenient means of smoothing out differences and adjusting common action between powers who respected one another—King, Church, Barons, and certain classes of the common people such as burgesses and knights. No one respected the villeins and they had no part in Parliament. Knowing that Parliament was hostile, 'labour,' as soon as it began to be self-conscious, preferred 'direct action' like the rising of 1381. But, setting the villeins aside, Parliament represented a friendly balance of power. The English people have always been distinguished for the 'Committee sense,' their desire to sit round and talk till an agreement or compromise is reached. This national peculiarity was the true origin of the English Parliament.

It was during the reigns of the first three Edwards that Parliament gradually acquired something like its present form. After his experiences in the time of de Montfort, Edward I saw in frequent national assemblies the best oil for the machinery of government. His object was not to limit the royal power or to subject it to the will of the commonalty. His object was to make the royal power more efficient by keeping it in constant touch with the life of the governed. And like Henry VIII, the only other monarch in our annals who did as much to increase the prestige of Parliament, he knew the value of the support of the middle classes in shire and town.

Edward I, therefore, decided to continue and popularize the experiment that had occasionally been made during his father's turbulent reign, of summoning representatives of the counties and boroughs to attend the great conferences of the magnates of the realm. He wanted, for one thing, to collect certain taxes more easily. The difficult as-

sessments could not be well made without the willing help
and special knowledge of the local knights and burgesses.
Their representatives would return from the presence of
King and assembled magnates, each to his own community,
awestruck yet self-important, filled with a new sense of
national unity and national needs. In that mood they would
help to arrange the assessments locally, and facilitate payment. And they would explain the King's policy to their
neighbours, who had no other means of information.

When there were no newspapers and few letters, and
when travel was difficult and dangerous, the King's rigid
insistence on the perpetual coming and going of ever fresh
troops of knights and burghers between Westminster and
their own communities began the continuous political education of Englishmen, and perhaps did more to create the
unity of the nation than Chaucer or the Hundred Years'
War. Nor, without such a machinery for the easy levy of
taxes, could the great Scottish and French wars of the
Edwardian period have been fought. It has been said that
it was not England who made her Parliament, but Parliament that made England, and there is an element of truth
in the epigram.

Financial need was not the only reason why the King
summoned the representatives of town and shire. Indeed
Edward I sometimes called them together on occasions
when he asked for no money at all. For he had another
end in view, to gather together the petitions and grievances of his subjects, so as to be able to govern in accordance with real local needs, and to keep a check on the
misdeeds of local officials. Thus a large part of the business
of these early Parliaments consisted in receiving piles of
petitions for redress, mostly from private persons or single
communities, but increasingly as the Fourteenth Century
went on, from the House of Commons as a whole. In the
reign of Edward I these petitions were directed, not to
Parliament, but to the King or Council. They were dealt
with in Parliament either by the King, by his ministers, or
by committees of councillors, judges and Barons, known as
'Triers.' The redress afforded to the petitioners in these

early times may now be regarded as either judicial, legislative or administrative; the distinction was not then made. But, as time went on, while many of the private petitions were referred to judicial processes in the Chancery Court or elsewhere, the more important class emanating from the Commons' House as a whole began in the reign of Henry VI to take the form of 'bills' to be passed into law by Parliament. Such was the origin of the right of the House of Commons to initiate legislation.

But we must not speak of 'Houses' of Parliament as early as the reign of Edward I. There was then but one assembly, presided over by the King from his throne, or by his Chancellor from the woolsack; the rest of the chief officers of State were present *ex officio*, together with the Barons, lay and spiritual, summoned each by special writ; there were also present, humbly in the background, the representative knights and burghers summoned through the sheriff of each shire, not likely to speak unless they were first spoken to in such a presence. This was the 'High Court of Parliament,' which is still visible to the eye in the modern House of Lords with its throne and woolsack, although the Chancellor alone of the King's Ministers can now attend *ex officio* even if he is not a peer, and although the throne is now occupied only when Parliament is opened or prorogued. Then, when the Commons flock to the bar to hear the King's words, we have the original Plantagenet Parliament reassembled.

In the reign of Edward I the representatives of the Commons were not yet a separate House. And though they often attended the sessions of the Parliament one and indivisible, their presence there was not essential for much of the important business transacted by the magnates. Their consent to legislation was not always asked. The great Statutes for which the reign was famous were some of them, like *Quia Emptores*, passed when no representatives of the Commons were in attendance. And it is probable that if knights and burgesses were present at all when high matters of foreign and domestic policy were debated by the

Ministers, Barons and Prelates, it was but as 'mutes and audience.'

The House of Commons as a separate Chamber originated in unofficial meetings of the knights and burgesses, discussing anxiously behind closed doors what collective reply they should give to some difficult question or demand with which they had been confronted by the higher powers. They were so careful to leave no reports of these proceedings that we know nothing of the internal development of the early House of Commons. We do not even know how and when the Speaker became its chairman. For the Speaker was originally the person appointed to 'speak' for the Commons in full Parliament, the other knights and burgesses being silent in presence of their betters. But until Stuart times the Speaker was a servant of the Crown much more than a servant of the House. As early as the reign of Edward III we find some of the King's household officers sitting as knights of the shire, very possibly to direct the debates and decisions of the House of Commons in the interest of the Crown, as Privy Councillors continued to do with very great effect in Tudor times. It was also in the reign of Edward III that the Chapter House of the monks of Westminster came to be regarded as the customary meeting place of the Commons.

The most important fact in the early history of our institutions is that the English Parliament, unlike analogous assemblies of the same period in Europe, divided itself, during the later Plantagenet reigns, not into three Estates of clergy, nobles and bourgeois, but into two Houses of Lords and Commons. The greater part of our constitutional and social history is in some sense either cause or effect of that unique arrangement.

In the continental system of 'Estates,' all the 'gentlemen,' as we should call them, were represented in the estate of the *'noblesse.'* But the *'noblesse,'* in the large sense which the word bears on the continent, was in the English Parliament divided in two. The *barones majores,* each summoned by special writ, sat in the upper house. The *barones minores,* even though tenants-in-chief, shared with knights, gentry and 'franklins' the liability to be elected as knights of the shire. Thus the forms of English Parliamentary life abolished the distinctions of feudalism. Even a tenant-in-chief might be found sitting and working with the burghers of the towns.

This strange and significant arrangement of the Fourteenth Century English Parliaments was rendered possible by earlier developments which we have already noticed. The active part taken by the smaller gentry in shire business had often brought them in contact with the burghers as well as with the humbler rural freeholders.[9] The English rule of primogeniture, which sent the cadets of a noble family out into the world, had given the inhabitants of castle and manor-house a friendly interest in trade and commerce. The inter-marriage of classes and the constant intercommunication of the upper and middling ranks of society were already much more marked in England than elsewhere. Ages long ago, before the battles of Bannockburn or Crecy, the House of Commons already reflected these English peculiarities. Already the knights of the shire, a semi-feudal class, were acting as elected representatives of the rural yeomen, and were sitting cheek by jowl with the citizens of the boroughs. That is why the House of Commons was able to assert its importance at a very early date, when burghers and yeomen had small political prestige unless they were acting in association with knights. That also is why the English Civil War of Stuart times was not a class war; and why the English of Burke's time could not understand what in the world the French Revolution was about.

Neither was any Estate or House of the Clergy formed

[9] See p. 223, above. The members of the Lower House, including the burghers, were all summoned through the sheriff, not by special writs directed to individual towns. This made a connection between burgher and knight—they were both in a sense representatives of the shire, in its rural and urban aspect respectively. The sheriff and the shire had played so great a part in royal government that the arrangement seemed natural to all.

as part of the English Parliament. Not only did the spiritualty refrain from drawing together as a separate clerical 'Estate' in Parliament, but they voluntarily abandoned all their seats among the Commons and many of their seats among the Lords.

In the Upper House, indeed, the Bishops and certain of the greater Abbots continued to sit in their secular capacity as holders of baronies in a feudal assembly. Moreover some of the Bishops were royal ministers and civil servants. But the Prelates who were churchmen first and foremost took little stock in Parliament. The majority of the Abbots and Priors, wrapped up in local monastic interests, disliking the trouble and expense of long journeys, and feeling more bound in duty to the Pope than to the King, would not be at the pains to attend. They fell out of the national life and abandoned their places in Parliament, with results that became apparent in the Parliamentary Statute Book of Henry VIII.[10]

So, too, the representatives of lower clergy did not become a permanent part of the House of Commons, and gradually ceased to attend Parliament at all. The business of voting the 'fifteenths' and 'tenths' of clerical property to the King was conducted instead in the Convocations of Canterbury and York. Those assemblies were and are ecclesiastical, not political. They were in no sense an Estate of Parliament like the French Clerical Estate which figures in the original session of the *États Généraux* of 1789. The English clergy, on the principle that the things of Cæsar and the things of God were best kept apart, deliberately stepped aside from the political life and growth of the nation in the later Middle Ages. But since they also preserved their great and envied wealth and many ancient privileges, which came to be regarded as abuses in a changed world, their position was one of isolation, peculiarly exposed to attack when the Reformation began.

[10] The number of Abbots and Priors attending Parliament declined from about 70 in the reign of Edward I to about 27 under Edward III and his successors.

From humble beginnings in the reign of Edward I the House of Commons attained in the next hundred and fifty years to a great place in the constitution. The consent of its members became necessary for all making of Statutes and for all extraordinary taxation; their own petitions very frequently received the assent of the King in Parliament; and even the highest acts of State like the deposition and election of Kings took place with the Commons as parties to the deed. Their constitutional power when the Wars of the Roses broke out was indeed more apparent than real, for the strongest forces in politics were Crown, Barons and Church, not Commons. But their recorded position in the public law of the country supplied invaluable precedents for the assumption of real power by the Lower House after the Tudor monarchs had clipped the wings of Church and baronage.

If in later Plantagenet times the Commons increased in real power much, and in nominal power more, the reason is not far to seek. They were a third party, holding the balance, and courted by the principals in the warfare of State. The constant struggle between King and Barons under the three Edwards, the equally constant struggle between the great families around the throne in the days of the House of Lancaster, put the Commons almost into the place of umpire. They were well fitted to take advantage of the position, because their interests were not wholly bound up with either Barons or King.

Edward I had probably looked to the Commons to support him against the baronage. But the townsfolk, too, had their own griefs against the King. It was his habit, when in need of instant supply for Gascony or Scotland, to seize a larger share of the exports of wool than was warranted by the 'customs.' These 'maltoltes' or 'ill takings' of wool were declared illegal, after the burghers, on a famous occasion, had joined the opposition of the Barons and clergy, who were suffering from grievances of their own with regard to the King's hasty demands. [1297.]

[1307.] Nevertheless, when Edward I died he was on the way to make himself absolute master of England and of Scotland both. He had in the last years of his life gone far to break the baronial opposition at home, and to tread out the embers of the fire that Wallace had kindled and that Bruce was trying to fan. An able successor might have destroyed constitutional liberty in England and national liberty in Scotland. Parliament might have become, not an opposition or a critic to be conciliated, but a useful cog in the machine of royal government—as no doubt Edward himself regarded it. The reign of his innocent-minded but lazy and incapable son, Edward II [1307–27.], saved the situation. It is not good to have an unbroken succession of great rulers like Henry II, Edward I, or the Tudors. John, Edward II, and the Stuarts had their appointed place in the destiny of Britain.

The lax rule of two people of such unbusinesslike and artistic temperaments as young Edward II and his friend Piers Gaveston, presented the Barons with another chance. Gaveston was by no means the first nor the worst 'upstart,' nor the most alien 'foreigner' who had risen to the head of affairs in England, but he had no prudence, for he gave nicknames to the leading Barons. In return, some of them took his life by treachery. [1312.] Edward II and Gaveston were perhaps as unfit to govern England as Charles I and Buckingham. But the leaders of the baronial opposition, especially Earl Thomas of Lancaster, were stupid, selfish and brutal men, swollen with the pride of birth. The King's next favourite, Despenser, was not an 'upstart' like Gaveston, but he developed into a tyrant. And yet the struggle between such unpromising opponents worked out to the advantage of the nation. The machinery of administration was improved, not by subjecting it to the clumsy control of the Barons, but by certain bureaucratic reforms. And the powers of Parliament were much increased, for on several great occasions it was called upon, now by Edward II, and now by the baronial opposition, to regularize their alternate victories by vote and Statute. In this new prestige of Parliament the Commons had their share.

The net result of the baronial tumults—they can scarcely be called baronial wars—during the reign of this unhappy

King was not to increase the power either of Crown or of baronage. Throughout the Middle Ages the Barons were never able, in spite of repeated efforts, to dominate the King's counsels on any regular plan, though they held that on feudal principles he ought always to be guided by their noble advice, instead of by the advice of trained clerks and civil servants whose only qualification was that of understanding the King's business. The Barons failed to establish their claim to govern, because government means steady application, which a Baron could seldom give. His castles, his hunting, his estates, his retainers, his habits of life, his manors scattered over half the counties of England, very properly took up his time. He could not be the King's responsible Minister or attend at the regular sessions of the Council, because he had other duties and other pleasures.

A second reason why the Barons failed to control the government except in moments of revolution was that the King's Court and household were too large and complicated to be easily subjected to control. If one office—say the Chancery with its Great Seal—was secured by the baronial opposition, the King could dive underground and still govern the country through the Wardrobe with its Privy Seal. The King's Court was plastic and adaptable in its organization, yet highly specialized as a civil service, full of trained and able men who went on quietly governing, while far over their heads fools or scoundrels like Gaveston and Thomas of Lancaster, Despenser and Mortimer, ranted and killed each other for the benefit of posterity and the Elizabethan dramatists. Meanwhile peaceful stone manor-houses could rise in quiet corners of the land, the export of wool could increase, the population could go up, all classes could grow less poor and less ill-fed, because all the while the King's Peace was indifferently well enforced.

In the reign of Edward III an addition was made to the State machinery, significant of much. Keepers or Justices of the Peace were set up in every county to help the central power to govern. Like the Coroners before them, they were not bureaucrats but independent country gentlemen. As typical of the rising class of knights and smaller gentry, the Justices of the Peace took over more and more of the work previously done by that great man the Sheriff, or by the Judges on circuit. The 'J.P.'s' seemed to strike root in the shire and grow as a native plant, equally popular with their neighbors and with the King's Council, between whom it was their task to interpret. For four hundred years their powers continued to increase, both in variety of function and in personal authority, till in the Eighteenth Century they were in a sense more powerful than the central government itself. This would not have happened if they had not responded to the needs and character of the English over a long period of time. According to Maitland, the respect in which the English hold the law was generated not a little by this system of 'amateur justice.' For the magistrate who expounded and enforced the law for ordinary people in ordinary cases may not have known much law, but he knew his neighbours and was known of them.

BOOKS FOR FURTHER READING: See p. 206, above. Also Rashdall, *The Universities of Europe*; Haskins, *The Rise of the Universities* (Holt, New York); Reginald Poole, *Illustrations of the History of Mediæval Thought*; Jessopp, *The Coming of the Friars*; Sabatier, *Life of St. Francis*; A. L. Smith, *Church and State in the Middle Ages*; Tout, *Edward I.*, and *Place of Ed. II. in Eng. History*; Maitland, *Year Books of Edward II.*, Introd. (Selden Soc.), and *Memoranda de Parl.*, 1305 (Rolls Series), Introd.; Pasquet, *Essay on the Origins of the House of Commons* (translated, 1925, Cam. Press); M. V. Clarke, *Mediaeval Representation and Consent*.

NOTE ON THE COURT OF CHANCERY: From the time of Edward I's friend Robert Burnell, if not before, the Lord Chancellor was the chief officer of the Realm, for his office, in charge of the King's Great Seal, was necessarily as much in touch with all departments of State as the Treasury in our own day. Until the Reformation, the Chancellor was frequently an ecclesiastic as well as a lawyer. In the course of the Fourteenth and Fifteenth Centuries, his Chancery Court became a definite tribunal where equitable remedies were provided for unforeseen abuses in the working of the courts of Common Law. His court, on behalf of the King's Council, answered petitions of the aggrieved subject in a judicial manner. Since Parliament now prevented the King from altering procedure or calling up cases by the issue of unauthorized writs, and since the Common Law was rapidly becoming a law unto itself, a rigid system independent of the King's volition—this equitable and correctional jurisdiction of the Chancellor was invaluable to the King as a method by which he could turn the flank of the common lawyers and of the Parliament men. But no strong objection was taken, because the relief it often afforded to individual subjects was so great. Before the accession of the Tudors the Chancery Court had become a recognized part of the Constitution, and was destined to survive later royal expedients for supplementing the Common Law, such as the Court of Star Chamber.

In the Fifteenth Century, Chancery had been a method of appeal to common-sense from the technicalities of the other law courts. Four centuries later, in the days of Eldon and Charles Dickens, it had become the slave of its own technicalities, and the subject's remedy lay rather in the modern habit of frequent remedial legislation by Parliament.

CHAPTER FIVE

Celt and Saxon. Attempts to Complete the Island Empire. Causes of Failure in the Middle Ages. Ireland, Wales, Scotland

The England of the later Middle Ages, the most highly organized of the larger States of Europe, lay alongside of Wales and Ireland, each a congeries of Celtic tribes, and abutted on Scotland, a poor and thinly inhabited Kingdom, racially divided between Celt and Saxon, but already becoming Anglo-Norman in language and institutions. In such circumstances it was inevitable that attempts should be made to round off the island empire on the basis of conquest by England.[1]

The Romans in Britain had been faced by precisely the same geographic problem. Their good genius prompted them to leave Ireland alone; they tried repeatedly and vainly to conquer Scotland; but they quickly subdued Wales by their system of military roads and forts, without,

[1] I use the word Celtic in this chapter, as elsewhere, to designate the mixture of Celtic and earlier 'Iberian' races.

however, inducing the mountaineers to adopt the Latinized civilization of the plains. Mediæval England had much the same measure of success as Roman Britain. More slowly indeed than the legions, English feudal chivalry with its network of castles made a military conquest of Wales, but the full adjustment of Welsh to Saxon civilization was left over till Tudor and Hanoverian times; the attempt to subdue Scotland was a complete failure; while beyond St. George's Channel, England effected not a conquest, but a lodgment in mediæval Ireland, and hung on like a hound that has its fangs in the side of the stag.

A main reason why the mediæval English failed in Scotland and Ireland, and never reduced even Wales to good order, is to be sought in their continental entanglements. Till the loss of Normandy in John's reign, the energies of the Norman and Angevin Kings of England had been occupied in the recovery or defence of provinces in France. The only time that the Plantagenet Kings were able to devote the best part of their thoughts and resources to purely British problems was during the century that followed the final loss of Normandy and preceded the outbreak of the Hundred Years' War. [1214–1337.] During that period there was only one great King, Edward I, and in his reign, as we should expect, the power of mediæval England in Wales, Ireland and Scotland reached its high-water mark. After his death, the incapacity of Edward II, and the preoccupation of all later Kings before the Tudors with the extravagant attempt to conquer France or with resultant civil troubles at home, destroyed English rule in all Scotland and in nearly all Ireland, and weakened it even in Wales.

When we last looked towards Ireland it was in the heaviest midnight of the Dark Ages, when the light of learning sparkled in that distant corner of the world, casting back gleams on the opaque ignorance of Scotland and England, Germany and France.[2] The saints, artists and learned men of Irish monasticism shone by their individual merits and were free from the bondage of organization. Institution-

[2] See pp. 81–82, above.

alism was as abhorrent to the early Irish Church as to the tribal system from which it sprang. It followed that the Irish clergy never helped, as the Saxon clergy had done, to organize their race in a united Church and a single State. When the zeal and inspiration of the early saints died away, they left nothing behind but memories, and Ireland was little less dark and distracted than she had been before.

Even the suzerainty formerly exercised over the other chiefs by the 'High Kings' at Tara had become in the Eleventh Century a mere title. The career of Brian Boru, King of Cashel in Munster, the racial hero against the Viking invaders, did not permanently strengthen the 'High Kingship' or unite the Celts. But the victory of Clontarf [1014.] on his death's day saved Ireland from the Norsemen and confined the Danes to the towns they had founded such as Dublin, Waterford and Limerick. Town life and trade had no attraction for the native. Cattle-feeding and cattle-lifting, tribal war and family feud, minstrelsy and a little agriculture still occupied the time and thoughts of the Celtic tribes, as of many other tribes all the world over for many thousand years in times gone by. It is a matter of opinion whether or not these simple folk were better employed than the new restless Europe with its Crusades and Hildebrandine movements, its stone castles and cathedrals, its feudalism, its charters, its trade-routes and all the stir of modernity. But for good or for evil the time had gone by when a European race could, with impunity, remain primitive. To eschew defensive armour, castles and feudalism in the days of Strongbow was as dangerous as to eschew machine guns and the industrial revolution in our own.

The Irish, therefore, were regarded as savages, almost outside the pale of Papal Christendom. It is true that in the first half of the Twelfth Century St. Malachy and other Irishmen began a movement for Church reform. The excessive number of Irish Bishops was reduced, in order to enhance the episcopal authority; a gallant attempt was made to rekindle the religious zeal of the laity, to enforce the payment of tithe, and approximate the Church a little to the Roman model. But it was the armed invaders from England who gave full power to the influences which in the end attached Ireland irrevocably to Rome. The reforming Church party in Ireland was willing, in the absence of any strong national feeling, to welcome and abet Strongbow and the English. Adrian IV, the only English Pope in history, had commissioned Henry II to conquer the island if he liked, as the best means of bringing it into the Roman fold.

[1169–71.] Henry II was too busy on the continent to take up the Irish question himself. The conquest was, however, begun in his reign by private adventurers from Wales, led by Richard de Clare, Earl of Pembroke, nicknamed Strongbow. His partners in this last of the Norman conquests were not pure Normans, nor pure Anglo-Normans. Many of them, like the famous Fitzgeralds, were sons of Welsh mothers. They were a special border breed, these 'Marcher Lords'; and their soldiers were many of them Welsh or Flemings. Perhaps the Celtic element in the blood and experience of these first 'English' conquerors of Ireland helped their descendants to mingle only too easily with the native Irish and adapt their own feudal institutions to the tribalism of the Celtic world beyond the Dublin 'pale.' Possibly pure Normans or Anglo-Normans might have stamped more of their own character and institutions on this land, as they did on so many others.

But no Norman intruders in England, Sicily or Scotland ever showed themselves superior in warlike efficiency to the followers of Strongbow. His chain-clad knights were supported by archers, whose skill was then the speciality not of England but of Wales. The unarmoured infantry of the Irish tribes, fighting with the Danish battle-axe and hurling stones and javelins, were helpless against the best archers and some of the best cavalry in Europe. The only refuge of the natives was the marshes, woods and mountains of their roadless and unreclaimed island. They knew all the arts of guerrilla war, using felled trees and earthworks to block the narrow passages through forest and bog. But the opposition to the invaders was not truly national. They found many allies both among tribesmen and churchmen. Dermot, who had invited over Strongbow, was not in his own life-time universally execrated as the traitor that he appeared in the distant retrospect.

Castle-building was the cement of Anglo-Norman rule in Ireland, as in the sister island. Here, too, the Celt was at a great disadvantage, for the only resistance behind perma-nent fortifications which the invaders had to encounter was in the port-towns of the Danes. But since the battle of Clontarf, the Danes in Ireland had become peaceful traders instead of warrior Vikings, and moreover they were few in number. Their towns were easily captured, and were transformed at a stroke from Scandinavian to English. The citizens of Bristol were given the right to inhabit Dublin. Dublin Castle, first erected by the Vikings, became the centre of Saxon rule in Ireland from the Twelfth to the Twentieth Century.

The Danes were massacred or returned to Scandinavia, making way for the conquerors, who henceforward held in these port-towns the keys of entry into the island. Celtic town life did not yet exist. Even towns like Galway in the far west were of Anglo-Norman origin. Only towards the end of the Middle Ages, the English inhabitants of the towns outside the Dublin pale gradually adopted the speech of the surrounding population with whom they bartered, and became by intermarriage and otherwise scarcely less Irish than English.

At the time of Strongbow's conquest and for long after-wards, national feeling did not exist, and foreign rule would have been accepted on its merits. All that was then neces-sary to put the races on a friendly understanding was strong and just government. But throughout the Middle Ages the government was neither strong nor just. Henry II, the father of rebellious sons, and the embarrassed ruler over half of western Christendom, had perforce to limit the liabilities which Strongbow had created for him, for he had neither time, money, nor men to establish his own rule in the island, in anything more than name. Yet, while he could not afford to keep up an effective royal government, he dared not let Strongbow or any of the feudal leaders obtain Viceregal authority. The adventurers therefore continued to prey on the natives, and to carve out baronies for themselves, fighting for their own hands without either proper support or proper control from the English King. For more than a century the Conquest went forward, slowly enlarging its boundaries westward, meeting no determined resistance from the natives, but divided and uncertain in its own purpose, and bringing in its train neither justice nor even a strong tyranny.

In these circumstances there grew up that three-fold division of the island which, with continual variation of boundary, held good throughout the rest of the Middle Ages. There was the 'Pale' round Dublin, where English law was administered as in an English shire. Far in the west lay the purely Celtic chiefs and tribes, threatened but still untouched by the invasion. And between these two Irelands, and intermingled with them both, lay the areas of mixed rule, the baronies where the descendants of the great adventurers bore sway from their castles over the native population. But their Norman-Welsh feudalism was gradually transformed into something very like the Celtic tribalism which it was intended to replace. If, long afterwards, with all the differences of religion, the descendants of so many of Cromwell's soldiers were quickly absorbed into the Celtic atmosphere around them, it is no wonder that the same evolution took place in the case of the Anglo-Irish Barons. Throughout the greater part of the island English rule had been built upon the foundation of an Irish bog.

In the reign of Edward I, the greater attention paid at that period to insular affairs enabled Ireland to enjoy a brief spell of prosperity, especially in Leinster and Meath where the English interest was strongest. Villages sprang up and agriculture spread under the protecting shadow of the castles. Trading towns like Dublin, Waterford and Cork pushed their commerce overseas.

Then came one of those rapid wrong turnings, so habitual in Irish history. Edward I's attempt to conquer Scotland led to reprisals under his feeble son. Immediately after Bannockburn the Scots under the Bruce brothers broke into Ireland through Ulster, where in all ages they have had strong connections. [1315–18.] The delicate prosperity of the new Ireland was destroyed with fire and sword, and the English influence never recovered for two centuries. The invasion of the Bruces was rather the occasion than the cause of the collapse. At bottom it was due to the character and power of the Anglo-Irish baronage, ever less distinguishable from the Celtic chiefs, and ever enlarging the boundaries of their rule at the expense of the genuinely English colony.

The Pale grew narrower both in space and in spirit. The English settlers and officials, increasingly conscious that they were a garrison in an alien land, cooped up and hard beset, drew in upon their own company and their own ideals of life. They came to regard almost everyone and everything outside the Pale ditch as belonging not to the 'English' but the 'Irish' interest. The distinction set the tone to a policy that for centuries was fruitful of mischief. The colonists drew ever more rigidly the line between the two races, and proscribed native law, language and custom, so far as their little power extended in pre-Tudor times.

The Hundred Years' War with France distracted England's attention yet further from the overseas possession where her real duty lay. In the interval between the two parts of that long struggle, Richard II came with an army to Ireland. Then he fell, and no English King set foot in Ireland again until William of Orange. The utter neglect of Ireland by the rival Houses of Lancaster and York completed the relapse to Celtic tribalism outside the Pale, and, in spite of the efforts of one section of the colonists, Irish language and custom spread among the English of the Pale itself. The native civilization had indeed profited by the conquerors whom it had absorbed. Town life had been started; most of the towns founded by Danes and English had become, in part at least, Irish-speaking; while the Anglo-Irish nobility presided over a native world that gave

Map 11   Ireland towards the close of the Middle Ages

in the Fifteenth Century signs of a rude social prosperity of
its own.

But the bare presence of England in Ireland prevented
any project of national unity from being pursued on native
lines. The scant footing maintained by the English in and
around Dublin, and the acknowledged claims of the English King as overlord, sufficed to prevent the union of the
country under one of the Anglo-Irish Barons. It is true that
in the last half of the Fifteenth Century there was a movement towards the government of the island in the name of
the King by Deputies chosen from one of the great Anglo-
Irish families, particularly the Fitzgeralds, Earls of Kildare.
But events in the reign of Henry VII showed that this arrangement, whatever its effect upon the internal condition
of Ireland, was incompatible with the safety of the King of
England, whose dynastic enemies used the Fitzgeralds and

the credulous Irish people as allies of Yorkist intrigues and for armed invasion of England on behalf of pretenders like Lambert Simnel. [1487.] 'Aristocratic Home Rule' therefore proved a failure, since a free Ireland was employed to attack and disturb her great neighbour. 'Poynings' law' put a term to the experiment, by decreeing the complete dependence of the Irish Parliament on the English executive. [1494.] The attempted solution had failed, but the actual reconquest of Ireland was not undertaken till the following century.

England had proved too weak to conquer and govern Ireland, but strong enough to prevent her from learning to govern herself. It is significant that the island which had once been the lamp to Europe's ignorance was almost alone of European countries in having no University when the Middle Ages came to an end. It was a sorry heritage overseas which the mediæval English handed on to the English of the Reformation. They had neglected Ireland for centuries when a forward and active policy might have saved the situation; when the policy of real conquest was adopted under the Tudors it was in an age too late, an age of religious cleavage, commercial competition and national self-consciousness all in their crudest form.

The relation of the Celt to his neighbour has proved more happy in Britain than in Ireland. And again we must look to mediæval history to see why.

[SEE MAP 4.] In the latter stages of the Anglo-Saxon conquest, the remaining territories of the Cymri or Welsh had been cut by the English advance into three separated parts —Strathclyde in the north, Wales in the centre, and the Devonian-Cornish peninsula in the south. Their collective power of racial resistance was greatly reduced by their geographic isolation from one another, which was rendered complete by their enemies' command of the sea from the Isle of Man, the Vikings' centre of operations, and from the great port-towns of Chester and Bristol. Before the Norman Conquest, Scandinavian settlers had already given a thoroughly Nordic character to the Lake District and North

Lancashire,[3] while Devon had been so far colonized by the Saxons of Wessex that it has ever since been regarded as an integral and characteristic part of the life of England. Cornwall remained as a pocket of Celtic race and language, but too small and isolated to give trouble on that score. Conquered in Anglo-Saxon times and closely annexed to the English Crown, it was subjected to Norman feudalism as Domesday Book records, and subsequently to mediæval English law. But it spoke a Celtic tongue of its own until Stuart times, and it preserves a regional and Celtic character in its population to this day.

The larger problem of Wales remained. The wide extent of its mountain area had brought the Saxon Conquest to a halt behind Offa's Dyke. But the mountains which kept back the English prevented the union of the Welsh. In Edward the Confessor's reign, Harold made headway westward, and secured the alliance of some of the Celtic tribes ever at feud with one another, thus opening a road to further advance under the Normans.

From William the Conqueror till the accession of Edward I the most successful efforts to subdue Wales were made, not by the Kings of England, but by the 'Marcher Lords' and their private armies, men of the type of Strongbow and the Fitzgeralds. In blood a mixture of Norman, English and Welsh, they represented feudal government and English economic penetration rather than the English monarchy. At one time there were reckoned to be 143 Lords Marcher, and wherever a Marcher Lord carved out for himself an estate with the sword, he built a castle and proceeded to exact feudal dues from the inhabitants, and to enforce in his own court feudal law, English law or fragments of Welsh tribal custom. Under his protection English-speaking colonists,—military, farming and trading,—settled on the land he ruled. He was in reality a petty sovereign, representing the intrusion of a new race and a more elaborate civilization.

The Anglo-Norman invasion conquered the lowlands and

[3] See note, p. 67, above.

penetrated up the valley bottoms, because the valleys were the only gates of entry into the roadless mountains, and because they contained the arable land. But as the valleys themselves were frequently choked up with forest and marsh, the process was slow. The English had to play the part of pioneer farmers, as well as of warriors ever on the alert.

Before the coming of the Anglo-Normans, the Welsh had been a pastoral rather than an agricultural people. They did not inhabit towns, villages or even houses, but lived in huts of boughs which they twisted together for a few months' occupation, as they followed their flocks and herds from winter to summer ground upon the mountain side. But whenever these simple tribesmen saw their valley dominated by a Norman castle of timber or stone, with a feudal court and an English-speaking agricultural village attached, one part of them fled higher into the neighbouring hills in pursuit of freedom. Others remained below as vassals of the new lord, but were often at heart faithful to the tribal chief exiled onto the neighbouring mountains, whence he was perpetually returning in destructive raids upon the vale.

To imagine such a situation in fifty different valleys is to get some idea of the chaos that Wales must have presented in the Twelfth Century. Tribalism and feudalism were struggling for the land. And mountain barriers separated district from district, increasing the tendency inherent in both tribalism and feudalism to divide political authority into fragments. In the hills tribe fought against tribe, and in the valleys Baron fought against Baron, while every baronial valley was at war with its tribal hills.

Yet civilization was advancing, however slow and however bloody the process. Time was on the side of the invaders, who were near to their own bases and were perpetually recruited by sea and land, unlike the forlorn hope of Anglo-Norman civilization, derelict among the bogs of Ireland. Ships from the great ports of Bristol and Chester commanded all the valley mouths of Wales that ran into the sea; while, inland, the upper valley of the Severn gave

The Principality (outlined in black) as delimited by Edward I, is in two parts, Gwynedd, and Cardigan-Carmarthen
All except the Principality and the English border counties may be regarded as normally Marcher Lordships
Names of some of the chief Marcher Lords in brackets thus:-(Bohun)

Map 12   Mediæval Wales

the invaders an easy route from Shrewsbury into the heart of the country, enabling them to overrun Powys and cut off Gwynedd in the North from Dinefawr in the South. Pembroke was planted from the sea by so many industrious English and Flemings that it lost the use of the Celtic tongue and became known as 'little England beyond Wales.' But even at the height of their power the Lords Marcher were never able to subdue the Gwynedd district centred round the impenetrable fastnesses of Snowdon.

The Lords Marcher represented a type of government more backward than that of England but more advanced than that of tribal Wales. Bohun, Mortimer and the other Marcher families were an element of disturbance in the English polity, because they were accustomed to fighting and feudalism while the nobles and gentry of England proper were becoming accustomed to peace and centralized government. But to the tribal Celts the civilization forcibly imported by the Marcher Lords meant progress. All through the Middle Ages the native Welsh, in imitation of their English lords and neighbours, were slowly taking to agriculture, erecting permanent houses, trading in market-towns built and maintained by English-speaking folk, and learning, though slowly, to cease from the tribal blood feud and to accept the English law. Yet they preserved their own tongue, which it was their boast should answer for Wales at the Day of Judgment; and they continued to elaborate their own bardic poetry and music, destined in our own day to save Welsh intellect and idealism from perishing in the swamp of modern cosmopolitan vulgarity.[4]

The warfare that went on for so many centuries both before and after the Edwardian conquest, resembled all warfare of civilized armies against hill tribes. Giraldus, the Welshman, has described how his countrymen would rush down with terrifying shouts and blowing of long war horns, to fling themselves, with indiscriminate valour, a half-naked infantry, against ironclad horsemen. If they were not at once successful their courage ebbed, and they would fly in disgraceful panic. But they as quickly recovered, and carried on long and stern guerrilla warfare, rendered doubly formidable by the character of their wooded

4 About 1200 A.D. Giraldus the Welshman wrote of his countrymen words which are equally true of them to-day: 'In their musical concerts they do not sing in unison like the inhabitants of other countries, but in many different parts; so that in a company of singers, which one very frequently meets with in Wales, you will hear as many different parts and voices as there are performers.'

mountains, their own savage hardihood and their indifference to agriculture and the arts of peace. The English had put up no such resistance to the Norman Conquest. The invaders of Wales were indeed invincible when they could charge on level ground, but there was little level ground in Wales, and much of that was swamp. Horses and armour are not easily taken up into steep hills covered by forest. The Anglo-Norman warriors had, therefore, to learn and borrow much from their despised antagonists.

Above all, the English borrowed from the Welsh the use of the long-bow. It was in the south-east corner of Wales, between the upper waters of the Wye and the Bristol Channel, that this famous weapon first emerged into local fame. As early as the reign of Henry II it had been known, in Welsh hands, to pin a knight's armoured thigh through his saddle to the horse's side. Eighty years later there were Welsh archers with de Montfort at Lewes, but they still attracted less notice in England than the crossbowmen. It was Edward I's experience in Welsh campaigning that determined him to adopt the long-bow as the special weapon of his infantry in his Scottish wars. It is true that in an Assize of Arms of Henry III's reign certain classes of English freemen had, for the first time, been required to possess bows of some sort. But it was the Welsh who taught Edward I and his subjects what a 'long-bow' really meant. Not till the Fourteenth Century can it fairly be called the English national weapon, when it crossed the seas to affright the feudal chivalry of Europe at Crecy and Poitiers.

In the early years of the Thirteenth Century a Welsh national revival took place. It was displayed not only in a fresh effervescence of bardic poetry, but in a movement to unite all the tribes under the hegemony of the Llewelyn princes, who ruled over Gwynedd, among the fastnesses of Snowdon and in the rich grain-bearing island of Anglesey, sheltered behind that lofty barrier. North Wales summoned all Wales to unite and be free. Llewelyn the Great [1194–1240.] reconquered much of Powys from the Marcher Lords. He was a prudent diplomatist as well as a great warrior, for while he called on his countrymen to

rally round him as the native Prince acclaimed by the
Bards, he never forgot that he was also a great feudal
magnate, owing allegiance to the Crown, and could as such
play a part in English faction most helpful to his other
rôle as Welsh patriot. By the judicious policy of joining the
Barons' party in England, he secured for Welsh rights three
clauses of John's Magna Carta.

His grandson Llewelyn ap Griffith [1246–83.] carried on
the same double policy and allied himself with Simon de
Montfort. He still further enlarged the area of his Welsh
Principality at the expense of the ever divided and quarrel-
some Lords Marcher, many of whom were forced to do him
homage. At length he began to dream of complete separation from England. He went out of his way to defy Edward I, who was more than ready to take up the challenge.
That was the beginning of the end of Welsh independence.

[1277.] In the greatest of Edward's numerous Welsh
campaigns he surrounded the unapproachable Snowdon
fastnesses by sea and land and starved Llewelyn and his
mountaineers into surrender. After another rebellion, provoked by harsh government regardless of Celtic laws and
susceptibilities, another war resulted in another conquest
and a better settlement. [1282–84.] Royal castles such as
Conway, Carnarvon, Beaumaris and Harlech rose to make
the King's authority in North Wales as secure as feudal
authority in the centre and south. Edward divided up
Llewelyn's 'Principality' into shires on the English model,—
Carnarvon, Anglesey, Merioneth, Flint, Cardigan and Car-
marthen,—and soon afterwards gave to his infant son, Edward, born at Carnarvon, the title of 'Prince of Wales.' But
the 'Principality' was not yet a part of England, and all the
rest of Wales remained to the Lords Marcher.[5]

Edward I would fain have abolished the feudal independence of the Marcher Lords, by subjecting their jurisdictions to a strict *quo warranto* inquiry. But he had not
the power to do it, and he had need of their co-operation

[5] The whole of Wales is now often called the 'Principality,'
but in Edward's time the 'Principality' contained only these
half-dozen counties.

to keep down the spirit of the Welsh, perpetually incited
by Bards recounting the glories of the House of Llewelyn.
Until the Tudor reforms, Wales remained divided between
the feudal territories of the Lords Marcher on the one
hand, and on the other the Celtic Principality, ostensibly
governed by English law, but with a large allowance for
tribal custom. In both districts English and Welsh were
slowly learning to mix and to co-operate. Civilization was
creeping forward with the growth of towns, trade and agriculture.

Nevertheless, by any standard of English comparison,
Wales in the Fourteenth and Fifteenth Centuries was a
scene of tribal feud, baronial violence and official tyranny
and extortion. In the troubled times of Henry IV, Owen
Glendower, reviving the policy of Llewelyn the Great,
made play with the rivalries of English factions while ap-
pealing to the hopes and grievances of his race. [1400–15.]
This wonderful man, an attractive and unique figure in a
period of debased and selfish politics, actually revived for
a few years the virtual independence of a great part of his
country, at the cost of wars that proved utterly disastrous
to the economic life of Wales, both in the Principality and
in the Marches. The Welsh and English districts, which
were then found side by side in the same county and even
in the same feudal manor, were again set by the ears, and
the necessary amalgamation of the two races into the modern Welsh people was further delayed. Even after the
death of Glendower and the re-establishment of English
rule, the King's Peace was but poorly enforced. Between
Celtic and feudal anarchy, Wales remained a paradise for
the robber and the homicide, so long as the Crown was
preoccupied with adventures in France and dynastic strife
in England.

The disorders alike of the Principality and of the March
lands preserved the military habits of the Welsh so long,
that even after the Tudor pacification poets still regarded
them as

An old and haughty nation, proud in arms.

They followed the military life not only at home but in the King's armies in Scotland and France, while in every English Civil War from Henry III to Charles I it was always found easier to recruit infantry among the poor of Wales than among the settled and peaceable English. The Wars of the Roses were to a large extent a quarrel among Marcher Lords. For the great Lords Marcher were closely related to the English throne, and had estates and political interests both in England and in the Welsh March. Harry Bolingbroke of Hereford and Lancaster was a great possessor of Welsh lands, as also were his rivals, the Mortimers. The House of York, Warwick the Kingmaker, and Richard III's Buckingham were all in one way or another connected with Wales and the Marches. Such men brought a fighting element into English constitutional and dynastic faction. Because mediæval England had left half done its task of conquering Wales for civilization, Welsh tribalism and feudalism revenged themselves by poisoning the Parliamentary life and disturbing the centralized government of its neglectful overlords. But when at length a Welsh army put a Welsh Tudor Prince upon the throne at Bosworth Field, Wales supplied a remedy to those ills in the English body politic which she had helped to create.

The history of Scotland presents yet another version of the contact of Saxon with Celt. Wales and Ireland were both eventually forced to submit to England's rule more completely and for a longer time than Scotland, yet they both remain to this day far more Celtic in character. The apparent paradox is explained if we remember that the wealthiest and most important districts inhabited by the Celt in Scotland had already adopted Anglo-Norman language and institutions before the struggle for national independence began in the time of Edward I. Resistance to England was not therefore identified with Celtic speech and tribal traditions, as in mediæval Ireland and Wales. The wars of the Edwards against Wallace and Bruce were a struggle between two kindred nations, each organized as a feudal monarchy. The analogy to Irish or Welsh mediæval history is to be found rather in England's conquest of the Highland tribes after Culloden.

It had indeed seemed likely, in the Dark Ages, that Scotland would emerge as a Celtic Kingdom with a Saxon fringe along the lowlands of her eastern coast. For the union of the Picts and Scots under the Scot, Kenneth Macalpine [844.], had enabled them to impose a name and a dynasty on the land from the Celtic capital at Scone. But history began to revolve in the other direction when Lothian, the part of Saxon Northumbria that lay to the north of Tweed and Cheviot, [SEE MAP 5.] was detached from its southern connections and converted into an integral part of Scotland.[6]

The change was a natural result of the dissolution of the Kingdom of Northumbria under the blows of the Viking invasions. After many generations of warfare between Celt and Saxon in the heart of Scotland, Lothian was acknowledged, in the time of Canute, to be a possession of the Scottish Crown. [1018.]

It was in the newly acquired territory of English-speaking Lothian, with its rich agricultural soil and its rock-fortress of Edinburgh, that the Scottish Kingship, which had been Celtic, tribal and North-Western in origin, became Anglo-Norman, feudal and South-Eastern by choice. Led or driven by the monarchy, Strathclyde and Galloway, though very largely Celtic in race, eventually adopted English speech and feudal organization. We can only notice one or two of the more obvious stages in that long, complicated and obscure process of evolution.

First, before the period of Anglo-Norman influence, came the period of purely English influence in the last half of the Eleventh Century. Malcolm III [REIGNED 1057-93.], before he dethroned Macbeth, had spent his boyhood in exile in the England of Edward the Confessor. The English proclivities of his education were enhanced in later life by his second marriage with the saintly and strong-minded Margaret, sister of Edgar Atheling. As Queen of

[6] See p. 113, above.

Map 13   Mediæval Scotland and North England

Scotland she did much to strengthen the English language
and the Roman ecclesiastical system against Celtic tradition. Her pertinacious efforts, far from popular with the

tribes and priests of Celtic Scotland, were helped by the catastrophe that had befallen her own race and lineage in England after the battle of Hastings. The first result of Norman conquest down south was to drive over the Border troops of Saxon and Scandinavian exiles of all classes, from Margaret herself to the hinds of Yorkshire and Durham fleeing from the red wrath of William and his 'harrying of the North.' The Nordic element in Scotland, based on the Saxons of Lothian, was greatly strengthened by these refugees.

English influence prepared the way for Anglo-Norman penetration that followed hard on its heels. David I [1124–53.], a worthy son of Malcolm and Margaret, took advantage of the paralysis of England under Stephen to build Scotland anew in the form of a Norman feudal monarchy, and to appropriate as much as possible of the disputed territories in Cumberland, Northumberland and Durham. His successes beyond Tweed and Cheviot were not permanent, and the Border between the two Kingdoms gradually took its present shape when England recovered her strength under the Plantagenets. But David's invasions of North England during the anarchy of Stephen had served to reveal how vain was the courage of the disorderly and savage clansmen of Scotland charging with their claymores, as compared to mail-clad feudal knights, whether of England or of Scotland. This had been demonstrated at the Battle of the Standard, near Northallerton. [1138.] There is no wonder that the Scottish Kings embarked on a policy of change deliberately aimed at the extinction of tribalism and Celtic institutions.

Warriors of Norman or English race, like the Bruces and Balliols, were invited over the Border by King David, and given by him baronies in Scotland, to be held on terms of feudal service. There was no large displacement of existing proprietors, as in conquered England after Hastings; for this was Norman penetration, not Norman conquest. Estates of the Crown and unused lands, both very extensive, enabled David to create baronies for the new-comers without resorting to wholesale confiscation. But the Celtic tribal inhabitants, or the colonists of newly occupied waste land, found themselves placed in a strictly feudal relation to their Anglo-Norman overlords, who knew how to make their new-fangled claims respected. Everywhere, as in contemporary England, rose the circular mound with the timber or stone tower on the top, whence the armoured cavalry ruled and judged the countryside.

And beside the castle rose the parish church, for the country was divided under Anglo-Norman auspices into parishes on the English system. The parish was often coterminous with the fief of the new lord. Religion as well as government was territorialized, and St. Columba's Church became a ghost and a memory, like the tribes to which it had ministered. King David and his nobility vied with each other in pious bequests and endowments of the feudal type. The Twelfth and Thirteenth Centuries were the great age of ecclesiastical architecture in Scotland. Stately Cathedrals and Abbeys rose, destined to perish at the hands of English moss-troopers or Scottish reformers. From the first the people resented the tithes and other novel burdens laid on them in David's reign for the benefit of an alien clergy. And ere long the attitude of the Barons to the Church became little more than a desire to secure the ecclesiastical endowments for their own families,—a desire gratified by many curious devices, such as warrior nobles masquerading as churchmen, until the Reformation introduced more direct methods.

David and his immediate successor, William the Lion, reproduced many of the features of the English State with remarkable success. The Shire system and the King's justice were brought in gradually, though much limited by the franchises of the Barons. Scottish 'burghs' received royal charters to elect their own magistrates, even more freely than the wealthier and more populous 'boroughs' of England.

The new Scotland was able to take shape and solidify, because she remained so long on tolerable terms with England. During the century and a half before the era of the wars of independence, the nobles of Scotland served King and country better than they ever did again. [1124–1286.] They and their vassals spread the use of the English language, nomenclature and institutions so successfully that these were the institutions for which Scots under Wallace and Bruce were prepared to die. The world of Celtic tribalism passed away out of the Western Lowlands, making less armed resistance than we should expect, save in fierce Galloway, where things Celtic lived longest and died hardest. With his formidable following of mail-clad feudal cavalry, the King could disregard those Celtic tribal chiefs who refused to become feudal lords. The old order gradually shrank into the mountain area of the Northern Highlands, where tribal Scotland survived intact until 1746. South and east of the Highland Line men gradually adopted the names, manners and language of the new regime.

While these great changes were in process, Crown and baronage were still necessary to each other, and both were still necessary to the best interests of the youthful nation. It was only when the war of independence against Edward I put that new-made nation to the test, that the Barons proved less responsive than the commons to the novel creed of patriotism, because feudalism is international, and their estates in England involved them in a dual allegiance. And it was only after the Scottish monarchy had established itself in the hearts and habits of the people, that the baronage became its constant and most dangerous foe.

[1286.] The golden age of mediæval Scotland came to an end when Alexander III's horse carried him over a sea-cliff. His surviving heir was his grand-daughter Margaret, 'the maid of Norway,' a girl who resided in Scandinavia during her brief reign. By the Treaty of Brigham it was arranged that she should marry the first English 'Prince of Wales,' afterwards Edward II of England. [1290.] The peaceable union of the whole island was close in sight. The crowns of Scotland and of England would meet on one head, but the two countries would be administered as separate realms, much as afterwards took place when James VI of Scotland became James I of England. But the course of history was not to be thus foreshortened. The Scots have seldom had luck with young Queens brought from oversea. That very autumn the Maid of Norway died in the Orkneys on her voyage home.

The chance of a peaceful solution died with the Maid. Edward I, pressing the claims of ancient English Kings to be overlords of Scotland, asserted his right to act as arbitrator between the various claimants to the vacant throne, of whom the chief were John Balliol and Robert Bruce. He decided in favour of Balliol, justly it would appear. But, not content with that, he treated Balliol as a puppet and Scotland as a subject land. Balliol, goaded to desperation, renounced his allegiance to his oppressive overlord. But he received little support from a divided and jealous baronage, and was easily deposed by Edward, who marched in triumph through the land, carried off the coronation stone from Scone to Westminster, and made himself direct King of Scotland. [1296.] The Ragman Roll contains the long list of the Scots nobles who did him homage.

All seemed finished. All in fact was about to begin. Deserted by her nobles, Scotland discovered herself. The governors whom Edward I left behind him were incapable and cruel, and the foreign soldiery made the Scots feel their subjection. In the following May a guerrilla chief of genius, a tall man of iron strength, who suddenly appears on the page of history as if from nowhere, defeated at Stirling Bridge end an English army under its blundering feudal chief the Earl of Warenne, of *Quo Warranto* fame. [1297.] Thence William Wallace broke ravaging into Northumberland and Cumberland.

This unknown knight, with little but his great name to identify him in history, had lit a fire which nothing since has ever put out. Here, in Scotland, contemporaneously with the very similar doings in Switzerland, a new ideal and tradition of wonderful potency was brought into the world; it had no name then, but now we should call it democratic patriotism. It was not the outcome of theory. The unconscious qualities of a people had given it reality in a sudden fit of rage. Theories of nationhood and theories of democracy would follow afterwards to justify or explain it. Meanwhile, it stood up, a fact.

Edward I had thought that he was going to yoke Scotland to England through the ordinary feudal apparatus of the time. His mistake was very natural, for by the accepted standards of the day, his proceedings were less abnormal than Wallace's amazing appeal to the Scottish democracy to save the Scottish nation. Nowadays, indeed, we expect as a matter of course to find both national feeling and democratic instincts in every part of Europe. But in mediæval times things were very different. Society was divided, not perpendicularly into nations; but horizontally into feudal strata. And Edward I had the feudal magnates of Scotland mainly on his side. Anglo-Normans, owning estates in England as well as Scotland, were excusably lukewarm in their Scottish patriotism and anxious not to quarrel with England's King, from whom they held their English lands.

But the Scottish people had national feeling and democratic feeling, both hitherto unconscious and unexercised. Wallace called them into activity. The burghers and peasants, led by the lairds or small gentry of whom Wallace himself was one, defied the power of England and when necessary defied the power of their own Scottish nobles. The 'schiltrons,' thick masses of plebeian spearmen, standing shoulder to shoulder, withstood on many a field the onset of the armoured English knights and their horses, who had made short work of the Celtic clan charge in Wales and Ireland. Here was a steadier spirit, and the discipline of a more settled civilization. But on other occasions the Scottish schiltrons were broken by the irresistible combination of feudal chivalry with Welsh or English longbowmen, whose arrows prepared a passage for the horsemen through the ranks of death. Falkirk, which put an end to the effective part of Wallace's career, was but the first of many English victories won by these tactics. [1298.]

But to defeat the Scottish army now and again was not to conquer Scotland. The common people were accustomed to the state of war, and every peasant was a warrior. In

that at least Scotland resembled rough Wales rather than
peaceful England. The Scots were ready to fire their huts
and lay waste their country in front of the invader rather
than give in, and again and again they were called on
to put this stern virtue into practice. Two things decided
the long-doubtful issue in favour of Scottish independence:
the personality of Robert Bruce, and after his death the
distraction of Edward III with the Hundred Years' War
in France.

Robert Bruce, grandson of the claimant of 1290, had
been brought up in no tradition of high-flown Scottish
patriotism. Both he and his father had adopted the trim-
ming politics common among the nobility; he had changed
sides more than once in the days of Wallace. But he was
betrayed into the path of duty and heroism by his own
fiery temper. When once he had cut the throat of the
Red Comyn in the church, he was a hunted outlaw, and
had no choice but to throw himself on the patriotic section
of the Scottish people, and revive the Wallace tradition.
[1306.] In that he found salvation for himself and his
country. To the democratic traditions of Wallace were now
added a much needed element of feudalism which Bruce
and 'the good Sir James' Douglas could supply, and an
element of true Kingship to be found in Bruce and in
Bruce alone.

When the timely death of Edward I [1307.] left the
Scots matched with Edward II, the desperate conditions
of their struggle for freedom became more equal. One by
one the castles from which the English held down the
land were captured and destroyed by those redoubtable
men of war, Douglas and Bruce. The crowning victory of
Bannockburn, in which the English failed properly to de-
ploy their masses of cavalry or to use their archers to
advantage, enabled the homely Scottish schiltrons to thrust
the English baronage and knighthood at the spear's point
into marsh and stream. [1314.] Never before or after was
there such a destruction of English chivalry. After that,
the English carried off the main of their archers and men-

at-arms oversea to southern lands where the peasantry had no such spirit.

The Border warfare of England and Scotland during the centuries that followed Bannockburn went best for the Scots when they fought it with guerrilla tactics. Some rude rhymes known as 'good King Robert's testament' handed on the supposed advice of Bruce to his people to avoid the open field,—in spite of the great exception of Bannockburn,—and to sacrifice their homes and property again and again to foil the invader. The conditions were indeed unequal for the Scots, demanding in them a marvellous patience, for while they could only raid the comparatively barren lands of Northumberland, Cumberland and Durham, the English moss-troopers and armies again and again harried the richest parts of Scotland, lying as they did within two days' ride of the Cheviot Border.

Scottish independence was won at a heavy price, as most things worth having are won. For two centuries and a half after Bannockburn, Scotland remained a desperately poor, savage, bloodstained land of feudal anarchy, assassination, private war and public treason, with constant Border warfare against England, with a peculiarly corrupt Church, with no flourishing cities, no Parliament worth calling such, and no other institutions that seemed to give promise of a great future. Her democratic instincts had prevented her from being annexed to England, who would have given to her wealth and civilization. But her democratic instincts had done nothing else for her politically, had not kept her feudal nobility in order, still less found expression for the national feeling in any representative system. Her alliance with France, useful militarily against England, was unnatural culturally, and could be no true substitute for the broken connection with her nearer neighbour. What then had Scotland gained by resisting England? Nothing at all,—except her soul, and whatsoever things might come in the end from preserving that.

BOOKS FOR FURTHER READING: Professor E. Curtis, *History of Mediaeval Ireland*; Stephen Gwynne, *History of Ireland*; Mrs. J. R. Green, *The Irish State to* 1014, and *The*

Making of Ireland; Giraldus Cambrensis, *Description of Wales* (trans. *Everyman* Library); W. Ll. Williams, *Making of Modern Wales*; Rhys and Jones, *The Welsh People*; W. Rees, *South Wales and the March 1284–1415*; Tout, *Edward I*; Hume Brown, *History of Scotland*, Vol. I.; Andrew Lang, *History of Scotland*, Vol. I.; Oman, *Art of War in the Middle Ages*; Scott's *Tales of a Grandfather*, Vol. I.

NOTE Lines from Bruce's 'testament': 'On fut suld be all Scottis weire, / By hyll and mosse themselff to reare. / Let woods for wallis be bow and speire, / [Let woods instead of castle walls be their weapons of defence] / That innymeis do them no deire. / In strait places gar keip all store, / And byrnen ye planeland thaim before. / Thane sall thai pass away in haist / When that thai find na thing but waist. / With wyles and waykings of the nyght / And mekill noyis maid on hytht / Thaim sall ye turnen with great affrai, / As thai were chassit with swerd away. / This is the consall and intent / Of gud King Robert's testament.'

But in spite of the first line, the Scottish picked troops, when they raided England, were a *mounted* infantry, riding to battle and dismounting to fight. Froissart has described them on these raids in the reign of Edward III, 'for they are all a horsbacke, without it be the traundals and laggers of the host who folow after, a foote. The knightis and squiers are well horsed, and the comon people and other on litell hakeneys and geldyngis; and they carey with them no cartis, nor chariettis, for the diversities of the montaignes that they must pass through in the countrey of Northumbrelande.' He goes on to describe how each horseman carries a little sack of oatmeal and a metal plate on which to cook it 'in manner of a cracknell or bysket, and that they eate to comfort of all theyr stomakis.' Otherwise they lived on the half-sodden flesh of the cattle they captured *en route*. (Froissart. Lord Berners' translation.)

Froissart also tells us how on one occasion in the reign of Richard II, when the French knights found the Lowlands apparently ruined by an English invasion, 'the people generally made light of it, saying that with six or eight stakes they would soon have new houses, and that they should have cattle enough for provisions from the forests, whither they had been driven for security.' This illustrates the working of the policy of 'Good King Robert's testament.' There was much more woodland in North Britain at that time than in the era of the Stuarts.

CHAPTER SIX

The Hundred Years' War. Its Causes and Effects.
The Birth of Nationalism. Archery and Yeomanry.
English Language and Patriotic Feeling

KINGS: Edward III, 1327-77; Richard II, 1377-
99; Henry IV, 1399-1413; Henry V, 1413-22;
Henry VI, 1422-61

It is sometimes held that the unity of mediæval Christendom prevented such wars as those which have devastated
Europe at intervals from the Sixteenth to the Twentieth
Century. But there was, in fact, no unwillingness on men's
part to wage war on one another, and the cruelty with
which war was waged was even greater than in our own
day. The desire to kill was under less restraint of conscience or of custom, but the means of killing were more
restricted. It was not the unity of Christendom but the limit
of man's control over nature, the inferior methods of loco-
motion, and the want of political, administrative and financial machinery to keep and feed large bodies of men in
distant campaigns that prevented wars on the colossal
scale. Europe, still very poor and with no elaborate system
of credit, could not pay for the withdrawal from agriculture of a large proportion of her youth to engage in destruction as a skilled trade. The small warrior class of feudal
Barons and knights were all-powerful, because they and
their paid followers held a monopoly in the profession of
arms. From the Eleventh to the Fifteenth Century, wars on
the continent were numerous and local, instead of few and
large like those of modern times. The arm of Mars was
short, but it was kept in continual practice, and the peasant
suffered more constantly from the soldier than he does to-
day.

[1337-1453.] Perhaps the first European war that can be
called national was the Hundred Years' War as waged by
England. The armies she sent year after year to lay waste

and plunder France were indeed very small, but their
efficiency was the outcome of a national organization and a
national spirit. England, on account of her insular and remote position, and her strong kings, had since the Norman
Conquest outstripped the rest of Europe in obtaining a
certain measure of internal peace, and was passing from
feudalism to nationhood. As soon as King and Parliament
had endowed her with administrative machinery and national self-consciousness, she exercised these new powers
at the expense of that clumsy giant, the French feudal
Kingdom. She became for a while the plunderer and bully
of her continental neighbours, not because she had less
conscience than they, but because she had more power.
In Tudor times the position was to be reversed, when
united France and united Spain became each more powerful than England; but her island position saved her from
reprisals, and suggested a more profitable outlet to her national energies in commerce and discovery beyond the
ocean.

The Hundred Years' War was therefore a question of
political dynamics. It is useless to idealize it. The fact that
the plundering expeditions of four generations of Englishmen were supposed to be justified by the genealogical
claims of Edward III and Henry V to the throne of France,
no more proves that the Middle Ages had respect for 'the
idea of right,' than the similar dynastic claims of Frederic
the Great on Silesia can help the Eighteenth Century in
like case. Froissart, much as he admired the English performance which it was his life's work to record, was under
no such delusion.

'The English,' he wrote, 'will never love or honour their
king, unless he be victorious and a lover of arms and war
against their neighbours and especially against such as are
greater and richer than themselves. Their land is more fulfilled of riches and all manner of goods when they are at
war than in times of peace. They take delight and solace
in battles and slaughter: covetous and envious are they
above measure of other men's wealth.' 'The King of England must needs obey his people and do all their will.'

Indeed no King could have constrained an unwilling people to wage war oversea for four generations. The Hundred Years' War was not, at bottom, the result of dynastic ambition, but of national, popular and Parliamentary institutions. The new England passed through a phase of expansionist militarism, profitable at first, in the end disastrous.

It was early in the reign of Edward III that English ambitions were diverted from Scotland to France. To pick the famous lily was an enterprise of more profit, ease and honour than to pluck the recalcitrant thistle. When English noblemen, younger sons and yeomen returned from oversea, each brought back his share of booty, perhaps the gold vessels of an abbey, the tapestry of a merchant's house, or a brace of wealthy French knights to ransom; and each had his stock of tales for an admiring audience, in days when tales held the place in society that books and newspapers hold to-day,—rich tales of adventure, battle, free quarters and free love in the most famous cities and best vineyards of Europe. That way a man cut a finer figure in his own and his neighbour's eyes than when he returned from harrying a thrice-harried Scottish moorland, where he had burnt some empty huts and a few stooks of oats or barley, but found nothing to carry away save the skin of a cow too lame to hobble to the hiding place in the wood.[1]

[1] Froissart's accounts of English proceedings in France and in Scotland, respectively, make this very clear. In the invasion of 1346 he tells us in great detail how 'by the Englishmen was brent, exiled, robbed, wasted and pilled the good, plentiful country of Normandy.' 'The soldiers,' he tells us, 'made no account to the King nor to none of his officers of the gold and silver that they did get. They kept that to themselves.' There is abundant evidence that the English armies of the Fourteenth Century frequently behaved like the Turkish bands to-day, robbing, massacring and burning. Yet the English were not specially inhumane. In mediæval warfare humanity and courtesy were not shown to 'your even Christian,' but only to members of the knightly class, male and female, and to clergy and nuns, who often, though by no means always, obtained respect for their persons, but less often for their property.

The modern mind, nursed on the theory and practice of racial nationalism, is astonished that the English should ever have thought it possible to annex France. But for many years the French resisted us less heartily and hardily than the Scots who spoke our own tongue. For Scotland was already a nation in spirit, while France was a loose collection of feudal fiefs. Moreover, when the Hundred Years' War began in 1337, Edward III and his nobles spoke French and were more at home in Gascony than in Scotland.

There were deeper causes of the breach with France than Edward III's dynastic claims to her throne. His possession of Gascony, the last wreck of the old Angevin Empire, was coveted by the French King, who aided the Scots against us. France, moreover, had designs in Flanders against the burgher democracy of Van Artevelde, and we could not brook French predominance in those parts because of our trade interests: our chief export, English-grown wool, was sold to feed the looms at Ghent, Bruges and Ypres, for our cloth manufacture at home was still in its infancy. At sea the English and French traders were perpetually cutting one another's throats, in the Channel and on the route across the Bay to fetch the Gascon wines. The first great action of the war was the battle of Sluys [1340.], won by the English merchant navy. After that, Edward III claimed to be lord of the English sea, and the gold noble he struck represents him standing armed and crowned in a ship.

Foure things our noble sheweth to me,
King, ship and sword and power of the sea,

wrote the author of the 'Libel of English Policie,' who in the latter part of the Hundred Years' War put out the first reasoned case for the necessity of sea-power to England. Sea-power was one of the objects of the war, but unfortunately not the chief object.

Because the struggle was much more than feudal or dynastic, it lasted intermittently for over a hundred years. John had failed to compel the English to fight in defence

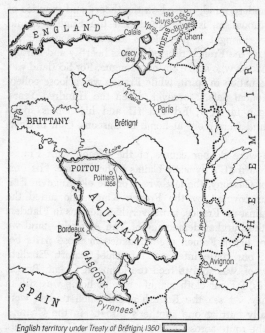

English territory under Treaty of Brétigni, 1360 [   ]
Boundary of French Kingdom   ....

Map 14 France: First Part of Hundred Years' War.
Height of Edward III's Power

of his Norman and Angevin possessions. But from Edward
III to Henry VI Parliament after Parliament voted supplies
for the war, and called to account Ministers who failed to
conduct it with success. Pride in the triumphs of the English archer 'for all the French boast,' the joy of seeing—

Our King go forth to Normandy
With grace and might of chivalry,

and return with the proudest princes and nobles of Europe
as captives in his procession through London streets, intensified the patriotic sentiment that united all classes of the
nation. Hatred of the French was even stronger among the
common folk than in the bi-lingual upper class. Therefore

we persisted so long in this disastrous enterprise, till our
own well-ordered mediæval society was ruined, and till
we had twice goaded the French themselves, once under
Du Guesclin and again fifty years later under Dunois and
Joan of Arc, to become conscious of their nationality and
to change the purely feudal tactics and spirit of their
armies. The Hundred Years' War was the diplomatic and
military aspect of the period of transition from the feudal
to the national, from the Middle Ages to the Renaissance.

As so often happens in war, the armies and tactics employed by the two sides respectively represented underlying social facts, and registered changes of more than
military importance.

France was a Kingdom in a very different sense from
England. She was not governed in shires by the King's
judges, sheriffs and coroners sitting in the King's courts.
She was governed in provinces and baronies by her feudal
princes and lords, each in his own territory. The peasant
serf was bitterly despised by the noble; and there was no
important middle class, no substantial yeomen, and no small
gentry accustomed to serve the Crown and carry on public
business in close connection with classes above and below
their own. France had indeed wealthy cities, but the links
were slender that connected the townsfolk with the exclusive feudal society around them; there was no co-operation between the burghers and the lesser *noblesse* as
in the English shire and the English House of Commons.

These social facts were reflected in the armies that suffered defeat at Crecy, Poitiers and Agincourt. They were
feudal hosts, called out under feudal obligations, and with
all the indiscipline, political and military, characteristic of
feudal pride. The King of France and his generals had the
same kind of difficulty with the units of their command as
Montrose or Prince Charlie with the Highland chiefs. The
feudal army had no idea of tactics except the unsupported
cavalry charge. Its shock had decided the issue of battle
for many centuries past, but the English archers put a term
to its supremacy on the day of Crecy. [1346.]

The best missile troops the French had were Italian mercenaries,—crossbowmen from Genoa. The French peasant, despised in peace, was little regarded in war. His part was to pay the ransom from the estate, when his lord had been carried off to an English manor-house, to hawk and flirt with his captor's family till the money arrived. This method of securing 'reparations' during the war itself, especially the ransoms extorted for the great haul of highborn prisoners at Poitiers [1356.], in addition to the terrible plunderings of the soldiery, goaded the starving peasants of France into the revolt of the *Jacquerie,* a gesture of mere despair. [1358.]

The English social system was no less faithfully reflected in the organization and tactics of the invading armies. In the England of the Edwards, Piers Plowman was in better plight than Jacques Bonhomme across the Channel. Even the villeins were relatively wealthy and well-fed, and the proportion of free-men agriculturists above the status of villein was on the increase. Indeed the Hundred Years' War covers the greater part of the period of servile emancipation in England. Now the Plantagenet Kings had compulsorily organized all the freemen for training in military service, not on a feudal system but on the principle of the Saxon fyrd brought up to date by the Assizes of Arms. A large body of militia were kept familiar with the use of those weapons which each man was compelled by the State to possess. The fact that so many of the common folk had arms in their cottages which they knew how to use, was a chief cause why the island atmosphere breathed something of political and social freedom.

In the Fourteenth Century the longbow became more and more the prescribed weapon, and the practice at the butts behind the churchyard became the chief sport and excitement of village life. Edward III encouraged it by royal proclamations, prohibiting under pain of imprisonment—

handball, football or hockey (*pilam manualem, pedivam, vel bacularem*); coursing and cockfighting, or other such idle games, which drew men away from the butts. In a later age Hugh Latimer used to tell from the pulpit the tale of his father the yeoman—

He taught me how to draw, how to lay my body in my bow, and not to draw with strength of arms as divers other nations do, but with strength of the body. I had my bows bought me according to my age and strength; as I increased in them, so my bows were made bigger and bigger. For men shall never shoot well unless they be brought up in it.

We may be sure that Crecy and Agincourt had been vicariously won by just such careful fathers as old Latimer. For the art of the longbow was so difficult that foreigners never learnt the knack that would send an arrow through plate-mail, and though the longbow was for more than a century the acknowledged master-weapon in European war, it never ceased to be an English monopoly. And even in England its gradual supersession by the less efficient hand-gun of Tudor times appears to have been due to the village neglect of archery for 'football and other lewd games,' or as Latimer thought, for 'bowling, drinking and whoring,'—Statutes and Proclamations notwithstanding.

In Edward III's time this formidable militia was at the height of its efficiency and could on occasion be called out. When in the year of Crecy [1346.] the Scots thought to make an easy prey of a land whose King and nobles were in France, the democratic levy of the shires taught the invaders, at Neville's Cross near Durham, the lesson they had learned at Northallerton and were to learn once more at Flodden, that England,—though she had no national motto to remind her of it,—can no more be 'provoked with impunity' than Scotland herself.

From this large body of armed and half-armed freemen, Edward III selected, by Commissions of Array addressed to each shire, a picked host to wage war oversea. For this purpose he resorted at first to conscription, eked out with volunteers. But as the French war went on, the Commissions of Array and the principle of compulsion were abandoned in favour of the system of hiring private 'companies' of professional warriors.

These 'companies' were the backbone of the long English warfare in France. They were not feudal hosts or conscript levies, but long-service professional soldiers, enlisted for pay by some noble or knight who had determined to push his fortunes in politics and in war. The King could contract with their leaders for their services at easy rates, because they counted on enriching themselves further with plunder, ransom and free quarters. Sometimes, especially during the intervals of truce between France and England, they fought and ravaged on the continent for their own hands, like the famous Hawkwood and his English Company in Italy. When driven back to England in the reign of Henry VI, the 'companies' became a chief cause of the social and political disruption at home, which provided them with fresh occupation as 'retainers' in the Wars of the Roses.[2]

The tactics of the English implied trust in the yeoman as a fighting man and in the longbow as a weapon. Those lessons had been learnt in the Scottish campaigns of the first two Edwards. The feudal warriors of the continent had taken no interest in such obscure and barbarous wars, and were stricken with amazement when, on the field of Crecy, the despised islanders revealed themselves as the masters of all Europe in the art military.

The lesson learnt in the Scottish wars had been twofold. At Stirling Bridge and Bannockburn the schiltrons of Scottish spearmen had shown that under favourable circumstances a self-respecting infantry could defeat feudal knighthood hand to hand, while the English victories, such as Falkirk, had taught the value of the longbow. From these two lessons of the Scottish war put together, the army chiefs of Edward III deduced a new method of war-

---

[2] Conan Doyle's *White Company* gives a spirited and well-informed if somewhat idealized picture of one of these 'companies' abroad, while Stevenson's *Black Arrow* describes Sir Daniel Brackley and his retainers at home, with a great measure of historical truth.

fare, combining the archer and the feudal knight in a single unit of battle, formidable alike for its missiles and its sword play. The English chivalry, perceiving that they had not the numbers to meet the French chivalry in the shock of horse and lance, consented to dismount and to fight in their full armour as a 'stiffening' to the line of half-armoured archer infantry, who were to win the battle by the rapidity of their penetrating volleys of cloth-yard shafts. Those of the French knights who struggled alive through the arrow-storm, came to hand grips with the English line, where the archer, drawing his sword, stood shoulder to shoulder with the armoured knights and nobles, sometimes behind a hedge or a line of portable stakes.[3]

The French were so hopelessly defeated by these tactics at Crecy that they determined so far to imitate the victors as to fight on foot. But that by itself was not the secret, as Poitiers proved. Their other remedy against the arrows was to increase the thickness of their armour and to substitute plate for chain mail over all parts of the body. But they lost as much in mobility as they gained in protection, and the absurd helplessness of the Fifteenth Century knight, in a case too heavy for him to carry, only hastened the decline of chivalry.

The French in fact never devised a means of successfully attacking the English infantry line, once it had taken up chosen ground with flanks protected. But the English system elaborated by the Black Prince had one great defect. It was not mobile on the field of battle, like the 'thin red line' of Wellington. It could not advance to attack the mounted knights without exposing itself to be outflanked and ridden down. In short it could only win victories when the French were foolish enough to attack it in position.

The first deliverance of France was made by Du

[3] The archer, when his value as a fighting man had come to be fully recognized, was often supplied with defensive armour and a horse, so that the whole army of mounted infantrymen would scour through France on their raids. But all from King to scullion, dismounted to fight if occasion demanded.

Guesclin, the man who grasped the full meaning of these
facts. It was he who, in the last years of Edward III
[1369–77.], overthrew the compromise treaty of Brétigni,
which in 1360 had assigned south-western France to England. [SEE MAP 14.] Du Guesclin hired the service of 'free
companies' instead of relying on the undisciplined feudal
host, and he avoided battle, except when he could surprise
the English or take them in some circumstance of special
disadvantage. His principal work was to besiege the castles
from which the English ruled the country, and in that the
French were our match, for they excelled in the early use
of cannon. Gunpowder, not yet used effectively in the open
field, was already revolutionizing siege operations. It
helped to liberate France, but it sapped the power of
feudalism, for the King, who could best afford to pay for
a train of artillery, would in the end put down the feudal
Baron, if he could blow a hole in his castle wall.

Yet even so feudalism died very hard in France. After Du
Guesclin had freed his countrymen by finding substitutes
for the feudal tactics which had failed at Crecy and
Poitiers, a growth of French national monarchy at the expense of feudalism might have been expected during the
generation of uneasy truce and intermittent warfare that
divided the two halves of the Hundred Years' War. But
no such development took place. When Henry V, on his
accession, [1413.] revived Edward III's pretensions to the
French Crown in order 'to busy giddy minds with foreign
quarrels,' the English, going out to fight with the tactics of
the Black Prince, found themselves opposed, not by the
proved methods of Du Guesclin, but by the idiotic feudal
array of Crecy and Poitiers. Agincourt was the natural
result. [1415.]

Indeed the similarity of the second to the first half of
the Hundred Years' War is extraordinary, as regards the
military methods of both sides. For a long time the French
refused to learn or to remember anything. Henry V, being
a great soldier,—he has been called 'the first modern
general,'—secured the English hold on Normandy as an
occupied province, and thence extended his power to the

banks of the Loire. The quarrel between the great feudal Houses of Orleans and Burgundy tore France in two, and brought about the alliance of Burgundy and Flanders with England, to the delight of wool merchants on both sides of the Channel. In 1420 Henry V was acknowledged heir to the French Crown by the Treaty of Troyes. Two years later he died, leaving his ill-gotten inheritance to an infant, who was acknowledged by Northern France.

During the minority of Henry VI came the second French revival, following tactically on the lines of Du Guesclin. His successor was Dunois, who had a harder task to face and was not his equal. But Dunois obtained a most unexpected and extraordinary ally. In one year of glory and one year of martyrdom [1429–31.] Joan of Arc evoked a national tradition and sentiment in France which has never since looked back. Spiritually she was the Wallace of France. But more than twenty years passed after her death, before the English power had been completely worn away by the Fabian tactics and siegecraft of the Dunois era. When English Talbot and his son perished in the last battle down in Gascony, the Hundred Years' War drew to a close [1453.]; its aftermath in England, the Wars of the Roses, began two years later at St. Albans. So little rest had England in the ill-governed Fifteenth Century.

What had we gained by the long, persistent endeavour to erect an English Empire in Europe? We had most justly earned the break-up of our own mediæval society and a period of anarchy and moral prostration. We had gained the port of Calais which we kept for another hundred years, the solitary pledge of England's foretime rule in France, as Berwick-on-Tweed of her lost Scottish dominion. Calais was used as a port of vent for our raw wool abroad, where it was gathered and taxed before sale. The staple was fixed there by the King of England for that purpose. But the use of the staple gradually declined with the increase of our cloth manufacture and trading enterprise oversea. Meanwhile Calais, the bridge-head firmly held in French soil, was a standing temptation even to prudent Yorkist and

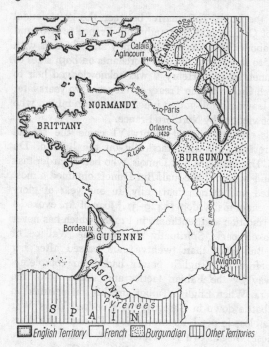

May 15   France: Second Part of Hundred Years' War.
Height of Henry VI's Power

Tudor Kings to revive their never abandoned claims on
France. Its loss under Mary was pure gain and helped the
Elizabethans to look westward for new lands.

Had the Hundred Years' War, then, done nothing but
harm to England? If it brought any compensating good it
was of the intangible and intellectual order—a strong national self-consciousness, more democratic than feudal;
great memories and traditions; a belief in the island qualities, which helped Englishmen to carry their heads high
in the coming century of eclipse behind the crescent mon-
archies of France and Spain. In Shakespeare we may read
the inspiration given by the memory of Agincourt to the

better-directed national revival under Elizabeth. In the days of good Queen Bess, Englishmen collectively had forgotten what the face of war was like; they had no memory of the bitter realities of the Hundred Years' War as they had been painted in Chaucer's vision:—

The carraine[4] in the bush, with throte ycorven,
A thousand slain, and not of qualm ystorven; [5]
The tirant, with the prey by force yraft;
The toun destroïed, there was nothing laft.

But the contemporaries of Shakespeare said proudly of the English yeomen:—

These were they that in times past made all France afraid. And albeit they be not called 'Master' as gentlemen are, or 'Sir' as to knights appertaineth, but only 'John' and 'Thomas' etc., yet have they been found to have done very good service. The kings of England in foughten battles were wont to remain among them who were their footmen, as the French kings did amongst their horsemen, the prince thereby shewing where his chief strength did consist.

From the Hundred Years' War onwards, the 'yeoman *motif*' runs through English thought, literature and politics with a potent and life-giving force, right down to the coming of the Industrial Revolution.

In earlier mediæval times hostility was normally felt against the natives of a neighbouring town, shire or village. This unneighbourliness diminished as insular patriotism enlarged the mind and pointed out the Frenchman or the Spaniard as the true 'foreigner.' The habits of thought and feeling that were contracted during the Hundred Years' War with France—a period of 'hate' less intensive but twenty-five times longer than our recent war with Germany—sharply defined the new patriotic feeling in the form of racial hatred of the French. It was intensified in the era of Du Guesclin by destructive enemy raids on our South coast and not unsuccessful warfare against our shipping. The feeling against the French outlasted the war, and helped to put an end to that subordination of

[4] Carrion, corpse.
[5] Not dead of sickness.

English to French culture which the Norman Conquest had established. From this time forward foreigners complained of the insular and surly exclusiveness of the English common people. In Henry VII's reign the Venetian envoy noted that:—

They think that there are no other men than themselves, and no other world but England; and whenever they see a handsome foreigner, they say 'he looks like an Englishman' and that 'it is a great pity that he should not be an Englishman'; and when they partake of any delicacy with a foreigner they ask him 'whether such a thing is made in his country?'

In the middle of the Tudor period a French visitor wrote:—

The people of this nation mortally hate the French as their old enemies, and always call us 'France cheneve,' 'France dogue.' (French knave, French dog.)

In the reign of Elizabeth these feelings were turned for awhile against the Spaniard. Yet there was often an element of good-nature in English nationalism. At the height of the Elizabethan struggle with Spain, Shakespeare's kindly caricature of Don Armado, 'a fantastical Spaniard,' in *Love's Labour's Lost*, does credit to the mentality of our people at war.

The upper classes followed more slowly in the wake of the common people in the repudiation of everything from beyond the Channel. Squire Western was in process of evolution, but not yet evolved. Ever since the loss of Normandy and the Angevin Empire, the French-speaking upper class had been cut off from estates and connections oversea, and their culture, severed from its roots in France, was clearly exotic. A hundred years before the days of Chaucer's Prioress, Frenchmen 'of Paris' used to laugh at the strange hybrid that passed for their tongue in the mouths of English gentlefolk. Yet, such as it was, it was their everyday speech till the reign of Edward III, and was regarded as the hall-mark of a gentleman, till the increasingly racial character of the war compelled all men to regard French as an enemy language.

Six years after Poitiers a statute was passed through

Parliament declaring that since the French tongue was 'much unknown in this Realm,' all pleading and judgments in the law courts should be spoken in the English tongue and enrolled in Latin. 'Men of lawe fro that tyme shold plede in her moder tunge,' it was said. 'Their mother tongue'! Here indeed is a new and significant order of ideas! If the statute was imperfectly obeyed at first, it was obeyed before long, although lawyers, with professional conservatism, long continued to write documents in the 'law French' in which their predecessors had addressed the court.

A still more fundamental revolution was taking place in regard to the language used in the schools. English was becoming once more the tongue of the educated and of the upper class, as it had never been since Hastings:—

Children in scole (thus wrote John of Trevisa in 1385), agenst the usage and manere of alle othere naciouns, beeth compelled for to leve thire own langage, and for to construe thir lessouns and there thynges in Frensche, and so they haveth seth (*since*) the Normans come first in to Engelond. Also gentil men children beeth i-taught to speke Frensche from the tyme that they beeth i-rokked in their cradel. . . . This manere was moch i-used to fore the first moreyn (*before the Black Death*, 1349) and is siththe sumdel (*since somewhat*) i-chaunged. For John Cornwaile, a maister of grammar chaunged the lore in gramer scole and construccion of Frensche into Englische; and Richard Pencriche lerned that manere teaching of hym, and other men of Pencriche. So that now, the yere of oure Lorde a thowsand thre hundred and foure score and fyve, and of the secounde Kyng Richard after the conquest nyne, in alle the gramere scoles of Engelond, children leveth Frensche and construeth and lerneth in Englische. . . . Here avauntage is that they lerneth ther gramer in lasse tyme than children were i-woned (*used*) to doo; disavauntage is that now children of gramer scole conneth no more Frensche than can thir left heele; and that is harme for them and (*if*) they schulle passe the see and travaille in straunge landes and in many other places. Also gentil men haveth now moche i-left for to teche ther children Frensche (*have much left off teaching their children French*).

Thus did these humble schoolmasters, John Cornwaile and

Richard Pencriche, prepare the road for Chaucer and Wycliffe in their own century, for Shakespeare and Milton in time to come, for the English Reformation and Renaissance, and the whole development of English national life and letters as something other than a northern offshoot of French culture. Some may regard the transaction thus casually recorded by the chronicler as more important than Magna Carta or the Declaration of Independence.[6]

During the formative period of the English language, the centuries after the Conquest when it was out of fashion with the learned and the polite,[7] in the chrysalis stage between Saxon caterpillar and Chaucerian butterfly, it was divided into many regional dialects, of which the chief were Wessex, Northumbrian, East and West Midland. The Wessex had been the Court language in Alfred's time, but the Norman Conquest had relegated it for ever to the cottage and the plough-furrow. It was the speech of the East Midlands that became the ancestor of modern English, triumphing over the other dialects, partly because it was spoken in London, Oxford and Cambridge; partly because it was employed by Chaucer, who enriched it with many French words, and by Wycliffe, who enriched it with many words from the Latin Vulgate. Both Chaucer and Wycliffe founded a school of imitators who used mainly the same dialect. Their writings and translations were for awhile widely circulated in manuscript. Then in the later Fifteenth Century came Caxton's printing press at Westminster, under the patronage of the Yorkist Kings; it further popularized Chaucer, and spread through the

---

[6] The linguistic situation about the year 1375 is thus summed up by William Nassington:—'Some can French and no Latin, / That have used courts and dwelled therein: / And some can of Latin a party, / That can French full febelly: / And some understandeth English / That neither can Latin nor French: / But lerid and lewid, old and young / All understanden English tongue.'

lerid and lewid=learned and ignorant.

[7] See pp. 179–80, above.

land translations of various works done into English of the same type.

In this way a standard of English was being formed for all those who could read, and for all, even beyond Trent and Avon, who wished to be regarded as educated men and women. In Tudor times the Bible and the Prayer Book in the same dialect—already regarded as 'the King's English'—obtained a diffusion and authority quite unparalleled by any works in earlier times, and firmly fixed the standard. During these two centuries from Chaucer to Elizabeth, the language in question, living on the tongues of men no less than in their books, was moving forward from strength to strength and from beauty to beauty, enriching itself with Latin words expressive of all the joy and learning of the Renaissance, until it fell into the perfecting hands of the man of Stratford. Since his day its adaptability to exact scientific statement has increased, and its poetic and literary quality has decreased, answering to the changes in the mind and life of the people who use it.

CHAPTER SEVEN

The Black Death. The Emancipation of the Villeins and the Fluidity of Labour. The Rising of 1381. The Church and the Laity. Wycliffe and Lollardry

In a previous chapter we considered the life of the mediæval English village.[1] We saw it, self-sufficing in its labour and its poverty; often suffering from famine but never from unemployment; little connected with the world beyond its own forest bounds, except through the personal activities and requirements of its lord; supplying nearly all its own simple needs; containing its own miller, craftsmen and spinsters; feeding itself by tilling, on traditional methods, the strips owned by the villeins in the open field, and by sharing the common rights over meadow and waste.

[1] See pp. 199–206, above.

We saw too that the village was a 'manor' held by some lord, resident or non-resident, lay or spiritual. We noted the relations between the lord and his villeins, who composed the great majority of the village, and by whose compulsory labour his domain was tilled under the supervision of his bailiff.

This system, found with variations all over feudal Europe, served no less than the sameness of religious observance to give unity to Christendom. In every land there was the same scheme of society resting on two pillars—the lord and his serf, and in every land the lord and the serf respectively had much the same outlook on life. Change and variation began with the rise of the yeoman, the free labourer, and a number of active and intelligent middle classes, towards the end of the mediæval period. The citizens of Paris differed widely from the citizens of London, the yeoman of Tudor England from the peasantry of Valois France. And so the feudal unanimity of old Europe was at length broken up into nations, each with a character of its own.

The manorial system had led England out of the Dark Ages and had enabled man to conquer the forest, subdue the soil, and colonize the land. In ages of brute force it had protected the weak behind the shield of custom, even while making them half slaves. It gave stability and peace, but checked progress and denied freedom. Its part in English history had been great, but its use was at length exhausted.

Already before the close of the Thirteenth Century the beginnings of change were perceptible. Lords and their bailiffs occasionally found it more convenient to take money rents of a penny or a half-penny instead of the day's work due. But the villeins who thus commuted did not necessarily become freemen in the eye of the law, and were in most cases still bound to the soil; indeed the commutation was often made in a form revocable by the lord. The change from servile to hired labour went quietly forward on some estates during the first half of the Fourteenth Century, but the old system was still prevalent though not

universal when in 1348-9 occurred the most appalling of
national catastrophes.

The Black Death, on its first visitation of Europe from
some mysterious fountain-head of disease in the undiscov-
ered East, swept off perhaps a third, possibly a half, of the
compatriots of Boccaccio, Froissart and Chaucer. The most
terrible feature of its first advent was its ubiquity. In the
most secluded English hamlets we often read, in the list
of vicars in the parish church, the names of *two* incumbents
under that fatal year. Some villages and hamlets ceased to
exist, the whole population having died. In the winter of
1349 the plague was stayed, but it remained in the island,
and was perpetually breaking out in one insanitary township after another. Its last appearance, as Charles II's
'Plague of London,' seems to have been little, if at all,
worse than several plagues that had devastated the capital
in Lancastrian, Tudor and Stuart times, with no Defoe to
celebrate them. Plague was a black cloud, ever hovering
over the filthy streets and brief lives of our ancestors. It
was a frequent sequel to the famine of a bad harvest year.

The reduction of the English subjects of Edward III, in
sixteen months, from perhaps four million to perhaps two
and a half million souls, precipitated the class struggle, and
embittered the process of emancipating the villein. In a
society accustomed to very slow changes in conditions of
life, the market value of labour had been doubled at a
stroke. The consequence was twofold. The labourer who
was already free struck for higher wages, while the villein
whose labour was not free struggled against the legal demands of the bailiff for customary services which were now
worth more to both parties; gradually he was led on to
demand his full freedom, the right to take his labour where
he would, to plead in the King's Court even against his
own lord, and to be free of irksome feudal dues.

Lords and bailiffs were in a terrible dilemma. Half the
domain land, half the rent-paying farms were lying un-
tilled, turf and bushes overgrowing the strips, the ploughmen dead, the thatch falling from their deserted hovels.
And the survivors were rising in open mutiny against law

and custom, and sometimes also against what was economically possible. The world seemed coming to an end, yet it never occurred to the governing class to stop the French war, which was still regarded as a source of profit and plunder. Poitiers followed Crecy, as though half the world had not died in the interval.

Part of their difficulties the landlords solved well and wisely, by substituting sheep-pasture for tillage. It was not till a hundred years later, when the population had nearly filled up the gaps left by the Black Death, that there was any need for landlords to evict ploughmen in order to make room for the shepherd. In 1350 death had evicted the ploughmen, and 'the deserted village' was ready to hand. In such circumstances, the multiplication of sheep-runs was pure gain to a community in distress. The export of raw wool to the Flanders looms, and the concurrent growth of cloth manufacture in England, aided by Edward III's importation of Flemish weavers to teach our people the higher skill of the craft, made demand for all the wool that English flocks could supply. In this way a national policy and distant markets were beginning to disturb and to improve the parochial economy of the old manor, and to offer alternative occupations for the emancipated or the runaway villein.

Other steps taken by the landlords in distress, though very natural, were less in harmony with the destined course of affairs. An endeavor was made to keep down wages and prices by law, to limit the mobility of the free labourer in search of highly paid employment, and to prevent the further emancipation of the villeins. But even in making these efforts to stop social and economic change, the landlords recognized the new and national character of the situation, for they legislated through Parliament. The conflict was moving away from the old manor court, which the peasant was learning to defy, to the arena of Parliament, which was already beginning to take over control of economic affairs from municipal and manorial authorities —a nation-making process completed under Queen Elizabeth. Unfortunately Parliament represented too exclusively the landed gentry and the employing classes of the towns. Their Statute of Labourers [1351.], following up the King's Ordinance of two years before, showed a desire to be fair, and endeavoured to fix not only wages but prices of provisions at the old standards. But no Statute could make two loaves or two labourers where there was only one. No Act of Parliament could repeal the Black Death or abolish the spirit of the age. The statutory limitation of wages, and the refusal to complete the emancipation of the villeins aroused a fierce struggle which lasted for the remainder of the century, and culminated in the drama of the Peasants' Revolt.[2]

Nothing is more remarkable than the change in the temper and mental activity of the lower orders during the Fourteenth Century. Professor Davis has summed up the reign of Henry III with the words: 'Of all the contrasts which strike us in mediæval life, none is so acute as that between the intellectual ferment in the upper class and the oriental passivity of their inferiors.' But in the reign of Edward III the peasants could no longer be accused of 'oriental passivity,' and the 'intellectual ferment' in their ranks reminds us of a modern labour movement. Village unions strike for higher wages, villeins demand freedom in return for 4d. an acre rent, and men ask each other in every field that deep-probing question—

When Adam delved and Eve span,
Who was then the gentleman?

The agitation was Christian in its form and language, but hostile to the Church authorities, whether as monastic landlords[3] or as royal Ministers. It had lost sympathy with

[2] Bertha Putnam, *Enforcement of the Statutes of Labourers, 1349–59 (Columbia University, Studies in History, etc.,* Vol. XXXII., 1908).

[3] There was no tendency on the part of the monasteries or other ecclesiastical lords to manumit serfs more rapidly than the lay landlords. Manumission of serfs was stigmatized as embezzlement of ecclesiastical property except when freedom was purchased as part of a business transaction. Corporate bodies, like monasteries, tended to a more con-

the mediæval order in Church and State, drawing its inspiration from the equalitarian element in earlier Christian
teaching. Some of the poor parish priests, some of the
friars, and some of the Wycliffite preachers helped to fan
the flame—Wycliffe himself maintaining a middle attitude
sympathetically critical of both sides, which contrasts fa-
vourably with Luther's heated partisanship in the very
similar case of the Peasants' Revolt in Germany.

Exalted by this new order of ideas, the peasants carried
on the struggle for their freedom. The free labourers attempted to ignore the Statutes fixing their wages, and
conducted strikes that were frequently but not always
successful. Those who had no land of their own often
emigrated to towns or manors where their illegal demands
were accepted. Their prosperity in good times is thus described in *Piers Plowman*:—

Labourers that had no land to live on but their hands,
Deigned not to dine to-day on night-old worts.
May no penny-ale please them, nor a piece of bacon,
But it be fresh flesh or fish, fried or y-baked,
And that *chaud* and *plus chaud* for the chill of their maw.
But he be highly hired, else will he chide, . . .
Then curses he the King, and all his Council after
For making such laws, labourers to grieve.

But the Justices entrusted with the enforcement of the
Statute of Labourers often succeeded in keeping wages
from rising as high as they would have gone in an open
market.

Meanwhile the villeins, still bound to the soil, slacked or
refused the unpaid labour which they owed on the lord's
domain. Some of them fled to the woods and became
Robin Hood bandits, helping to build up the legend of
that friend of the poor peasant and enemy of rich churchmen. Other villeins fled to distant estates, where in the
general dearth of hands they were received as free labourers, no questions asked. Their former masters strove to
drag them back to servitude and to exact the ancient dues

servative, though not necessarily a more oppressive policy
than individual lords.

from those who had remained behind, by employing the
'rusty curb of old father antic the law.' The activity of
the lawyers and well-to-do juries on the side of the landlords exposed the learned profession and its satellites to
the popular hatred, as not a few judges and jurymen learnt
to their cost in the days of June 1381.

The dramatic events of that summer had their roots in
social rather than political causes, though the revolt was
precipitated by the Poll Tax, a method of taxing the
poor for the French war at a moment when it was singularly
unsuccessful and therefore for a while unpopular. The
incompetent government of Richard II's minority was
hated and despised. But what chiefly brought the men
of East Anglia and the Home Counties trooping up to London was their own grievances and ambitions as peasants.
It was a rising, more or less concerted and prepared by
John Ball and his agents, against the gentry, the lawyers
and the wealthy churchmen. The rebels' chief demand
was the commutation of all servile dues throughout the
land for a rent of fourpence an acre; many of them also
demanded the disendowment of the Church, free use of
forests, abolition of game laws and outlawry—a 'Robin
Hood' programme suggestive of the life recently led by
some of those who were taking a leading part in the revolt.

The rising took the upper class by surprise, and for some
days there was little resistance, either central or local. Admitted into London by the 'prentice mob and by certain
democratically minded aldermen, the rebels held the capital and the government at their mercy. [JUNE 13, 1381.]
The King was in the Tower, which his subjects proceeded
to blockade. The situation was saved—but by very base
means. Richard II was sent to a conference at Mile End
with the rebels, where he made them promises of pardon
and emancipation from villeinage, which his counsellors
had no intention of carrying out. [JUNE 14.] It was easy
thus to beguile the moderate section of the rebels, who
had a simple-minded belief in the King as distinct from
his Council, Parliament, lawyers, Church and knighthood.

Yet in fact the Crown of England was identified with those interests.

Having received grants of emancipation and pardon hastily drawn up by the King's clerks, many of the insurgents set off home to their villages, deceived and happy. But meanwhile others had broken into the Tower and executed Sudbury, the Archbishop of Canterbury, on Tower Hill before a vast concourse of people who greeted the ferocious act with yells of triumph. They were incensed against him as Chancellor and chief Minister of the King, but the fact that he was Archbishop gave him no sanctity in their eyes. The relation of Church and people had undergone a profound change, since the ancestors of these same men had knelt beside their ploughs to pray for the Holy Martyr, Thomas Becket.

Other murders stained the rising, both in London and in the country, but there was no general massacre of the upper class such as characterized the French Jacquerie twenty years before. For the Jacquerie had been a gesture of savage despair, but the English revolt was the offspring of hope and progress, and was designed to hasten the advent of a freedom already on the way. It was one of the growing pains of the new England.

The forces of order were now beginning to rally. Another conference in the presence of the King, held in Smithfield, resulted not in further concessions, but in the slaying of a rebel leader, Wat Tyler, by the Mayor of London. [JUNE 15.] After that, the insurgents soon dispersed before a mixture of force and cajolery. The revolt went on spreading over the country till it reached from South Yorkshire to the South-Western counties. But when it had lost its hold on London it was doomed.

Whether the rising of 1381 actually hastened or retarded complete emancipation it is difficult to say. The immediate result was a strong and cruel reaction, when every promise made to the peasants in the hour of need was broken, and a bloody assize made mock of the pardons granted by the King. But a class that could give its rulers such a fright could not ultimately be held down. As compared to Peterloo, or to the rick-burning and the 'peasants' rising' in 1830, the revolt of 1381 was extremely formidable. Thistlewood talked about taking the Tower, but John Ball took it. For the peasant of the Fourteenth Century was not unused to arms and archery; he had the leasehold farmer in his ranks instead of against him, and he was in close touch with the turbulent democracy of the towns. In the battle for the preservation of order at home, the feudal class of the Hundred Years' War had no such allies and no such organization as the gentry in the time of Castlereagh and Wellington.

The failure of 1381 by no means ended the strikes, labour troubles and riots against serfdom. It must have been difficult to get a good day's work on the domain out of such surly fellows. Partly for this reason, partly in obedience to the general economic tendencies of the age, landlords gradually ceased to work the domain by the forced service of villeins, and let it instead to farmers who produced for the market, and so obtained money to hire free labour. In most cases the villeins bought their emancipation from serfdom, a process facilitated by the growing wealth of the country and of the peasants, and by the increasing quantities of coin of the realm. The emancipation took place mainly in the Fifteenth Century, and was completed under the Tudors. It was hastened by the changed attitude of the King's law courts, which became surprisingly liberal, and 'strained the law in the interests of the humbler classes.' [4]

The emancipated villein filled many rôles in the new society. He became a small yeoman farmer, whether freehold, leasehold or copyhold; or else he became a labourer

---

[4] Holdsworth, III. 505. On the whole question of emancipation see 'Oxford Studies in Social and Legal History,' Vol. V., Black Death, etc., by Miss Levett and A. Ballard, with introduction by Vinogradoff. Also T. W. Page, End of Villeinage in England, and Maitland, History of a Cambridgeshire Manor (Collected Papers, Vol. II.).; Ashley, Economic Organization of England, Chap. III.; G. G. Coulton, The Mediaeval Village, especially Chaps. XII., XIII., on monks and serfs.

for hire, or else he drifted into the towns or village work-shops, or took to the wars or to the life of the high seas. He retained valuable rights of his own in the open field and the waste, to induce him to stay in the village: but he was now free to go if he wished. 'The world was all before him where to choose,' and the modern English proved themselves great adventurers, both in the material and the spiritual world.

The fluidity of labour had come, altering the whole out-look of economic society. The change from the fixed and limited rights and duties of the serf to the competition and uncertainty of the open labour market was by no means wholly to the labourer's advantage, though for a hundred years after the Black Death the dearth of labour enabled him to command a high price. But in the later part of the Fifteenth Century, when the population had recovered, wages fell. Under the modern regime, though famine was more rare and the average standard of life was raised, the horrors of unemployment became known, and the 'sturdy beggars' of Tudor times had little joy of their freedom. But the change was necessary if the English race was to be anything better than a race of serfs, if it was to make vast increase in numbers, wealth and knowledge, if it was to take to industrial and maritime adventure and people the lands beyond the ocean. The power, liberty and prog-ress that we associate with modern England, America and Australasia, required as a precondition the emancipa-tion of the serfs. Emancipation and the consequent fluidity of labour formed the necessary prelude to the growth of trade, manufacture and colonization, as well as to the intellectual and political developments of Tudor and Stuart England.

One feature of the old village economy lasted on in whole districts until the reign of George III. In the best wheat-growing belt of the midland and eastern shires, the open village field, with its queer strips, involving enforced adherence to early Anglo-Saxon methods of cultivation, survived in many places to shock the sensibilities of Arthur Young and his 'improving landlords.'

If the Fourteenth and Fifteenth Centuries saw the emancipation of the serf and the birth of English language, literature and national feeling, they witnessed also, in consonance with those great movements, the failure of the cosmopolitan Church of the Middle Ages to meet any longer the conscious requirements of the new nation.

It may be questioned how far the loss of moral and intellectual leadership by the Church was due to greater corruption or inefficiency than of old. It was not so much that the clergy had sunk as that the laity had risen. In Norman and early Plantagenet times, when the Church reigned supreme in the minds of men, the mass of the clergy had—as compared to the modern English clergy whether Protestant or Catholic—been very ignorant and often very irregular in their lives. The ecclesiastical machinery was not strong enough to enforce the full programme of Hildebrandine celibacy upon the unwilling English priests. But in those days the laity were even more ignorant and brutal than the clergy, and probably even more immoral. A more or less barbarous Church had easily maintained its leadership over a laity still more barbarous. But times had changed. In the days of Chaucer, though neither laity nor clergy led very reputable lives, there was a more widely diffused standard of civilized conduct, much more learning and a more intellectual outlook. It was a sign less of clerical decadence than of general progress that a new generation of laymen were alienated by abuses in the Church that were not new: orthodox Gower and Langland and humanist Chaucer were no less severe on the churchmen than Wycliffe the heretic.

In earlier days, whatever the average priest may have been like, the Church had supplied the intellectual and moral leaders of the country, from Lanfranc and Anselm to Langton and Grossetête. But in the course of upward evolution this had ceased to be the case. It reflects no discredit on the Church that she had so well played her part as schoolmistress of the nation that her scholar was beginning to think for himself. Except Langland, the most influential literary men of the new era, such as Chaucer and

Gower, were not clergy at all, while Wycliffe and his Oxford following, though clergy, were heretics in the eye of the Church. The lawyers, the gentry and the rising middle classes of town and country had not the unquestioning minds of their forefathers. They were beginning to think for themselves. The pious Langland tells us:—

I have heard high men eating at table
Carpen (talk) as they clerkes were, of Christ and his might,
And laid faults upon the Father that formed us all
And carpen against clerkes crabbed words—

to the effect that we ought not to be damned for the fault of Adam.

At meat in their mirth when minstrels be still
Then tell they of the Trinity a tale or twain,
And bringen forth a bald reason and take Bernard to witness,
And put forth a presumption to prove the sooth.

Times were ripe for ecclesiastical reform and religious growth, no less than for social and political change. But whereas Parliamentary institutions and servile emancipation were developing apace, religious reform was impossible. The Church in England had no power to reform herself, because she had no autonomy. She was part of a cosmopolitan organization centred abroad, of enormous prestige and power, knowing nothing of English needs and of set purpose to resist change. If in England the Church had retired step by step before the rising tide of lay emancipation, there would have been no violent overturn in Tudor times. But pent waters gather force. In the Fourteenth and Fifteenth Centuries the Church refused every concession, effected no reform, and called in brute force to repress heresy. If an opposite course had been followed; if the rights of sanctuary and benefit of clergy had been modified; if ecclesiastical property had been redistributed more fairly to the poor parson; if priests had been permitted to marry their wives as in Saxon times; if the Pope had ceased to job rich places of the Church for foreign favourites; if the ecclesiastical authorities had withdrawn their countenance from the sale of pardons and relics and other superstitious practices that revolted the better sort of laity, orthodox as well as heretic; if the Church courts had ceased to make a trade of spying on the lives of the laity in order to extract fines for sin; and finally if Lollardry had been tolerated as Dissent, there would have been religious evolution spread over several centuries, instead of the religious revolution which we know as the Reformation.

But the doctrine of persecution was an integral part of mediæval Christianity. To the men of the Middle Ages, life outside the Church in disobedience to her doctrines was no more conceivable than life outside the State in disobedience to its laws. Religious persecution was therefore as much a matter of course as civil police. It was a tradition some thousand years old, and only a long course of very bitter experience has in modern times gone far to eradicate the doctrine of persecution from the Christian mentality. It is necessary to understand this before we can be fair to the conduct of any of our ancestors in the terrible religious struggles that began for England with the rise and suppression of Lollardry. There was never any serious question of tolerating Wycliffe's doctrines, if he could not get them accepted by the Church. There is no need to ascribe evil characters to the energetic Kings and Bishops who persecuted the Lollards, any more than to the members of the court that sentenced Joan of Arc. But neither is there any need to approve of the doctrine of persecution, because it was at that time very ancient, very respectable and universally held. It was none the less erroneous, and was destined to cause incalculable evil for centuries to come. That we should ever have cast out so deeply ingrained and so specious an error, is perhaps the most solid piece of human progress to which Europe can point.

We may, on similar principles drawn from the history of the case, understand why the Church refused to make concessions to the laity on points of clerical privilege, and why the monasteries and the highly endowed clergy refused to redistribute tithe and endowment for the benefit of the parish priest, before the Tudor squirearchy laid hands on the spoil. Men cannot so easily shake off the past. In the Dark Ages that followed the fall of the Roman Empire, the Church, struggling for existence in a world of barbarous and lawless force, had learnt how to bring the enginery of excommunication and the whole power of the united Church of Christendom to defend every right claimed by the clergy and every piece of property acquired by any specific clerical corporation, as if the foundations of Christianity were involved in their conservation. In an age too late the Church still held to these customs, which had become a part of her nature. She would not treat with the State on the basis of concession. She would not reform herself from within. The complete triumph of the State over the Church was needed to effect any appreciable measure of change.

The Church of England, indeed, was in no position to reform herself, had she wished, because she had no independence, and indeed no corporate existence. All the friars and most of the monks in England were subject not to the English Bishops, but only to the Pope; to him, not to the Church of England, they owed loyalty and obedience. Ecclesiastical law was the Roman Canon Law which the English Church was not competent to change. Appeal in ecclesiastical causes lay to the Papal courts. The Bishops were therefore without power to set the English house in order.

Nor in any case did the episcopal bench contain men fitted for such a task. Appointed by collusive arrangement between the King and the Pope, many of the Bishops were royal civil servants—like William of Wykeham, the great builder of colleges, and the Chancellor Archbishop Sudbury, the victim of the rebels of 1381. They were excellent and useful men, but they served the State rather than the Church,—Cæsar rather than Christ as contemporaries said,—and their eccesiastical duties were often committed to subordinates. No one could look to them to reform the religious life of the country.

The Papal nominees were even less adapted to such a

task. The Pope no longer sent men of the stamp of Theodore of Tarsus or Stephen Langton to govern the English Church. His modern favourites were most numerous in the ranks of the higher clergy just below the episcopate; many of them were foreigners who resided abroad and regarded England as a source of income.

While plurality and simony were rife among the upper clergy, native or foreign, the best element in the Church in the last two centuries before the Reformation were the poor parish priests. Miserably starved as many of them were for the benefit of the monks and higher clergy to whom the tithe was 'appropriated,' and often very ignorant, they were in close touch with their flocks, and not a few of them, no doubt, resembled Chaucer's poor parson. Would that we had their annals!

The collusion between the Pope and the later Plantagenet Kings was injurious to the Church, which had no defence at all if the King deserted her. And the collusion was highly unpopular with Parliament. Yet it continued more or less until Henry VIII's change of front. The Pope, who alone had the power to reform the Church, was deeply interested in the ecclesiastical venality and corruption of which Englishmen, orthodox and heretic alike, complained. The chief centre of the traffic of simony was the Papal Court, held during the Fourteenth Century at Avignon on the borders of France, where the association of the Pope with the national enemy during the first part of the Hundred Years' War helped to turn English national feeling against the Papacy and all its works. Nor did the schism that followed between rival Popes increase respect for the institution.

But so long as mediæval theories of the relation of Church and State held good, England was without a remedy. She might grumble, but no one at Rome or Avignon cared. The 'English asses' might bray, but they must still bear the load. Parliament might pass Acts of Provisors and Præmunire to limit the Papal power as against the rights of the Crown. But these laws were largely inoperative, and at the most served the King as an asset in his perpetual bargaining with the Pope. They were, however, a remarkable sign of the movement of opinion among the laity, and formed a precedent for much stronger action to be taken some day by the King in Parliament.[5]

John Wycliffe, a Yorkshireman by birth and an Oxford don by profession, pointed out to England a remedy for her griefs, and found what had hitherto been lacking, a theoretic basis for denying the Papal authority. His 'theory of dominion' taught that the authority of the wicked could not come from God. The Pope's power was derived from the Cæsars of Rome, not from Christ or Peter. It is remarkable that an academician whose methods of thought and expression were involved in the technical labyrinths of later mediæval philosophy, should have foreseen so accurately many of the general lines of development which England was destined to follow between one and two hundred years after his death. The Anglican, the lay[6] and the Protestant positions are all prominent in Wycliffe's teaching, and it was by a mixture of these three different points of view that the affairs of Church and State were ultimately rearranged in England.

[5] The Statute of Provisors (1351) protected the rights of English patrons against Papal 'provisions' to English benefices. The Statutes of Præmunire (1353, 1365, 1393) were of much more limited scope than was supposed in later times. So far as they went they provided a machinery to check Papal interference with royal rights in England.

[6] 'Erastian' in the strict sense of the word Wycliffe perhaps was not. 'He was no Erastian,' Dean Rashdall writes, 'since while he held strongly a distinction between the clergy and the laity, he asserts very emphatically the priesthood of the laity, and insists that he is only calling on one part of the church to remove the evils due to the misconduct of the other.' But he did so call on the laity to reform the Church, as occurred in Tudor times, and many people would call that Erastianism. The tendency of his argument was to make the King the head of the Church, though he does not say so definitely. But the stress he lays on the individual conscience or priesthood of every lay person would have left him dissatisfied with the 'Tudor' solution.

The first important stage of Wycliffe's career as a reformer, in the last years of Edward III, brought him in touch with politicians. He was employed to state the case of the nation against Papal encroachments, and his attack on the 'possessionate' and 'Cæsarean' clergy not only won him much popular support, especially in London, but found for him powerful but unpopular allies in John of Gaunt, Percy of Northumberland and the party of lords and knights who were already nosing after the spoils of the Church. [1377.] And at this stage he also found defenders where he was afterwards to find his bitterest enemies; the friars[7] were always on bad terms with the rest of the Church in England and were still theoretically advocates of poverty and therefore of disendowment. Some of them found in Wycliffe an ally against the landed classes of monks and Bishops, until his denial of transubstantiation and his attacks on their patron the Pope became more than the mendicant orders could endure.

The peasants' rising in 1381, in which he was not involved on either side, did not directly affect Wycliffe's position, except by removing from the world the mild Archbishop Sudbury who had shown no desire to persecute him. The new Primate, Courtenay, was his bitter and energetic enemy, and the period of active repression was at hand. At the same time the Reformer broke with John of Gaunt, the politicians and the friars, by arguing against transubstantiation. His propositions as to the nature of the sacrament were indeed very moderate, but for those days bold in the extreme; his followers in the next generation went farther.

In the last years of his life Wycliffe became less political and less strictly academic. He retired from Oxford to his last home, the Rectory at Lutterworth, in Leicestershire, and there developed further his popular methods of appeal, through English tracts written either by himself or his companions. [1382–84.] He attacked, and taught his disciples to attack, the Pope, the monks, the friars and the

---

[7] On the friars see pp. 246–49, above.

'Cæsarean clergy,' and many of the religious practices of the day such as the worship of images and relics, sale of pardons and masses for the soul. He appealed for the direct relation of the individual to God without mediators, declaring that 'each man that shall be damned shall be damned by his own guilt, and each man that is saved shall be saved by his own merit.'

He demanded a service in English, and he produced, chiefly through the agency of his Oxford follower and secretary, Purvey, the first full English translation of the Bible, an admirable and scholarly piece of work, a great event in the history of English language as well as religion. The Bible was not to Wycliffe, as it was to some later Protestants, the sole basis of his doctrine and his sole canon of appeal. But his doctrines led him to perceive the practical need of a diffusion of the Scriptures in modern English, and the reading of the English Bible became the distinctive practice of his sect. The Church, which permitted under special licence the use of vernacular versions to wealthy persons and to nuns, continued during the Fifteenth Century to deny its possession to the laity in general and to make possession of the Scriptures in English a charge against Lollards.[8]

Meanwhile a great disaster had befallen Wycliffism, which was in origin an Oxford movement. The University, and even its officers, were to a large extent Wycliffe's partisans, at least in regard to many of his theses. The monks and friars of Oxford were now solidly against him, but the secular clergy and undergraduates were largely on his side. Archbishop Courtenay intervened in the quarrel, and with the help of the King overrode the liberties of the University and silenced or expelled the Wycliffites. [1382.] This purge, which had to be repeated in the reign of Henry IV, cut off Lollardry from its roots in the best culture of the day, and helped to turn it into a popular evangelicalism, hiding from authority and propagating it-

[8] On this question see Deanesly, *The Lollard Bible* (Cam. Univ. Press, 1920), in answer to Cardinal Gasquet's *The Old English Bible*.

self among the poor. Courtenay's suppression of the liberty of academic thought doomed the University to a hundred years of intellectual stagnation, in curious contrast to its great productivity in the relative freedom that it had enjoyed during the first two centuries of its existence. No single act had more to do with the barrenness of English mental and spiritual life in the Fifteenth Century.

Yet the dragooning of Oxford and Cambridge by the orthodox had one good side. It afforded an additional motive for the foundation and endowment of Colleges, because they were useful for secluding the students from heretical contagion.[9] The peculiarly English growth of the College system within the University made great strides in the period between William of Wykeham and Wolsey. The foundation by Henry VI of King's College, with its magnificent chapel, was one of the events that tended to bring Cambridge into prominence as a rival to the senior University. At the Reformation this famous rivalry became every day more marked.

Even after the intellectual roots of the Wycliffite movement had been cut by the hand of authority at Oxford, the influence of Wycliffe increased in the land till it was said, though with gross exaggeration, that every second man you met was a Lollard. Parts of Wycliffe's doctrines no doubt found favour with many who would have repudiated other parts. Thus in the reign of Henry IV the knights of shire in the Commons proposed that the King should seize the Temporalities of the Church to relieve taxation and the poor, and endow new lords and knights—the policy of Henry VIII. But they do not appear to have opposed the Statute *De Heretico Comburendo*. [1401.] The Lollard movement was suppressed by persecution in the days of Henry IV and Henry V, who sought security for their questionable dynastic claims in the powerful support of the Church. Some heretics were burnt, more recanted under threat of burning. During the rest of the Fifteenth Century Lollardry survived underground in the towns and

9 See page 244, above.

villages of England. In the reigns of Henry VII and Henry VIII the recrudescence of this native heresy began to alarm the orthodox and to provoke a very active persecution, marked by many martyrdoms, before it became merged in the return wave of Protestantism from Luther's Germany. But every important aspect of the English Reformation was of native origin. All can be traced back as far as Wycliffe, and some much farther.

BOOKS FOR FURTHER READING: See notes pp. 315, 319, above, on rural problems.
Vickers, *England in the Later Middle Ages*; Kingsford, *Henry V*; Coulton, *Chaucer and his England*; Trevelyan, *England in the Age of Wycliffe*; Dean Rashdall's article in *Dict. of Nat. Biog.* on Wycliffe; *The Lollard Bible*, Margaret Deanesly (Cambridge, 1920), especially Chap. IX.; R. Lane Poole, *Wycliffe and Movements for Reform*; Rev. H. B. Workman, *John Wyclif* (Oxford Press, 1926).

CHAPTER EIGHT

Parliamentary Development from Edward III to Henry VI. Aristocratic Anarchy. Some Aspects of English Life in the Later Middle Ages. Wars of the Roses. The Yorkist Kings

KINGS: Edward III, 1327–77; Richard II, 1377–99; Henry IV (Lancaster), 1399–1413; Henry V, 1413–22; Henry VI, 1422–61; Edward IV (York), 1461–83; Edward V, 1483; Richard III, 1483–85

Between the accession of Edward III and the deposition of Henry VI,[1] the English Parliament became fixed in its bicameral form, and acquired the outline of its modern procedure, while the House of Commons developed its financial and legislative powers and even asserted an occasional control over the executive by impeachment of Ministers before the Lords, and by insisting that redress of grievances should precede supply. [1327–1461.] In all

[1] See pp. 257–266, above, for Parliament under the first two Edwards.

these ways precedents were furnished for the future use of Stuart Parliaments, no less valid than the precedents of an opposite tenor quotable by royalist lawyers.

But at the close of the Middle Ages the Lower House was not yet an independent power representing the chief political forces in the country, as it was under Charles I. The mediæval nobility and the mediæval clergy stood between Commons and King, and dwarfed the stature of both. The Lower House enjoyed, indeed, great influence in the State, but only on condition of becoming to a large extent the tool of rival factions among the nobility who were fighting each other for the control or possession of the Crown. At the close of Edward III's reign, the 'good Parliament' of 1376 aided the triumph of the popular cause of the Black Prince and the Earl of March, and impeached their enemies, but the next year's Parliament was packed by the opposing faction of John of Gaunt. Similarly in Richard II's reign [1377–99.] the Commons had no consistent policy of their own, but were made the instrument of a series of State convulsions, contrived by the higher powers in deadly strife with one another. In the following century the premature experiment in Parliamentary control of the executive ended in the aristocratic anarchy which we know as the Wars of the Roses.

Before the Commons could aspire to take authority out of the hands of the King, an interlude was necessary of increased royal power under the Tudors, to strengthen the framework of the State and reduce the nobles and clergy to the level of other subjects. But there was never any complete break in the forms or in the spirit of the 'mixed' English Constitution. The most masterful of the Tudor monarchs used Parliament as the instrument of a revolution in Church and State which would, under the so-called 'Parliamentary' regime of the House of Lancaster, have been regarded as utterly beyond its competence. The complex forms and the free spirit of English government persist from century to century with continuity in change.

The Hundred Years' War, following on the Welsh and Scot-

tish campaigns, rendered it more than ever impossible for
the King to 'live of his own,' for in time of war the State
expenses could not be met from the proceeds of the royal
estates, law courts, feudal dues and other customary levies.
It was found increasingly convenient for all parties that the
King should raise extraordinary taxation, not by bargaining
with individual merchants, cities and counties, but by meeting their spokesmen in the national Parliament. The voting
of taxes on the wool trade, then the easiest way of collecting large sums in a hurry, gave to the burgher representatives a certain importance, in an age when they had no
desire to meddle in affairs of State, or even, if they could
help it, to attend Parliament at all. The financial importance
of the modest burghers increased the financial and political
importance of the knights of the shire, at whose side they
sat in the Westminster Chapter House.

The success of the warfare waged against France and
the power of the Commons who voted the taxes depended
upon one another, no less in the days of Sluys, Crecy and
Agincourt than in the days of La Hogue, Blenheim and
Waterloo. Only when the King bade fair to become ruler
of France in good earnest did the Commons take momentary alarm at the prospect: what indeed would become of
the liberties of England if her monarch ruled Western
Europe from Paris? [1420.] But the sudden death of Henry
V and the career of Joan of Arc saved the British Constitution.[2] [1422–29.]

The mediæval English Parliament was not only a tax-
voting and law-making assembly; it was also 'the High
Court of Parliament,' charged with judicial functions, not
all of them distinguishable in those days from its legislative
powers. The lawyers practising in Westminster Hall regarded the national assembly, so often held in their neigh-

[2] In 1420, when the French had acknowledged Henry V
as heir to their throne, the English Commons withheld a
money grant till the King returned from France, and called
for a republication of the Statute of 1340, guarding against
any subjection of the people of England to their King quâ
King of France. The danger was much greater in 1420
than in 1340.

bourhood, as the greatest of all law courts, and were, for that reason, the more ready to assist its development. The alliance of the common lawyers with the Parliament men can be traced back to Plantagenet times.

The lawyer-like respect for precedent and procedure that has always characterized the House of Commons was a great strength to it from the first. It began its life, not as a mere 'debating assembly,' but as part of the King's 'High Court' of Parliament, with the formality and the privilege of a law court. By the help of the lawyers among them and around them, the knights of the shire learnt many indispensable arts, foremost among these the drawing up of well-drafted 'bills' ready to become Statutes, instead of mere petitions for redress. This change seems to have begun towards the end of Henry VI's reign, and gave the Commons greater control over the Acts to which their assent was asked, and even some power of initiation. Without the active help, continuous down the ages, of some of the best legal brains in the country, the House of Commons could never have become the principal source of legislation, nor have argued the constitutional case against the Crown lawyers and the royalist judges in the century of Coke, Selden and Somers.

The early connection of the Inns of Court with the House of Commons increased a tendency, apparent in students of the English Common Law, to regard the King himself as subject to law, and not as the absolute monarch envisaged by the Roman Code and its students. And so, at Richard II's deposition, it was formally imputed against him as a crime that he had declared the laws to be 'in his own breast,' and himself alone competent to frame and change them at will. This issue was not finally decided until the revolution that drove James II from the throne, but a preliminary judgment was passed upon it when a similar fate befell Richard Plantagenet.

These two revolutions [1399, 1688.], separated by almost three centuries of time, have an extraordinary likeness in their constitutional, and to some extent in their personal and accidental circumstances, although the great religious and international issues which make 1688 an era in European as well as English history were lacking in the quarrel between Richard and his subjects. Three years before the event, neither revolution could have been prophesied by the keenest observer, without an exceptional inner knowledge of the King's character. In 1396 Richard, as in 1685 James, still had a tolerable public record, strong partisans and adequate popularity, and though each had bitter enemies, those enemies had been subdued. Richard, indeed, had already governed well for half-a-dozen years, so long as his violent passions had been restrained by his affection for his first wife, Anne of Bohemia.[3] But after her death some obscure psychological change destroyed his nerve and judgment, just as advancing years, sudden power, and religious fanaticism seemed to make another and a worse man of James.

Three years sufficed to unite against either monarch his old friends and his old foes. For each suddenly entered on a course of open tyranny; each, after packing Parliament in vain, tried to govern without it; each broke law on law, and finally frightened every freeholder in the country by depriving people of their estates, without pretence of right. 'Richard the Redeless' was not more bloodthirsty than the clique of domineering nobles whose power he had quelled in former years. But for ill-advisedness, not even the ejection of the Fellows of Magdalen by James surpassed Richard's seizure of the estates of the House of Lancaster, a family, till then, by no means inveterately hostile to his person. The light-hearted folly of the act is heard in the jingle of Shakespeare's rhyming couplet:—

Think what you will: we seize into our hands
His plate, his goods, his money and his lands.

The return of Henry of Lancaster from abroad, claiming his paternal estates, rallied the whole country round him,

[3] It is supposed that some of her Bohemian (Czech) countrymen who came over with her, must have taken back copies of Wycliffe's works to Bohemia—with the result of the great Hussite movement there in the Fifteenth Century.

like the coming of William of Orange. Richard, like James, made every possible mistake at the crisis, could get no one to fight for him, and was deposed by Parliament on the express ground that he had broken the fundamental laws of the Kingdom. And Henry, like William, was called to the empty throne partly indeed by hereditary right, but yet more by Parliamentary title, for neither Henry IV nor William of Orange was the nearest heir.

The result of the Revolution of 1399 was to set the power of the two Houses of Parliament on ground at once higher and firmer than ever before. They had not only deposed a King—as had happened when Edward II was forced to yield the throne to his son—but this time they had chosen the successor. The Lancastrian, like the Hanoverian Kings, ruled by Parliamentary title, and under them the power and privilege of both Houses must needs be respected.

It is not, therefore, surprising to find that the political theories of the Fifteenth and of the Eighteenth Centuries both lay great stress on the legal limitations of the Crown's power, and proudly contrast the freedom of the English subject to the slavery of the French. Such was the constant theme of the contemporaries of Hogarth, Blackstone and Burke, and such, three hundred years earlier, was the boast of the typical common lawyer of the Fifteenth Century, Chief Justice Fortescue, a patriot who loved his country as being the land of liberty. Though he was driven into exile with the Lancastrian party after Towton [1461.], he sat down abroad to write the praises of the English constitution: 'For the King of England,' he writes, 'cannot alter nor change the lawes of the Realme at his pleasure. For why, hee governeth his people by power, not only royall, but politique'—'constitutional,' as we should say. The spirit of the English Common Law, writes Fortescue, is repugnant to the theory of the Civil or Roman law, dominant in other countries, that 'The Prince his pleasure hath the force of a law.' He goes on to contrast, from personal observation, the misery of the French common people, continually robbed and insulted by the King's soldiers and servants, to the 'Realme of England, where no man sojourneth in an other man's house without the love and the leave of the good man of the same house'—in other words, the Englishman's house is his castle.

It is very remarkable that Fortescue should have used such language at the height of the Wars of the Roses, and the more so since he was bitterly conscious of what was wrong in contemporary England. He diagnosed the 'lack of government,' tracing the evils of the day to their true source in 'the perils that come to the King from overmighty subjects,' and he demanded a richer and stronger monarchy and poorer and less powerful nobles. He foreshadowed, in some detail, the policy actually carried out by Henry VII.

The great nobles and their satellite gentry, who disturbed the England of the Fifteenth Century with their lawless brawls, had at least accepted the fact of the unity of the national State. They did not aspire to govern whole provinces with feudal or princely sway, like the French nobles whom it was the task of Louis XI to subdue after the final departure of the English invaders. In England the rival King-makers did not seek to destroy or divide the royal authority, but to control and exploit it. They did not even attempt to restore the now obsolete 'franchises' or private courts which de Warenne had so noisily maintained against Edward I's *Quo Warranto* enquiry.[4] The latter-day noble knew how to get what he wanted in the King's courts, by bribing and intimidating county jurors and royal Judges and Justices of the Peace. Indeed, the law-breakers often held the King's commission in the shires. The records of the period sometimes give a curious picture of a set of country gentlemen now enforcing the King's Peace and the Statutes of Labourers, now charged with robbery, piracy and murder, now sitting on the Bench, now sent to prison.

While too many of the smaller gentry acted in this fashion in the country-side, their patrons and paymasters, the great nobles, were quarrelling with each other for the

[4] See pp. 256–57, above.

control of the central government, as the fount of power, honours and wealth. The battlefield was the King's Council, where the executive power was lodged. The nobles regarded the Council as a body representative of the forces in the State, or at least of the higher aristocracy, a sort of Parliament in permanent session, where each of the great lords had a personal right to sit whenever he felt so disposed. The King, on the other hand, regarded the Council as personal to himself, to be filled by whom he would, not necessarily by great nobles; under a foolish King this meant the rule of favourites, under a wise King the rule of trained, professional experts.

Conflict between the King's view and the nobles' view of what the Council should be, had often led to strife, particularly in the reign of Richard II. And in a sense Henry IV's wars with the Percys, Mortimer and Scrope [1402–5.] had been fought on the same issue, complicated by Welsh and northern border problems, and by the dynastic question never wholly at rest. But neither the royal nor the aristocratic theory as to the proper constitution of the Council had completely extinguished the other, for each had a solid basis in the actual needs and forces of that age. Only during the long minority of Henry VI [1422–37.] the Council inevitably fell into the hands of the great nobles, and when Henry grew to manhood he lacked ability and character to resume authority as Richard II had in like circumstances done. The personal feuds of the great nobles with each other for supremacy at the Council board and in the bedchamber continued as before, until at length they plunged the country into the Wars of the Roses. [1455.]

The weakness of the saintly Henry among the rival factions in the Council was translated into lawless violence in the countryside by the privileged clients of the great families. Parliament should have supplied a remedy, and strengthened the power of the King against the nobles. But it did not even attempt the task. In Henry VI's reign the mediæval House of Commons reached its highest point of constitutional privilege, but failed to use it for the benefit of the nation. There was no friction between Parliament and Council, because both were controlled by the same aristocratic cliques, whose only contests were against one another.

In 1430 an Act of Parliament took away the county franchise from the general body of freemen suitors in the Shire Court, and limited the right of voting for knights of the shire to the class of forty shilling freeholders. So the letter of the law remained until the Reform Bill of 1832. But in Lancastrian times a freehold worth forty shillings a year was a much higher qualification than it became after the value of money had fallen. For some generations, therefore, the disfranchising law of 1430 excluded, as it was confessedly designed to exclude, almost everyone below the small gentry, and the result of a diminished county electorate was to increase the power of the great nobles over Parliament. The House of Commons, in aristocratic leading strings, was getting ever more out of touch with the people, while driving the theory of Parliamentary government to extremes in an age too soon. Because the nobles could use the House of Commons for their purposes, they were not jealous of its growth. Here again, we find a parallel, in certain respects, to the Eighteenth Century, when the power and prestige of the House of Commons were on the increase, at the very time that it was becoming an aristocratic assembly on the basis of a franchise tending to become rather less than more popular.

It is significant that the last of the English were driven out of France in 1453 and that the Wars of the Roses began only two years later in the streets of St. Albans. The return of the garrisons and armies from oversea filled England with knights and archers, accustomed to war, licence and plunder, and fit for any mischief. The unemployed and starving veteran was dangerous enough, but yet more dangerous was the 'company' of warriors in private employment, kept together by its paymaster when the French war was over, to further his political ambitions or his designs upon his neighbours' estates.[5]

Nor was the Hundred Years' War injurious to English society only when it came to an end. Throughout its whole course it had bred habits of lawlessness and violence at home. The Parliaments of Edward III had complained of estate-jumping, carrying off of heiresses and breach of the peace by gentlemen and their retainers as a new and growing evil. And to the influence of the foreign campaigns must be added the older and more permanent influence of the Welsh and Scottish Borders, where the Marcher Lords in their castles, like Mortimer in Wigmore and Percy in Alnwick, lived constantly under arms, preserving the feudal customs and spirit that had disappeared from the more civilized South and East. Wales and the North between them caused the troubles under Henry IV; and the Wars of the Roses were to a large extent a quarrel between Welsh Marcher Lords, who were also great English nobles, closely related to the English throne.[6]

A characteristic feature of this revival of anarchy in a civilized society was the combination of legal chicanery with military violence. It was an age of litigation tempered by house-breaking. In Stephen's reign the barbarous Barons had had no need to be lawyers; but under Henry VI every ambitious noble, and every country gentleman who aspired to found the fortunes of his family, was well versed in the processes of law as well as in the siegecraft of forcible entry into a moated manor-house. Such a man kept in his pay not only archers but lawyers and jurymen. The correspondence of the Paston family has made us familiar with the type in reality, and Stevenson's Sir Daniel Brackley in fiction. The law-breakers were often Justices of the Peace, and some of the worst 'ambushes' were committed by royal judges and by nobles high in office. The operations of purely private war were some-

[5] See p. 302, above, for the 'companies' in the Hundred Years' War, who now became the 'retainers' at home.

[6] See p. 283, above.

Names of great families with Influence in a district are in brackets thus:- (PERCY)

English Miles
0 10 20   40   60   80

SCOTLAND

Hedgeley Moor
IIII X 1464
Alnwick Castle

(PERCY)

Hexham   Newcastle
1464 X

(NEVILLE)

I. of Man   (CLIFFORD)   (NEVILLE)
(STANLEY)

York
X Towton, 1461

DUCHY OF
LANCASTER)   Ravenspur
                                        Henry IV landed 1399
(STANLEY)   R. Humber   Edward IV   1471

(LANCASTER)

(OWEN
GLENDOWER)   Stoke
                1487
                X   (YORK)   Caister
WALES   Shrewsbury   Bosworth   Cas.
             IIII X 1403   X 1485
AND   (LANCASTER)   Norwich
ITS   Lutterworth
MARCH
(MORTIMER)   Cambridge

Wigmore
Castle   Tewkesbury
(STAFFORD)   1471   St. Albans, 1455, 1461
                            Westminster   Barnet, 1471
Milford   Oxford
Haven   Eton   London
Henry VII landed 1485   R. Thames
             Bristol   Windsor Blackheath
                                    1497
             R. Severn

(BEAUFORT)   Winchester

Plymouth
Warwick landed 1470

EMERY WALKER LTD. SC.

Map 16   England in the Fifteenth Century

times on a scale that matched the more regular dynastic
struggle. In 1469 a dispute over Sir John Fastolf's will led
to a five weeks' siege of Caister Castle by the Duke of

Norfolk with 3000 men, finally ended by cannon to breach the walls—and this in East Anglia, the richest and most settled part of the island.

Juries were as regularly intimidated in Fifteenth Century England as in Nineteenth Century Ireland. 'Maintenance' was the recognized duty of the great man to protect his client in the King's courts from the consequences of illegal action, and since the English courts already insisted on the unanimity of the twelve jurymen, it was seldom possible to get verdicts against the friend of a great man. Maitland has expressed the opinion that more injustice was done at this period by wrongful acquittals than by wrongful condemnations. The subsequent Tudor practice of making jurors answer for their verdicts before the King's Council, though incompatible with the full freedom of the subject, was at one time regarded as a much needed reform. At the outbreak of the Wars of the Roses the grievances of quiet people were summed up in these rude verses:—

In every shire with jacks and salads[7] clean
Misrule doth rise and maketh neighbours war.
The weaker goeth beneath, as oft is seen,
The mightiest his quarrell will prefer.

They kill your men alway one by one,
And who say aught he shall be beat doubtless.
For in your realm Justice of Peace be none
That dare aught now the contesters oppress.

The law is like unto a Welshman's hose,
To each man's legs that shapen is and meet;
So maintainers subvert it and transpose.
Through might it is full low laid under feet.

What are we to think of this outbreak of savage wrongdoing in the highest ranks of a society so far emerged from feudal barbarism, and artistically so much the superior of our own in the arts and crafts of daily life? But contrast is the essence of social history, and particularly of mediæval history. We think of the Fifteenth Century as the era of chivalry: for did not its knights wear the

[7] Cuirasses and helmets.

plate armour in which modern artists depict Sir Galahad
with his pure, schoolboy face, and was it not the century
when Sir Thomas Malory produced his 'Morte Arthur'?
[1470.] But the actual contemporaries of Malory would,
at close quarters, have seemed to us singularly deficient
in 'chivalry' according to modern notions. It was not that
in England 'chivalry' any longer looked with unmitigated
scorn on burgher and villein, as it still did in the yet more
'chivalrous' society of France and Flanders recorded by
Chastellain. Peasant emancipation, burgher wealth and the
prudent mixing and intermarriage of all the well-to-do
classes were in England tending to fill up the chasm that
elsewhere divided the gentles from common folk. But
'chivalry' was, in England as elsewhere, compatible with
brutal violence and calculating materialism, not least in
the treatment of women.

Wife-beating was a recognized right of man, and was
practised without shame by high as well as low. The
woman's defence was her tongue, sometimes giving her
the mastery in the household, but often leading to muscu-
lar retort. One of the Fifteenth Century English translations of the fashionable manual of the Knight of La Tour
Landry thus describes the proper treatment of a scolding
wife:—

He smote her with his fist down to the earth. And then
with his foot he struck her in the visage and brake her
nose, and all her life after she had her nose crooked that
she might not for shame show her visage it was so foul
blemished. . . . Therefore the wife ought to suffer and
let the husband have the word, and to be master.

Similarly, the daughter who refused to marry the
gentleman of her parents' choice was liable to be locked
up, beaten and flung about the room, without any shock
being inflicted on public opinion.[8] Marriage was not an

[8] Locking up a daughter to force her to a loathed match
was not impossible in squires' families as late as the middle
of the Eighteenth Century, as we know from Squire Western's proceedings in the case of a daughter to whom he
was much attached. A Fifteenth Century Squire Western
would have beaten Sophia into the bargain.

affair of personal affection but of family avarice, particularly in the 'chivalrous' upper classes. 'For very need,' complains a member of the noble family of Scrope, 'I was fain to sell a little daughter I have, for much less than I should have done by possibility.' Betrothal often took place while one or both of the parties was in the cradle, and marriage when they were scarcely out of the nurse's charge. It was sometimes difficult to get a little fellow to say the necessary words of the ceremony, before running back to his toys.

The elaborate literature of love, French in origin, of which Chaucer's *Troilus and Cresseyde* was the finest flower, was concerned with marriage principally as a disturber thereof, though the old ruling of the Court of Love 'that no married pair can really be in love with each other' admitted in the world of reality of countless exceptions. And, indeed, Chaucer, who saw human nature not merely through the stained glass of literature, has drawn in his *Franklin's Tale* a beautiful picture of wedded faith and love alongside of the professional 'lover's' torments. And though child-marriage and forced marriage were accursed customs, there were cases of young people successfully defying the heartless plans of their elders, even in the prosaic society of the Pastons. Side by side with the violence and materialism of mediæval life, there was much also of the 'good nature and integrity of the English people' which was not a thing of yesterday.

Civilization and knowledge were all the while encroaching on the realm of ignorance. For although Oxford in the Fifteenth Century decayed in intellectual vigour prior to the blossoming of the New Learning, the end of the Middle Ages was a great period for the foundation of schools, besides William of Wykeham's Winchester and Henry VI's Eton. Guilds and private persons were constantly endowing chantries with priests to say masses for souls, and schools were often attached to them. Other schools were being founded on an independent basis, sometimes with lay headmasters. All this was over and above the Collegiate, Cathedral and parish church schools of earlier foundation.

Reading and writing, therefore, had quite ceased, in
the days of York and Lancaster, to be the monopoly of
the clergy. Not only the merchants but the bailiffs of
manors kept good accounts and often wrote tolerable
Latin in their business documents. Members of landed
families like the Pastons corresponded with one another
by letters written in their own hands, usually on legal
or other business or to convey political news.

For several generations after Chaucer's death in 1400
English literature remained under Chaucer's domination.
The chief poets were of his school, and in the latter part
of the century Caxton made haste to print him for a public
that could not get enough copies of him in manuscript.

The works of Chaucer and his numerous imitators expressed to the satisfaction of the society of that age its
delicate sense of the beauty of natural sights and sounds
in the orchards and artificial gardens where it passed so
many hours of dalliance, or in the wild wood beyond. To-
day we like our gardens and parks to appear wild, because
we have so terribly tamed the land outside, but from the
Fifteenth to the early Eighteenth Centuries they liked
artificial gardens because they had so much of wild nature
elsewhere, in which their souls rejoiced no less than in
the gardens. The song of birds, the run of water, the
flowers in bloom and the woods in leaf gave those country-
dwellers a joy of which they were fully conscious. It is
in nature that the lover seeks ease from his 'love-longing':—

And the river that I sate upon
It made such a noise as it ron,
Accordaunt with the birdës' armony
Me thought it was the best melody
That might ben heard of any mon.

The medicine recommended for the wounds of despised
love is—

Go looke on the fresh daisie!

Or again—

A wind, so small it scarcely might be less,
Made in the leavës green a noisë soft,
Accordant to the fowlës song aloft.

The beauty of the domestic architecture of the manor-houses, then coming to perfection in stone or the new-fangled brick, the artistic merit and originality in dress, furniture and articles of common use for farm, barn and household, enriched life with joys that have disappeared from it, both for the craftsman who created and the owner who used his creation. Altogether a marvellous place was England at the end of the Middle Ages, so full of what we have lost, so empty of what we now have, and yet, as Chaucer and the Pastons have written and shown us, so English and so like us all the while.

[1455.] When the Wars of the Roses at length broke out in form, no question of principle or even of class interest was involved in the quarrel between Lancaster and York. It was a faction fight between the families allied to the royal house, contending for power and wealth and ultimately for the possession of the Crown. On each side was ranged a group of great nobles. And each noble had his *clientèle* of knights, gentry, led captains, lawyers and clergy, some attached to his person, some living in distant manors, but all conscious that their fortunes were involved in the rise or fall of their 'good lord.' Changing of sides was more frequent in this civil war than in others, because there was no principle to desert. The mass of the people looked on with indifference, the towns and villages only bargaining that they should, as far as possible, be spared the horrors of war. Even London, for once, remained neuter in the civil strife convulsing England. In return, the armies were much less destructive than in France, because their chiefs knew well that if the neutrals were roused by ill treatment they could soon dispose of the few thousand partisan soldiers, who scoured the country in hot pursuit of one another from Plymouth to the foot of the Cheviots, making and unmaking the short-lived fortunes of Lancaster and York. So in spite of the wars, which were at the worst inter-mittent, the neutral majority suffered little, and trade followed its usual course along the rivers and riding tracks

with not much more than the usual amount of disturbance
from highwaymen and water-thieves.[9]

But the actual combatants suffered severely. The fighting nobles were savage in their treatment of one another.
There were many sudden turns of fortune's wheel, and
each meant a fresh confiscation of great estates, and a new
batch of noble heads for the block, over and above the
heavy proportion of leaders killed upon the field of battle.
The Crown was enriched by these confiscations and the
nobles were impoverished, while their numbers, never
great, were much reduced. The way was thus prepared
for the Tudor policy of bridling 'overmighty subjects.' The
Wars of the Roses were a bleeding operation performed
by the nobility upon their own body. To the nation it
was a blessing in disguise.

The hosts engaged in battles like Towton, Barnet and
Tewkesbury were partly professional mercenaries, partly
friends and tenants hastily called out; they were serving
under private paymasters, at whose behest they marched
under the banner of York or Lancaster. The tactics were
those employed by the same leaders in the recent French
war. Cavalry fighting was the exception rather than the
rule, the normal soldier being a mounted infantryman.
Cannon and the new hand-guns were sometimes used in
the field, but the longbow was still the lord of weapons.
The archer still fought on foot, in line beside the knight.
But the battles had not the same character as Crecy or

[9] In the Middle Ages roads were little more than riding-
ways, but rivers were deeper and more navigable than
now. York, Lincoln, Doncaster and other inland towns depended on the water for their trade. As early as the Fourteenth Century, London consumed coal as its normal fuel,
because it could come by sea from Tyneside. The traders
of the English towns had a great interest in keeping the
rivers on which they stood open to barges, by removing
weirs and bridges that impeded traffic. Partly for this reason fords or ferries were preferred to bridges even when,
as seldom happened, money was available to build a bridge.
In the Middle Ages to travel by land meant to walk or
ride, and to cross a stream or river meant to splash through
a ford or to hail the ferryman.

Agincourt, because in England there was little to choose between the archery on the two sides, and rather than stand long under the arrow-storm, men came as soon as possible to close quarters and hacked out a decision with sword and bill.

The figure that rose victorious from the murderous mêlée of the Wars of the Roses was Edward IV, [1461–83.] heir of the House of York, the best soldier produced by those rough-and-tumble campaigns. The battle of Towton, fought in a blinding Yorkshire snowstorm, placed him on the throne. He was the first English Prince of the Renaissance type, so familiar to us in Louis XI of France and the Tudor Henrys, though Edward was too lazy and self-indulgent to have served Machiavelli for a perfect model.

These faults once cost him dear. Warwick the King-maker, of the great House of Neville, type of the noblemen who were England's bane, had done much to set Edward on the throne of the incompetent saint of Lancaster. [1461.] Ten years later, in a fit of jealousy for unrewarded service, analogous to the jealousy of the Percys against Henry IV, Warwick dragged Henry VI out of the Tower and made him King once more. [1471.] But in the campaign of Barnet and Tewkesbury the luxurious Edward showed that when aroused he was still the better soldier. The deaths of Warwick and of Henry VI and his son were the results of the affair, leaving the House of York firmer than ever on the throne, whence nothing could have dislodged it but its own intestine broils and treacheries.

Edward IV's policy was a faulty and incomplete rehearsal of the policy afterwards pursued by Henry VII. Edward had no desire for 'overmighty subjects' in his kingdom, least of all on the steps of the throne. His own brother, 'false, fleeting, perjured Clarence,' soon followed Warwick to the further shore of the Styx, where the shades of England's noble and royal families were collecting in troops. And since Edward had made good his claim rather by conquest than by Parliamentary title, he had not the Lancastrian respect for Parliament, nor is there any evidence

that people thought the worse of his rule for that. It was
indeed, a dangerous moment for Parliamentary institutions
Edward seldom summoned the Houses, and he began t·
rely less on taxes voted by the Commons and more o·
carefully modulated 'benevolences' or forced gifts from in
dividual subjects.

A chief instrument of aristocratic power under Henry V
had been the King's Council.[10] It was, therefore, in littl·
favour with Edward IV until in the latter part of his reig·
he saw reason to revive it as the instrument of the King'·
personal rule, a policy carried much further by the Tudor:
after him.

Edward had less inclination to the society of the grea·
nobles than to that of the merchant princes of the rising
plutocracy. London, 'the flower of cities all' as it was now
becoming in the whole world's esteem, was growing in
wealth and outward beauty and inward intelligence, while
the nobles were cutting each other's throats and the
Church was losing its moral and intellectual leadership.
The monastic scribes could no longer meet the nation's
needs, and indeed the abbey chronicles were growing
more meagre than of old. A new class of 'scriveners' or
'stationers' copied books in an attempt to keep level with
the growing public demand for poetry of the school of
Chaucer, and for chronicles, histories and other works in
prose. In these circumstances the setting up under Edward IV's patronage of Caxton's printing-press at Westminster was perhaps the greatest English event of the
century. Edward, who wanted the money and liked the
company of intellectual men and sprightly women, both
from policy and choice lived much with the great citizens
of London and their wives.

But with all this Princecraft of the modern order, Edward IV failed to establish the King's Peace in the counties,
and to 'bridle stout noblemen and gentlemen.' That great
work was left to the Star Chamber of Henry VII. No effective plan for strengthening the executive in the enforce-

[10] See p. 337, above.

ment of order was conceived by the House of York. Private war, maintenance, and estate-jumping flourished only a little less after Towton and Tewkesbury than while Henry VI still sat on the throne. Moreover, Edward IV, instead of being content to govern through a professional civil service of clergy, lawyers, bourgeois and gentry, made the mistake of raising up his wife's relations, the Woodvilles and Greys, as parvenu nobles.

On Edward's death [1483.], the jealousy felt by the remnant of the old nobility against the upstart Woodvilles and Greys, enabled Edward's brother, Richard Duke of Gloucester, to usurp the throne. Edward V was a child, and his mother and her relations were odious to the nobles and not popular with the nation. This intestine feud was the ruin of the House of York. Richard was no monster born; there is no clear evidence that he was more responsible for the deaths of Henry VI and Clarence than the rest of the Yorkist party, nor, prior to his usurpation of the throne, was his record as treacherous as that of his brother Clarence or as bloody as that of his brother Edward. But the glittering bait of the crown ensnared his soul: he murdered his two nephews under trust, and the disappearance of the Princes in the Tower, following on the violence of the usurpation, lost him the loyalty of the common people. [1483.] The English had not been wholly debased by the wars and murderings of their ruling class, and the revulsion of feeling against Richard was the beginning of better things.

The claimants to the reversion of the throne, Yorkist and Lancastrian alike, had disappeared so fast in the battles and executions of twenty-five years that, on the death of Edward V, a Welsh gentleman named Henry Tudor, Earl of Richmond, was able to put up a very respectable case for himself on the Lancastrian side. After the custom of opposition leaders in those brisk times, he had sought refuge abroad, first in the Court of Brittany, then in France. Taking advantage of the unpopularity of the child-murderer, he landed with a slender and untrustworthy force, at Milford Haven, on the coast of his native Wales. The racial enthusiasm of the Welsh for a descendant of their ancient British Princes,—marching, as Henry was careful to march, under the red-dragon standard of Cadwallader,—broke out into prophecy and song, and enabled him to raise in little more than a week a small army of zealous supporters as he traversed that ever warlike land. They, with the help of a few French and English adventurers, won Bosworth Field [AUG. 22, 1485.] against a King for whom the mass of his English subjects were ashamed to fight. Here, indeed, was one of fortune's freaks: on a bare Leicestershire upland, a few thousand men in close conflict foot to foot, while a few thousand more stood aside to watch the issue, sufficed to set upon the throne of England the greatest of all her royal lines, that should guide her through a century of change down new and larger streams of destiny, undreamt of by any man who plied bow and bill that day in the old-world quarrel of York and Lancaster.

BOOKS FOR FURTHER READING: C. L. Kingsford, *Prejudice and Promise in 15th Century England* (Ford lectures, 1925); James Gairdner, *Richard III.*; Sir James H. Ramsay, *Lancaster and York,* 2 vols.; Vickers and other works already mentioned, pp. 206 and 330, above; Stubbs, *Const. Hist. of England,* Vol. III.; Chrimes, *English Constitutional Ideas in the 15th Century,* 1936.

INDEX

Lee

377 – 8873